COCKER SPANIELS

AN OWNER'S COMPANION

Jennifer Lloyd Carey

The Crowood Press

First published in 1992 by
The Crowood Press Ltd
Ramsbury, Marlborough
Wiltshire SN8 2HR

© Jennifer Lloyd Carey 1992

British Library Cataloguing in Publication Data

A catalogue record for this book is available from the British
Library.

ISBN 1 85223 488 1

Throughout this book, 'he', 'him' and 'his' have been used as
neutral pronouns and refer to both males and females.

Acknowledgements

My thanks are due to those who have provided information
and photographs or in other ways helped with the production
of this book, especially George and Joyce Caddy, John and
Anne Daniels, Tracey Daniels, V.N., Enid Dickson, Thelma
Dulley, Yvonne Horrocks, Maureen Johnson, Tracy Morgan,
Paul Rawlings, Ian Scott, Wilson Stephens, Rosemary Timms,
Gordon Hampton (Australia), Kate Romanski (USA), Franca
Simondetti (Italy), H. van Wessem (Holland), and Prudence
Walker (Canada).

Front cover: Falconers Theseus of Ware, photographed by Tracy Morgan.
Back cover: photograph by Alan Carey.

Line-drawings by Annette Findlay.

Typeset by Acorn Bookwork, Salisbury, Wiltshire
Printed in Great Britain by Redwood Press Limited, Melksham, Wiltshire

Contents

Forewords

By HSH The Princess Antoinette of Monaco

I am delighted that Mrs Jennifer Lloyd Carey has written this very special book about Cocker Spaniels. It is going to be of such interest and use to all those lucky people who own Cocker Spaniels and will enable them to understand – and cope with – every aspect of Cocker welfare.

Cocker Spaniels were my first love, and when the Second World War broke out I owned eight goldens, some of whom were excellent workers. One dreamed of some day owning a dog from the of Ware kennel of Mr Lloyd, whose word was law to all us Cocker lovers.

I hope the owners of today will make good use of this lovely book and thus be able to do their best for the delightful breed for which Mr Lloyd and his daughter have done so much.

Antoinette de Monaco, Mrs John Gilpin
President of the Monaco Kennel Club, and
Vice-President of the Kennel Club of Great Britain

By Leonard Pagliero

Jennifer Lloyd Carey is the third generation of a family which is, perhaps, more identified with the Cocker Spaniel than any other. The kennel was founded in 1875 by her grandfather, who bred the first of Ware champion, Crown Prince, more than a hundred years ago.

She has written this book from a fund of practical knowledge and experience. However, she would be the first to own that much of this knowledge was gained from her father H. S. Lloyd, who must surely be regarded as the doyen of the breed, and the book would be incomplete without some reference to him. As one who knew him well, perhaps I may be forgiven for using this foreword to pay my small tribute.

His record of Best in Show winners at Crufts is unassailable. He achieved this award in four successive Crufts, which is almost beyond belief, with Exquisite Model of Ware in 1938 and 1939 and then, after the wartime break, with Tracey Witch of Ware in 1948 and 1950. This must be a record that will remain for all time.

But that is only part of the story, for the successes in the show ring of the of Ware Cockers, not only in this country but overseas as well, during a sustained period of more than three decades, gave Bert Lloyd a supremacy that was virtually unchallenged. There were successes in field trials too, including wins in the Kennel Club's Cocker Spaniel Championship. Even that was not the end of it, for in 1934 he was invited by the Home Office to establish a Police Dog Experimental School, and during the war years of 1939–1945 he was appointed by the War Office as technical adviser to the Army War Dog School for which service he was made an MBE.

In every sense Bert Lloyd was a 'dog man'. Real dog men are few. They are born and not created. They stand out and their memory is indelible. Bert Lloyd was one of them. His knowledge of dogs was second to none. He bred them, showed them and trained them with a skill that is given to few. He had a genius for producing outstanding Cocker Spaniels with unfailing regularity. He could recognize them in the nest, and his judgement never seemed to be wrong.

He had an uncanny affinity with his dogs. To watch him show one was a revelation. I never saw him 'handle' a dog in the ring. Every one he exhibited showed itself, with Bert apparently just holding on to the end of a slack lead, and always his dogs were the epitome of the 'merry Cocker', evincing character, intelligence, animation and inevitably that wagging tail. He was the showman supreme.

It is from this background that Jennifer's book is written. It will make an important contribution to canine literature, and I strongly commend it to its readers.

Leonard Pagliero
Vice-President of the Kennel Club
Chairman, 1976–1981

Introduction

In writing this book, I have kept in mind the roles that Cocker Spaniels fulfil. Most are domestic pets, but many are used for breeding and showing, while some are working gundogs. There is something for all in these pages: guidance for the potential purchaser, help for the pet owner, information for the breeder and an overview of active pursuits.

Basic advice is offered and, where it is enlarged upon for the show dog, the exhibitor should read both parts in conjunction. As with any recommendations, owners must judge for themselves the suitability or safety of a particular method or product for their own dog.

Sufficient historic detail is given to enable the owner who has appropriate pedigree information of his own Cocker Spaniel to trace his family all the way back to Champion Obo, born in 1879.

Exhibitors are aware that the quality of a breed is assessed and maintained through competition, and from their involvement in showing comes for many an aspiration to judge. The chapter on judging will help exhibitors understand what is required and guide those who have the opportunity to take on this responsibility.

While compiling this *Owner's Companion*, I have noted that the standard of pictures in club year books has deteriorated. Intrusive hands, feet, shadows and backgrounds fail to do the dogs justice. It is worth using the services of a professional photographer, since such publicity reaches a worldwide readership. Some sections of Cocker Spaniel society are hungry for printed material, as well as old pedigrees in any condition, so please ensure that unwanted literature and documents will be passed on to addicts or breed clubs.

I hope you find this book both enjoyable and informative and that it helps you to appreciate the lovely breed. Perhaps, too, it may inspire those who begin with a family dog to progress to the many other pleasures that a Cocker Spaniel can offer.

1

The History of the Breed

Origins

It is generally accepted that spaniels are dogs of great antiquity – probably the oldest members of the canine family – and, as the name implies, their origins lie in Spain. It is believed that all varieties of spaniel, including the toy, have come from the same ancestry, and that the setter was derived from the spaniel. Although the spaniel's purpose was to help the falconer in his quest for game, it seems that he was also highly thought of as a companion; early writers talk of friendly dogs who were faithful to their masters.

One nineteenth century writer explains:

> No dog appears to us to become so personally attached to his master or mistress as a Spaniel: it cannot endure to be absent; it will come to the room door and scratch and whine to be admitted, and even patiently wait for hours, until entrance be granted. We had a small high-bred female of the Cocker breed a few years since, which displayed towards her mistress the strongest affection. This dog was remarkable for beauty, having long glossy hair like silk, and for admirable symmetry; she was, besides, as spirited as elegant: she would kill a rat in an instant, and attack a cat with the courage of a Bulldog.

The falcon and net were superseded by the gun, but the spaniel continued its usefulness as far as the sportsman was concerned. At the beginning of the nineteenth century, two kinds of spaniel were described, the larger being the Springer and the smaller becoming known as the Cocker. The dogs were required to hunt and flush birds from cover but not, at that stage, to retrieve.

Writing of sporting spaniels in the 1860s, 'Stonehenge' refers to them all under the general heading of Field Spaniels; those known as Springer included Sussex, Clumber and Norfolk Spaniels, and others were called Cocker since they were 'chiefly used for wood-

7

cocks, though also good for general purposes'. He claims that the King Charles and Blenheim Spaniels originally belonged to the division of Cockers, though they were chiefly kept as pets only.

A requirement at that time was that the dog should give tongue with a 'musical but not noisy' sound, as the masters of a good spaniel could distinguish by the note the kind of game located. However, noisy dogs were in due course discouraged because they gave early warning of the sportsman's approach. Springers were considered slow and heavy compared with the smaller and more active Cocker, who seemed to enjoy his work with greater enthusiasm.

There were apparently many varieties of Cocker in different parts of Great Britain. C. A. Phillips and R. Claude Cane in *The Sporting Spaniel* (Our Dogs, 1906) recalled the Devonshire Cockers of earlier days as being very hardy and with excellent working qualities. The Welsh Cocker was probably an old variety and more carefully bred, with red and white as the usual colour. They also had a good reputation as working dogs.

Early Showing

There seem to be no pedigree records going back to the early part of the nineteenth century, and the first strain appears to be that of Mr Footman of Lutterworth in Leicestershire. It was on this strain that Mr Burdett founded his kennel of Cocker Spaniels, and it is likely that present-day Cocker and Field Spaniels can be traced back to this source. Burdett's dog Frank, and Mousley's bitch Venus, produced Burdett's Bob, who was born in 1856 and won a first prize at the first show where spaniels were exhibited, held at Birmingham in 1859.

In the early days of showing, spaniels were classified by weight. Classes were put on for Field Spaniels over 25 lb (11.5 kg) and Field Spaniels under 25 lb, the latter being commonly known as Cockers. Dogs from the same litter could compete in different classes, one being designated a Field Spaniel, another perhaps a Cocker. This caused confusion amongst breeders, as did the fact that when dogs changed hands, they sometimes changed their names and had a new entry in the Kennel Club Stud Book. Even greater confusion was caused because different owners used the same names for their dogs.

Criticism was expressed that fancy show points were taking over from the working qualities to the detriment of the breed. Judges were looking for a sleek-coated dog who was long and low, and often one with crooked legs could get by provided his coat was not curly or wavy. The weight limit was a handicap for breeders who would perhaps reject a good type dog a little over the limit in case his offspring were oversize. Type seemed to be of minor importance, and with the weight restriction the breed made little headway.

It was not until the Spaniel Club was formed in 1885 that Breed Standards were drawn up for the different breeds, so that breeders could aim at a specified type. A Scale of Points was suggested for judging, totalling 100 positive points. On the negative side, a dog with a top-knot (termed 'fatal') would be marked down 20 points!

Differences of opinion were expressed among the show and sporting fraternity. Field trials were suggested by the Spaniel Club as a means of improving the breed, but it was thought that there were too many difficulties, partly because sporting estates worked spaniels in teams and also because judges would have problems in satisfying the owners!

However, while the Spaniel Club was dithering, a rival club, the Sporting Spaniel Club, was formed and proved that trials for spaniels were possible by actually holding them. Significantly, for many years some stakes were indeed run for brace and for team.

Recognition

By 1893, the Kennel Club had separated Cockers from the other spaniels in the Stud Book, and it can be said that from that date the breed was recognized in its own right. It was, however, the Spaniel Club which was responsible for the eventual abolition of the weight limit. On a proposal from Colonel Claude Cane and Mr J. J. Farrow, a resolution was passed to this effect, and the specialist club's recommendation was confirmed by the Kennel Club in 1901. The restrictions on breeding which the weight rule imposed had hindered rather than helped the Cocker Spaniel, and with the lifting of this ban the breed was ready to progress into the twentieth century. The Cocker Spaniel Club was set up in 1902 and 'descriptive particulars' based on those previously devised by the Spaniel Club were established as a guide for breeders.

At the same time, Springer Spaniels were receiving their own recognition, a separate register in the Stud Book of 1903 being granted with sub-divisions for English and Welsh. The latter had been known in Wales for generations as the Welsh Cocker. They were shorter in the ear and lacked the ear fringes of the rest of the family, and, if the dog Corrin of Gerwn is anything to go by, they were considerably larger than the average Cocker. Overnight, the Cocker Corrin of Gerwn, KCSB (Kennel Club Stud Book) Number 1391F, became the Welsh Springer Corrin of Gerwn, KCSB Number 894G. Even today there are some orange-and-white Cockers with shorter ears lacking fringes, and it is to be assumed that this is a legacy from their forebears of the last century.

Ancestors

Mr Farrow had begun making a name for himself in 1873 when his little black dog Emperor won a class at the Manchester Show. Exhibited at this and other shows were dogs from strains which were important in the history of the Cocker Spaniel. These included some bred by Phineas Bullock and by W. W. Boulton whose Beverley kennels were well known. In 1880, Mr Farrow's Obo went into the ring for the first time. He was a black dog whose parents were given as Fred and Betty. Fred was sired by Bebb who was a direct descendant, through Burdett's Bob, of Frank and Venus. Obo was soon a champion and is claimed to be the foundation of all Cocker Spaniels both here and in America. His grandsire Bebb was regarded in those days as an important sire, but it was Ch. Obo himself with his power of transmitting his qualities to his descendants who was, through his many champion offspring, to influence future generations and to be regarded as a pillar of the breed. As will be seen, the Cocker Spaniel of today can claim direct descent from him.

The railways were much used by breeders, and it is recorded that J. W. Robinson travelled from Newcastle via London with a bitch to visit Mr Farrow. The result of the union of the liver roan Tyneside Fancy with ten-year-old Ch. Obo was the black dog Rio. When Rio was put to the liver, white and tan Beauty III, a blue-roan dog later named Rivington Bluecoat was produced, both mother and son passing into the possession of C. A. Phillips when their owner gave up breeding.

Mr Phillips and his Rivingtons helped to pioneer an improvement in the breed based on the principles of a robust and capable working dog. He admired the strain of Cocker Spaniels owned by James Freme of Wepre Hall in Flintshire, and when on the death of their owner they came up for auction, he was able to obtain a black-and-white bitch who became known as Rivington Sloe. She was by Obo out of a bitch called Fan, and he put her to a black dog, Bredaboy (who was by Keno, a son of Obo and Young Rhea), to produce the black Rivington Signal, a dog who was to become important in the breed.

He also purchased from the Welsh border a black-and-white dog he named Rivington Jock. Although the dog had no papers, Mr Phillips was strongly of the opinion that he was from the same Wepre Hall blood. Jock was the sire of Rivington Blossom (black and white) who, when mated to Rivington Signal, produced the black-and-white bitch Rivington Bloom. From her, when put to Rivington Riot (a double grandson of Obo), the liver-roan Rivington Redcoat resulted. Redcoat was in due course sold to Monsieur Hazard in Paris, but later returned to this country and went into the kennels of Richard Lloyd at Ware in Hertfordshire, where he eventually finished out his days. It was said that Mr Lloyd 'fully reaped the benefit of this close and valuable infusion of the Obo blood in his coloured Cockers'.

Mr Lloyd founded his strain in 1875, though the of Ware affix was not adopted until a later date. It was based on the old Beverley and Bullock strains and descended from Burdett's Frank. He had bred a black, tan and white dog called Little Prince, whose liver daughter Myrtle, when mated to Rio, produced a liver bitch afterwards named Braeside Bizz. She was mated to his black dog Viceroy, who was by Toots (a direct descendant of Obo) out of a black bitch by Rivington Signal, and was sold in whelp to J. M. Porter. In the resulting litter, born in July 1894, was Braeside Bustle, a dog who was to become much in demand. He was described on his stud card as 'a very handsomely marked black and white flecked with black and blue, and often referred to as a blue roan', and was one of the earliest of that colour of any significance. He had many successes in the show ring and was described as 'a thorough, keen, hard worker, with plenty of stamina'. He transmitted the colour to nearly all his progeny and by the time he was five, his offspring were winning all over the country and on the Continent.

Braeside Bustle and Rivington Bluecoat were said to be of para-mount importance in establishing the coloured Cocker Spaniels (the blacks having been popular and dominant up to that time, with some black and tans and variations of liver). The black, white and tan Rivington Dora was produced from the lines of those two dogs and Rivington Redcoat on her sire's side, and on the dam's side a combination of the old blood of Alonzo, Ch. Fop and Alva Dash, who went back via Bebb to Frank and Venus but not by way of Obo.

The older history of the Cocker Spaniel is well documented in *The Sporting Spaniel* by C. A. Phillips and R. Claude Cane (Our Dogs) and *The Cocker Spaniel* by H. S. Lloyd (Our Dogs). In his book, Mr Phillips included the extended pedigree of Rivington Dora going back eighteen generations. How could he have guessed at its interest to students of pedigree nearly a hundred years on?

From Dora came Ch. Rivington Ruth, who was to have a considerable influence on the breed – solids as well as particolours. She was a liver, white and tan bitch who was higher on the leg than others being exhibited at the time. From her liaison with Ch. Doony Swell came, within four generations, Peacemaker of Ware, and from her later union with Fielding Blue Boy she became the great grandam of Corn Crake. Both Peacemaker and Corn Crake had important parts to play in the development of the show and working Cocker.

At about the same time as Braeside Bustle was making a name for himself, a dog who must surely be one of the earliest imports from North America arrived on the scene in the shape of a little black Cocker called Toronto. A visitor from Canada was asked by Mr Phillips to find him a suitable stud for his bitches, who he felt were beginning to lack in foreface. After surviving the adventures of a shipwreck, the puppy duly arrived in this country and, being strong in Obo blood, he subsequently fulfilled the demands made of him.

Braeside Bustle figured prominently in the pedigrees of the dogs owned by R. de C. Peele. He was the sire of Ch. Ben Bowdler, who in turn sired Ch. Bob Bowdler. Bob's son Ch. Dixon Bowdler was in his day considered to be the best blue roan ever seen, and he and Ben's other notable son, Ch. Doony Swell, were to become great grandsires to Fairholme Rally.

The owner of the Bowdlers, Mr Peele, had seen a black Cocker bitch named Schwab Powder running at trials, and he was so enamoured with her good looks that he purchased her and renamed her Jetsam Bowdler. Like Rivington Ruth, she was higher on the leg than those of the day, and it was Jetsam's entry into the show ring which initiated the progress of the more modern balanced type. When Mr Lloyd judged Cocker Spaniels at Crufts Show in 1905

Ch. Dixon Bowdler, from a painting by F.T. Daws, c. 1907.

(assisted by his son, the young H. S. Lloyd, as ring steward) he awarded the Challenge Certificate (CC) to Jetsam Bowdler, and it was often claimed later that his temerity in breaking away from the long, low type, which caused a sensation at the time, proved the turning point for the breed. Jetsam was, incidentally, entered in

The Gentlewoman, H.S. Lloyd's first Cocker Spaniel, bred by his father in 1901.

13

the 1905 Kennel Club Stud Book under Cocker dogs! However, by 1908, Ch. Jetsam Bowdler is credited with being the dam of Jock Bowdler (later Champion), also black, who through his great-grandson Rocklyn Magic was a forebear of the solids of today.

Meanwhile, Mr Phillips and Mr Peele had jointly purchased a big liver-and-tan dog, Lucky Traveller, of Field Spaniel blood. He was mated to Ch. Rivington Reine, who was by Heir Apparent, a grandson of Toronto. Two black bitches from the resulting litter were Rivington Arrow and Fan Bowdler, who formed respectively the foundation of the solid and particolour lines. Arrow was mated to Hampton Guard, a black dog imported from America by Mr Phillips and H. S. Lloyd, and carrying American and Obo blood. The result of this was a black dog, Ch. Rivington Rogue, who was the maternal grandsire of Rocklyn Magic. The sister, Fan Bowdler, was mated to the blue roan Dixon Bowdler, and from this union Fairholme Rally emerged in the third generation.

Achievement and Progression

The Cocker Spaniel made strides and was becoming popular at shows as well as at field trials, and a good many of the show dogs were useful gundogs too.

Jetsam Bowdler's type became the one to aim for. A reaction to the craze for elongated specimens had occurred and, with the advent of field trials, a more workmanlike active dog evolved. By then, the Cocker Spaniel was expected to retrieve game as well as to hunt. Because of Braeside Bustle, particolours came to the fore, and as many of them as blacks were winning. Up to this time the blacks had been almost invincible.

Women were beginning to take an interest in the breed, and soon more women than men were showing, and some were also training their dogs for trials. At Crufts Shows, even before the First World War, Cocker Spaniels had the biggest entry of any breed, entries of 120 being recorded.

The beautiful heads which had been in danger of being lost were again a feature of the Cocker Spaniel, exemplified in the black bitch Galtrees May, born in 1910, who was considered the most beautiful specimen up to that time produced. Her sire was Rivington Regent, a closely bred dog by Ch. Rivington Rogue, and her dam was Galtrees Nell, by Hampton Guard, thus doubling up on the imported line. But it was two of her sisters, the liver Galtrees Flora and the black Doony Dora, who were to leave their mark: the former as grandam of Ch. Pinbrook Scamp, and the latter as dam of Ch. Hampton Marquis whose blood contributed to the success of the Fulmer kennel.

Ch. Doony Swell was a great influence on type and Grindon Gerald, his blue-roan grandson from the union with Ch. Rivington Ruth, created records. Gerald and Galtrees May were examples of the more balanced, compact type that was by then becoming established, and such Cockers were the fruit of the struggle of the pioneers of the breed. From systematic selection from the limited and mixed material available, they had developed a dog possessing many of the characteristic points of the smaller type, combined with much of the beauty of the larger spaniels. The Cocker Spaniel had evolved from interbreeding with all varieties of the sporting spaniel, a task which was undertaken for a specific purpose and with the utmost patience, for breeding cannot be hurried. The objective had been to create a sporting dog with liberty of movement and emphasis on a merry, working character, and the result was a distinct and popular variety of spaniel.

Shows in 1913 and 1914 had large entries and judges found sufficient numbers of consistent type to fill the awards. Breeders were congratulated on the 'uniform excellence' of the exhibits.

The Falconers of Mrs Jamieson Higgens and the Fulmers of Mrs Fytche were becoming kennels to be reckoned with. Fulmer Peat must have made an impression on Mr Farrow, for when he awarded him a CC, he described the dog as 'hot stuff', a somewhat modern expression from a Victorian gentleman who was exhibiting in the 1870s! Many of the Fulmers were piloted by Charles Griffiths, whose own kennel was Colinette, and whose son Jack was known to a later generation of breeders as a respected Championship Show judge.

Naturally the breed suffered some setbacks because of the war, and afterwards good stud-dogs were scarce. However, the black Rocklyn Magic, belonging to Miss G. Lloyd, proved a useful sire. He and F. Gordon George's blue-roan Fairholme Rally were extensively used. Solids of the present day trace back to Rocklyn Magic through his great-grandson Dominorum D'Arcy, and particolours trace back to Rally through his grandson Ch. Invader of Ware. Rally was successful at trials, and both he and Magic had immense influence on field trial and show pedigrees. As there was no great choice of

Mrs Jamieson Higgens with Falconers Chita (13 CCs) and Falconers Careful (8 CCs).

stud-dogs, particolour stock in particular was closely bred to Rally for the next few years. He had many good points which he passed on to his progeny and uniformity of type was soon regained, but hindquarters were not his strong point and breeders had to give attention to them for some generations.

During the 1920s, the breed collectively appeared level in main essentials, but dogs in the ring were rather statuesque, perhaps subdued by modern handling methods. Their predecessors were considered superior in action, their characteristic animation and restless movement being one of the special features of the breed.

Liver roans were again becoming popular and some really good ones were produced, such as the multiple CC winners Langmoor Flora and Daphne of Dunkery. Another was Church Leigh Bess who had ten CCs to her credit. Although she was mistakenly recorded as blue roan in the KCSB, contemporary evidence proves otherwise. The prior unpopularity of the colour was attributed to the difficult coat, but with careful grooming discoloured shading could be avoided. Certainly the dogs in old photographs did not carry the dead hair which some exhibitors now leave on their dogs as feathering. A glaring light eye often accompanied the colour, but in the best specimens this had been bred out.

16

More people were becoming interested in the breed, and Cocker Spaniels were creeping up the registration table. In 1923 they were fourth on the list with 2,718 dogs registered. A top winner of those days, with twenty CCs, was Fulmer Ben, by Fairholme Rally. Others included three who had qualified for the title, namely his son Ch. L'ile Beau Brummel, Ch. Pinbrook Scamp, and Ch. Invader of Ware who proved an exceptional stud-dog and stamped his likeness on his progeny for generations to come. He was never beaten in the show ring and, together with his litter-brother Illuminator of Ware, achieved a unique double. They both won CCs at simultaneous shows, one at Edinburgh and the other at Brighton, a feat that is unlikely to be equalled now that the Kennel Club calendar is so strictly regulated.

Influences

Ch. Invader of Ware's pedigree is an interesting one. He descends on his sire's side through Fairholme Rally from Fan Bowdler's mating to Ch. Dixon Bowdler. On the dam's side, there is a double line back through Grindon Gerald to the Doony Swell and Rivington

Ch. Invader of Ware, Luckystar of Ware and Whoopee of Ware. (Fall.)

Ruth link. Invader was claimed to have given his progeny the neck and shoulders breeders were seeking, so that Cocker Spaniels were better able to carry out retrieving work in the field, a task which their ancestors had not been expected to do. This feature was assumed to have come through his dam's sire Barnsford Brigadier, a good working dog, whose sire, Peacemaker of Ware, was a great-grandson of Ch. Dixon Bowdler and Ch. Tissington Frocks, both owned by Mr Peele in the early years of the century. Tissington Frocks was an English Springer Spaniel, sired by Tissington Silence, also classified as a Springer. Little was recorded of the history of Tissington Silence and though his parents were given as Dash and Flush (unregistered), a question mark always hung over his true origins. His very name gave an air of mystery, and setter blood was suspected. Writers stated that English Springer blood contained a setter cross, but it was not until some years after the time of Ch. Invader of Ware that information emerged, from a source close to the Tissington kennels, confirming the suspicion that the sire of Tissington Silence was indeed an English Setter, namely Carew Rollick. Perhaps with the changing of names which occurred in the past, Carew Rollick might have been the same Dash who appeared in the breeding of many setters. With the mixing of blood that took place in the early days, it is not unlikely that such a mating occurred, and this would indeed account for the improved neck and shoulders in Cocker Spaniels. At any rate, with his physical and working attributes, Invader was the dog to set the seal on the modern type started off by Jetsam Bowdler.

The year 1924 is marked by the Kennel Club introducing a separate Field Trial Championship Stake for Cockers for the first time, and this was won by F.T.Ch. Elibank Attention, a grandson of Rocklyn Magic. Twenty-three sets of CCs were awarded, and the blue-roan dog Southernwood Critic took top spot at the Kennel Club show, going Best Exhibit against all breeds, an honour he was to achieve again a few years later. He was from the kennel of F. C. Dickinson, the owner of the Rocklyn affix.

The sire of Southernwood Critic was Corn Crake, a blue-roan dog born in Ireland, by Dyrons Bluecoat, who was a grandson of Ch. Rivington Ruth when mated to Fielding Blue Boy. Corn Crake had a tremendous influence on the breed and was an ancestor common to both solids and particolours. The solid influence in his own pedigree was not far back, Fielding Blue Boy being by the red Ch. Rufus Bowdler, and his dam descending from the Arabian strain.

H.S. Lloyd's Dominorum D'Arcy. (Fall.)

At the Bath Show in 1925, the judge D. McDonald praised the high all-round quality of the exhibits, especially the puppies. He remarked on three of them just making their appearance: Cobnar Critic, Dominorum D'Arcy and 'a gem of a tricolour' Falconers Cowslip who won the CC on the day. Cobnar Critic, a blue roan, was by Southernwood Critic, Dominorum D'Arcy was by Corn Crake, and Falconers Cowslip, bred by H. S. Lloyd, was by Ch. Invader of Ware. All three were destined to have an impact on the breed. Cobnar Critic, owned by C. V. Barraclough, was bred by Mrs Higgens from her old-established strain, and he and Cowslip together were responsible for a further important line of Falconers bitches; Critic was also the grandsire of the blue-roan Luckystar of Ware.

The black dog Dominorum D'Arcy became a great stud and also figured in the early breeding of the Oxshotts and Misbournes. He was the grandsire of Bazel Otto, who was the starting-point for the Treetops and other later kennels, and to whom solids of today trace allegiance. D'Arcy's dam, Dominorum Diana, was a product via Rocklyn Magic of the descent from Obo via the solid line of Toronto and Rivington Arrow; but Corn Crake, to whom she was mated, can be traced down the particolour line from Obo via Braeside Bustle and Rivington Ruth.

Ch. Invader of Ware also came from Obo via Braeside Bustle and Rivington Ruth, then Peacemaker of Ware on the dam's side, but via Toronto, Fan Bowdler and Fairholme Rally on the sire's side.

Corn Crake and his grandson Cobnar Critic, together with Invader, formed the foundation upon which future breeding of both particolours and solids was established.

Differences

During the 1920s, there was some controversy regarding the matter of 'Pocket Cockers'. Size had long been a debatable issue, but when some innovators attempted to breed Cocker Spaniels of ridiculously small proportions, devotees were up in arms. Dogs who were the misfits from Field Spaniel litters of the past, the small and weedy ones, had been termed Cockers, and it had taken breeders many years of patience and hard work after the abolition of the 25lb weight limit to consolidate the breed at the standardized level it then enjoyed. They were not going to allow it to be ruined by miniaturization, which the Cocker Spaniel Club regarded as retrograde and detrimental to the breed.

A weight recommendation of 25–28lb (11.5–12.5kg) had only in 1921 been inserted into the Standard. The breed was stable within that guide, and the Cocker Spaniel was able to meet the needs of a sportsman who wanted a single dog to last all day. The Club took a stand and a resolution was passed at the 1925 Annual General Meeting to the effect that the Club would not offer specials or guarantee classes at any show where 'Pocket Cockers' were scheduled, and that members should not exhibit or judge at such shows.

Nonetheless, the Cocker Spaniel made progress. He was popular in the ring and as a housedog. As a gundog, he had proved that he could carry out the work required of him as ably as any larger spaniel. There were still pleas to preserve the working instincts of the dog along with his good looks, in the belief that the future of the breed lay in a dog with beauty and brains. But a gulf was beginning to separate the show fraternity from practical shooting men and in the next decade, by the time of the Second World War, this division was more or less complete.

The Glorious Age

From the beginning of the 1930s, it was the particolours who were to become the big names and take the breed before the public eye as never before. Luckystar of Ware emulated his forebear Southernwood Critic by winning Best in Show at one of the major events, but this time it was Crufts in 1930. With Charles Cruft's skill for staging the spectacular, and with royal patronage too, the winners of his shows had their picture in every newspaper and journal in the land. Luckystar of Ware accomplished the feat a second time, and with his likeness appearing on all manner of objects and souvenirs, the Cocker Spaniel soon became familiar to all.

The breed's disposition and looks resulted in its becoming more and more popular with the public, and more people were taking an interest in the Cocker Spaniel as a show dog. Records were being created within the breed, and individuals were taking top awards against all varieties. The blue-roan Whoopee of Ware won fifty-six CCs, a record which stood for twenty years, and his grandson Silver Templa of Ware, another blue roan, was also highly successful. Whoopee of Ware, who was probably the most prepotent sire at the time, was a grandson of Ch. Invader of Ware through his sire Ch. Churchdene Invader; his dam Foxham Minx was by Corn Crake. Silver Flare of Ware, the sire of Silver Templa, was a grandson of Southernwood Critic.

There were more good dogs about than ever before, probably as a result of improved transport and more shows, which enabled owners to see and use a wider selection of studs. Regional breed clubs were formed to foster enthusiasm. The Midland Club, still flourishing today, started twenty years earlier. Satisfaction was expressed at the growing popularity of the Cocker, but protectors of the breed warned that too great a popularity could lead to decay.

The Oxshott, Blaedown and Sixshot kennels were already well established; Captain R. George (Nene Valley) and A. B. Nicolson (Glenbervie) were notable Championship Show judges, and the black bitch Valerie of Misbourne was winning CCs for Miss Dorothy Hahn and her mother.

Exquisite Model of Ware, a tricolour daughter of Whoopee of Ware, took the breed to the heights again when she reigned supreme at Crufts both in 1938 and 1939 and won a total of fifty-three CCs. Her kennel companion was the striking black, white and tan dog, Sir Galahad of Ware, a multiple CC winner who was described

21

Exquisite Model of Ware, from a painting by Frank Aveline exhibited at the Royal Academy 1939.

as the most perfect Cocker Spaniel yet produced. Probably more than any other dog, he influenced the future of the particolour, and it is likely that all today's particolours of show breeding can trace their ancestry through him. His was a remarkable achievement in a short space of time as he was exported to India when only four years old. He was by Manxman of Ware who was by Whoopee of Ware, and his mother was Falconers Confidence, a Silver Flare daughter. He was bred by Mrs Higgens from generations of Falconers matrons. Mrs Higgens was a very conscientious breeder who bred carefully to type and retained mainly bitches with whom she was very successful in the ring. She often passed the males to the kennel of H. S. Lloyd and in due time used Sir Galahad to her bitches, producing in particular Falconers Padlock of Ware and Falconers Wisdom. From Wisdom she bred Falconers Mark of Ware, and both he and Padlock became important studs.

Sir Galahad of Ware. (Fall.)

H.S. Lloyd's Bazel Otto. (Fall.)

Treetops Talkie, sire of Treetops Terrific. (Fall.)

Meanwhile, the reds and goldens had made headway, and Treetops Turtledove played her part in bringing the breed to the fore when she was awarded Best in Show at the Blackpool Championship Show in 1938. (Strangely, despite their later popularity, only one other Cocker Spaniel of this colour is recorded as going best against all breeds at a Championship Show.) The black Treetops Treasure Trove, a daughter of Bazel Otto and Felbrigg Hortensia, had laid the foundation for Judy de Casembroot's Treetops strain which was to become famous worldwide, the owner in due time gaining a singular reputation as an international judge of many breeds.

During this period, other notable kennels were appearing which were to become household names to Cocker Spaniel lovers at a later date. Affixes such as Colinwood, Ide and Weirdene were registered at the Kennel Club, and the Merryworths started breeding with Falconers bitches. The Lochranza and Broomleaf strains had much to thank the Treetops for in securing their own foundations. Treasure Trove was grandam to Treetops Terrific, sire of Sixshot Black Swan. Black Swan, a grandson of Bazel Otto on his dam's side, won CCs and, although his show career was cut short because of the war, he made his name as a stud force.

The Red Cocker

Looking back into the history of the Cocker Spaniel, we find that blacks have long been numerous, and blue roans, too, since the days of Braeside Bustle. Variations of liver have often been present, but there has been little said about the reds. Mention occurs of the colour at odd times in history, and a debate on both sides of the Atlantic in the American Press in the early 1900s as to the supposed origin of the colour makes fascinating reading; but during the developing stages of the breed the colour was hardly taken up.

Way back at the turn of the twentieth century, some reds were bred from a red-and-white bitch, possibly of Welsh Cocker origin, mated to a black Cocker dog. One of them was Molly of Gerwn, a well-known field trialler. Rouge Bowdler and Ch. Rufus Bowdler apparently just turned up. Reds were not looked upon favourably, and the only people to further them seriously were Mr and Mrs Trinder who had the Arabian strain. Their breeding was based on Toronto and an imported red dog called Canadian Red Jacket; Rufus Bowdler (whose sire Blue Peter was by Braeside Bustle) was also involved. The later import Hampton Guard, who came from a red male line, also produced some of this colour and helped in their development. Unfortunately, other breeders who were keen on the colour bred red to red with a disregard to type; reds were poor in conformation and were rarely seen in the ring.

It was not until after the First World War that interest was taken with the intention of improving them. Breeders had to strive to correct throatiness, big feet, heavy heads and straight hocks. H. S. Lloyd imported from Canada a black dog he named Broadcaster of Ware who was descended from Ch. Obo, and he proved beneficial. He had a well-chiselled head with definite stop, cleanness of cheek, good depth of brisket and powerful quarters.

In the 1920s, Judge Townsend Scudder in the United States acquired a dog called Blackstone Chief, from the Obo line. From Chief he bred Robinhurst Foreglow, and these two created a great impression on the breed there. Robinhurst of Ware, a grandson of Foreglow and already a proven sire before being shipped, was selected as likely to help in correcting faults in reds in the UK.

Although a deep red of Irish Setter hue had been the usual colour, lighter shades were coming into favour, so when a club was formed in 1928 for the encouragement and furtherance of the colour, it wisely took the name of the Red and Golden Cocker Spaniel Club.

The solid-coloured breeding stock available at the time was partly made up of blacks descended from Rocklyn Magic and Ch. Pinbrook Scamp. Added to this was the influence of the imported dogs, and the occasional infiltration of the particolour blood of Fairholme Rally and his grandson Ch. Invader of Ware. With this material and the support of the Club, kennels such as Byfleet, Sorrelsun, Lightwater, Garnes, Ottershaw, Woodcock, Waldiff and of Sauls were able to make improvements in succeeding generations. Their perseverance and careful breeding overcame various disappointments and tribulations, so that in the early 1930s no fewer than six of the colour were able to win CCs at the shows. Prior to this, Pinbrook Amber, born in 1924, Fairholme Kathleen, born 1909, and Ch. Rufus Bowdler, 1900, were the only reds to have achieved the award.

Not averse to using particolours to strengthen their lines, breeders used the blue-roan dog Luckystar of Ware, whose mother Wildflower of Ware was sired by Ch. Invader of Ware (who carried solid blood on both sides going back to the Arabian strain). A red son of Luckystar, Lodestar of Sorrelsun, proved important as a sire. In particular Lodestar's daughter, Golden Glory of Byfleet, became the grandam of Treetops Turkey Trot, who in turn was the grandam of Lochranza Lotinga. Lotinga was the dam of the black Ch. Lochranza Latchkey, the first of Miss Joan Macmillan's big winners.

During the 1930s, reds came on in leaps and bounds, and with Treetops Turtledove, Treetops Tristan and a few more adding to the number of ticket winners, the red or golden Cocker Spaniel was certainly here to stay.

Popularity Maintained

As war approached, it was hoped that some breeders would be in a position to maintain their strains in a limited way, and they were advised to retain young bitches for their bloodlines rather than for individual virtue. Experience gained from previous restrictions had taught its lesson: one able dog could serve many, but good bitches were scarce. As it turned out, shows were not prohibited, but only restricted or radius events took place. With the help of public interest in their stock, breeders had been able to keep strains going, and when the first Championship Show was held after the war their efforts were rewarded.

Mr A.W. Collins's tricolour dog Blackmoor Brand. (Thurse.)

This event was the Cocker Spaniel Club Show of 1946 which proved very successful with a record entry of 715. The level of quality was so good that authorities considered that it was on a par with pre-war standards and that the breed in general had not altered a great deal in thirty years. Kennels that were beginning to have successes would become the substance of the breed in the future. Into the ring came dogs whose names would go down in history.

By winning CCs early and gaining a qualifying certificate at a field trial, the tricolour Colinwood Cowboy soon became the breed's first post-war champion. He was a prolific and successful sire, and his descendants have gained distinction in many parts of the world. He was from Ottershaw and Blackmoor breeding; and through his sire Blackmoor Brand, he was a great-grandson of Sir Galahad of Ware and was to form one of the major links to the present day.

He was soon followed to the title by a trio belonging to Joe Braddon: Golden Rod of Ide (golden), Blue Flash of Ide (blue roan) and Rodwood Lass of Sandover (tricolour). Then came Ch. Broom-

Ch. Broomleaf Bonny Lad of Shillwater.

leaf Bonny Lad of Shillwater (golden), Ch. Oxshott Marxedes (a blue roan who won twenty-eight CCs) and Ch. Lochranza Latchkey (black) – all names to conjure with. Tracey Witch of Ware, a daughter of Falconers Padlock of Ware, took the breed to the heights yet again by winning Best in Show at consecutive Crufts in 1948 and 1950. It was recorded that in the year 1950, Witch made only four appearances in the ring. She won four CCs, was Best in Show all breeds at three of them and runner-up at the fourth. She had a good run over the years, taking her fifty-second CC when almost eight years old.

In the early days, dogs of any breed who had won three CCs could be called Champion. However, in 1909 it was ruled that dogs of gundog breeds must obtain a qualifying certificate at work in the field before being granted the title. The rule still stands today. Some full champions were duly made up, but with social changes people from many walks of life were beginning to take an interest in dogs

Falconers Careful, dam of Falconers Padlock of Ware. (Fall.)

and showing and few were in a position to have their dogs trained to the gun. Many big winners were deprived of their recognition. Old pedigrees and literature will show many famous dogs, in fact with numerous CCs to their credit, who because of their lack of working qualification, not necessarily of ability, did not have the right to a title. It was not until some years later that the Show Champion title was introduced.

Mr Phillips (Rivington) and Mrs Higgens (Falconers), both of whom had worked so hard for the breed, were gratified to see it at the standard it had by then attained. The breed suffered a great loss at their passing. To say that their knowledge and guiding influence had played an important part in the moulding and development of the Cocker Spaniel through the previous half-century or more is an understatement. The Falconers bloodline was bequeathed to H. S. Lloyd and is maintained in the present day by his heirs.

2

Modern Times

The overall standard of the breed had been well maintained and the Cocker Spaniel continued its universal popularity; registrations still exceeded those of any other breed and entries at shows were high. In 1950, with no restrictions on the number of dogs competing, the Cocker Spaniel entry at Crufts reached 1,008 from 432 dogs.

In 1914 there had been 400 Cocker Spaniels registered; in 1935, the figure had risen to 7,656 and on to an astounding 27,096 in 1947. Kennel Club registrations have always been regarded as a popularity poll for dogs, and in the 1930s and 1940s, the Cocker Spaniel was right at the top. This in fact brought problems, as back-street breeders exploited the market with anything that resembled the country's most wanted pet. Thankfully, registrations dropped back to around 7,000 and remained so for some thirty years, but this nonetheless ensured to this day a continuing place in the top ten. It was believed, though, that half of those born remained unregistered and when, in 1989, new rules required the whole litter to be registered, numbers indeed jumped to over 12,000.

A glossy magazine *The Cocker Journal* was published monthly, providing breeders with news, comment, advertising and features. It had a big overseas circulation, but was badly supported here. Even after extending its coverage to include a gundog review, it was unable to maintain publication and ceased in 1956 after only seven years. However, bound copies became collectors' items and those who possess them, particularly in the United States, regard them as an invaluable source of history and information.

In 1958, the Kennel Club decided, after consultation with interested parties and in accordance with the wishes of the majority, to retain the qualifying certificate for dogs to become full champions. In addition, because of overwhelming support for alternative recognition, the title of Show Champion was introduced. It was understood that the title could be used retrospectively.

Criticism was made that gundog breeds would be ruined and that they would lose their sporting instincts. It was also thought that exhibitors, once their dog had one title, would not bother to undertake the process of achieving the outright title of Champion. The Kennel Club did not agree and, in view of the support for the proposal, were happy to grant the new title which they hoped would be regarded as an intermediate one.

In the ten years up to 1958, twenty Cocker Spaniels qualified in the field and gained the full title. Of these, six belonged to Joe Braddon (of Ide) and five to A. W. Collins (Colinwood). Regrettably, in the thirty years after the introduction of the Show Champion title, only fifteen further Cocker Spaniels became full champions. These figures perhaps bear out the views of the critics, since owners appear content to settle for the Show title alone. Five of those fifteen dogs were owned by Arthur Mansfield, whose achievements were remarkable. His Lucklena kennel usually housed no more than four or five dogs, yet six full champions in all were made up in different generations. Mr Mansfield took pride in his breeding, always presented his dogs immaculately in the ring and, despite living in an urban area, managed to train his own dogs to their qualifying certificate. Others were exported and became champions in various countries, including Australia, Argentina, Sweden and Bermuda.

On the Right Lines

Mrs K. Doxford's Broomleaf Black and Tan (a retrospective Show Champion) created a sensation when she became one of the few of her colour before or since to win a CC. She was from a solid to particolour mating, by the red dog Ch. Broomleaf Bonny Lad of Shillwater, and out of the blue-roan-and-tan Butterfly of Broomleaf. Bonny Lad, a great grandson of Treetops Terrific, sired numerous other winners too, and his influence on the solid colours was considerable. One of his outstanding daughters was R. H. Wylde's golden bitch Ch. Solinda of Traquair, who became a matron of the breed and in particular was responsible for Lochranza Eldwythe Exceed, the sire of Sh.Ch. Lochranza Dancing Master. Dancing Master started off an unbroken string of successes for Joan Macmillan. Her Lochranza solids dominated the show ring for the next fifteen or so years, and she turned out one champion after another, all from the same mould. Many breeders in all parts of the world are indebted to Miss Macmillan for stud-dogs and foundation stock.

31

Sh.Ch. Pickpocket of Misbourne. (Fall.)

Another by Bonny Lad was the black Sh.Ch. Pickpocket of Misbourne. On more than one occasion, he and his black daughter Sh.Ch. Wendayle Valjolie of Misbourne fought it out for Best of Breed having taken both tickets for their owner Miss Hahn.

Rivalling Bonny Lad as a sire were Mrs V. Lucas-Lucas's red Sixshot dogs, Willy Wagtail and his son Sh.Ch. Woody Woodpecker, both of whom contributed greatly to the breed. In fact, amalgamations of Sixshot and Broomleaf lines were often made by breeders with much success. Willy Wagtail was a son of Sixshot Black Swan. Both kennels continued to produce many winning dogs and bitches of key importance to the breed.

The Colinwood kennel of A. W. Collins housed numerous dogs, both particolour and solid, who were very successful in the ring and at stud. Several became full champions and some, like Ch. Colinwood Son-of-a-Gun, gained their qualifier for the title in actual competition at a field trial. The Colinwood fame spread worldwide,

Sixshot Black Swan. (Fall.)

particularly through Ch. Colinwood Cowboy, sire of many champions at home and abroad, including Ch. Colinwood Firebrand and Sh.Ch. Ronfil Regent.

The Colinwood reputation was further enhanced with the success of the great Ch. Colinwood Silver Lariot, a blue roan who dominated the ring for several years. His total of fifty-seven CCs created a new record for the breed, which still stands for a male. He was also nine times Best in Show at All-Breed Championship Shows, an achievement unrivalled by any Cocker Spaniel since.

He was sired by Joywyns Blue Flash out of Truslers Misty Morn who was by Firebrand. It is interesting to note that Blue Flash was litter-brother to Sh.Ch. Joywyns Blueboy of Ware, a light blue, admired especially for his elegant head carriage and his style. Through Cartref dogs, these two were line-bred to Falconers Padlock of Ware. Interestingly too, their dam Cartref Charmer was a granddaughter of Blue Bonnet of Broomleaf, who was a half-sister to Sh.Ch. Broomleaf Black and Tan. To get Blue Bonnet, Mrs Doxford had put Butterfly to her lovely liver, white and tan dog, Bumble of Broomleaf. Both Silver Lariot and Blueboy were in

Cornbow Myosotis. (M.G. Jones.)

demand at stud, and between them formed much of the background to particolour breeding right down to the present day.

Though much-travelled as a judge on the Continent and in Scandinavia before and after the war, H. S. Lloyd could never be persuaded to judge in Britain during his highly successful showing years. However, he finally gave in to a request by the Midland Cocker Spaniel Club and judged bitches at their Championship Show in 1954. His choice on the day for the CC was a golden bitch, Cornbow Myosotis, owned by the Clarke brothers. She was of Treetops breeding and, being by Treetops Foxbar Cognac, was descended three generations from Sixshot Black Swan. In time she was mated to Broomleaf Bonny Lad, and from this the Cornbow line increased in strength. The present generation can all be traced back to Myosotis. Her red daughter Cornbow Miss Ottis was dam of Cornbow Mint Tea, who was carefully line-bred to Bonny Lad to produce the black dog Cornbow Manfred, the significance of which will be shown later. His sire Sh.Ch. Quettadene Mark, jointly owned by Mrs E. Woodbridge (Quettadene) and Leslie Page (Dellah), was by that great black dog Sh.Ch. Lochranza Merryleaf Eigar, a son of Dancing Master. Eigar's family history is interesting in that his maternal grandam, Merrythought Flare, was born in the United States. His breeder, Mrs K. R. Farquhar, was a good friend of Mrs L. Collier Platt, a former secretary of the English Cocker Spaniel Club of America, and as a result of an interchange of dogs across the Atlantic, Flare found a home with Mrs Farquhar. She must be one of the few modern Cocker Spaniel imports to Great Britain, although her lineage had close ties with England. She was out of Am. Ch. Broomleaf Ballet Skirt and her sire, Am. Ch. Merrythought Jiggs, was a grandson of Am. Ch. Surrey On Time Morse Code, a particolour-bred black grandson of Merryworth Mariner. In due course, Merrythought Flare had a daughter, Merryleaf Corinne, by Bally Atom of Broomleaf, and as a result of Corinne's visit to Dancing Master, Sh.Ch. Lochranza Merryleaf Eigar was born. Bally Atom was descended many times from Bonny Lad and Sixshot Willy Wagtail.

Another son of Eigar was the red Sh.Ch. Astrawin April Fire, whose dam was by Sh.Ch. Valjoker of Misbourne, a son of Valjolie. April Fire came from a line of Astrawin bitches, a strain established by Mr and Mrs S. Wise and continued by Phyllis with success

Bally Atom of Broomleaf. (Fall.)

35

to the present time. The black Valjoker was a successful sire of the day, his black daughter Sh.Ch. Colinwood Bunting being outstanding.

A grandson of Valjoker, the golden dog Val of Lochnell (later Show Champion) provided Mrs Marjorie Cameron, after many years in the breed, with her first CC win in 1963. After breeding Cocker Spaniels in Scotland for shooting, she moved south after the war and built up a strain of show Cockers, starting with Motala and Ulwell stock. Lochnells of all colours proliferated and many won honours abroad and at home in the hands of other people. Particularly noteworthy was the black Sh.Ch. Colinwood Jackdaw of Lochnell (line-bred to Dancing Master), who notched up a fine tally of thirteen CCs for Miss Phyllis Collins (later Mrs Woolf).

Some years earlier Mrs Cameron had bred the bitch Black Jade of Lochnell who became a show champion for Jimmy Auld's Glencora kennel in Scotland. From Black Jade, Mr Auld bred Sh.Ch. Glencora Black Ace (by Sixshot The Black Cockatoo, a son of Willy Wagtail), who became significant in the future of the solid-colour Cocker Spaniels. One of Black Ace's progeny was the golden bitch Sh.Ch. Lochdene Pepper Pot, bred and owned by another exhibitor resident in Scotland, Mrs P. G. Tosh (later Mrs Shaw), who always has a number of high-quality Cockers in her kennels who are infrequently exposed to the show scene.

Another old-established Scottish kennel is Noslien which has had successes over the years, including the distinguished achievement of taking both CCs at Crufts, in 1966, with the black dog Sh.Ch. Noslien Nathaniel and the red bitch Sh.Ch. Noslien Naughty Nineties.

Also in Scotland is Weirdene, a prominent kennel established as far back as 1927. Housing all colours, it came very much into the limelight in the 1960s when one champion and no fewer than five show champions were in the kennel at one time. With a kennel of this quality, it was not unusual for the names of five or six of Richmond Weir's dogs to appear in the list of CC winners in one year. Of particular influence on particolours was the black-and-white dog Sh.Ch. Wells Fargo of Weirdene, who was a grandson of Sh.Ch. Joywyns Blueboy of Ware. The lovely orange-roan Sh.Ch. Cochise Circe was just one of Wells Fargo's successful children and the first of several champions bred by Lt.-Com. and Mrs H. Blake. Weirdene and Noslien are close behind winning Lynwaters of today.

36

Sh.Ch. Joywyns Blueboy of Ware. (Fall.)

Singing the Blues

The next link in the particolour line was a grandson of Sh.Ch. Wells Fargo of Weirdene, the light-blue-roan dog Sh.Ch. Courtdale Flag Lieutenant, owned in South Wales by Mrs Sylvia Jones. His sire, Courtdale Colinwood Seahawk, was by Ch. Colinwood Silver Lariot (as was Sh.Ch. Cochise Circe's dam). Flag had a successful show career and made a great impression on the breed. His influence was considerable worldwide and his descendants numerous. He produced over thirty champions at home and abroad, including two full champions, Ch. Light Music of Lucklena and Ch. Scolys Showpiece, and five American champions. His name can be found behind a great deal of today's particolour breeding. (His pedigree is given in Appendix 3, page 251.)

He was followed by the outstanding blue-roan dog Ch. Ouainé Chieftain who ended up with a total of thirty-two CCs. Apart from gaining his full title here, he also won in Southern Ireland to become an Irish champion. He became a predominant sire in particolours.

He was carefully bred in 1968 by Mrs Joyce Caddy from a combination of Joe Braddon's champions to her original bitch line, thus consolidating on the old Falconers strain. Chieftain can be easily traced back to the Sir Galahad link. To take a random example, his grandsire Ch. Domino of Ide was a son of Ch. Rodwood Lass of Sandover who was by Falconers Mark of Ware. On the dam's side his maternal grandmother Ouainé Pandora was by Sh.Ch. Dellah Merrymaker of Wykey (seventeen CCs), one of the sons of Sh.Ch. Joywyns Blueboy of Ware.

Another son of Blueboy who had made an impression on the particolour line was the black-and-white dog Goldenfields Minstrel Boy. From his liaison with Craigleith Heathermaid (by Ch. Colinwood Silver Lariot), Mrs Mollie Robinson bred her blue-roan favourites Ch. Craigleith Cinderella and Craigleith The Boy Friend. The descendants of these two and their tricolour brother, Can. Ch. Craigleith Vagabond King, are scattered around the world.

Probably the greatest impact on Cocker Spaniels at the time was made by a light-blue-roan son of Goldenfields Minstrel Boy, Ch. Scolys Starduster, who was widely used at stud. Chief among his children was the light-blue-roan bitch Ch. Bournehouse Starshine

Ch. Scolys Starduster (Anne Roslin-Williams.)

who must surely be classed among 'the greats'. She was owned and bred by Gordon Williams from a daughter of Sh.Ch. The Mataroa of Merrybray (a son of Sh.Ch. Courtdale Flag Lieutenant). She was often handled by Mrs Marion France (Peelers), and was a great favourite with the ringside, displaying happy Cocker character with typical bustling movement. She won the Group at Crufts in 1976. While accumulating CCs, she had many a battle for Best of Breed with two black Lochranza dogs, Newsprint and his son News-reader. Her final total of sixty CCs was a new, and as yet unbroken, record for the breed.

About this time Mrs Phyllis Masters took on a young black-and-white dog from his former pet home, to become Sh.Ch. Chrisolin Cambiare of Styvechale and a prominent sire of his day. He was a great-grandson of Wells Fargo, and he and Styvechale Stormcloud feature prominently in the breeding of today's particolours.

The name of Sh.Ch. Leabank Levity, a blue-roan son of Ch. Scolys Starduster, appears in many pedigrees, both on his own account and through his blue son, Sh.Ch. Dearnewood Star Ven-

Mr and Mrs R. Richardson's Sh.Ch. Dearnewood Star Venture.
(Anne Roslin-Williams.)

ture who was widely used in the 1980s. Star Venture sired two show champions, Mistfall Mood Indigo and Remola Zola at Dearnewood, as well as several champions overseas. In 1991, his son Okell Outward Bound became a full champion (*see* page 240).

The successful Bitcon line of Moray Armstrong has been built up from his first show champion, Bitcon Blue Model, a Levity daughter born in 1972. Taking his bitches to such dogs as Sh.Ch. Crosbeian Cascade and Sh.Ch. Ramiro of Ronfil, he has bred a succession of show champion bitches culminating in the winning of the CC at Crufts in 1991 with his first dog title holder Sh.Ch. Bitcon Pacific Blue. Pacific Blue (by Ouainé Silver Buck) was out of Sh.Ch. Bitcon Shy Talk, who was by Mistfall Meddler (a Star Venture grandson), out of a daughter of Cascade and Blue Model. Cascade was sired by an inmate of the Colinwood kennel, Glencora Moyhill Mallory, who was by Mr Auld's Sh.Ch. Colinwood Cobbler, a grandson of Cowboy; his dam was by Thornfalcon Foxtrot, a grandson of Sh.Ch. Tracey Witch of Ware. Sh.Ch. Ramiro of Ronfil by Dutch Ch. Yardew Constellation, a son of Starduster, was owned by Mrs T. M.

Sh.Ch. Cilleine Echelon. (Hartley.)

Bebb in Wales. He was from her successful Ronfil bitch line, and had nineteen CCs to his credit.

Undoubtedly one of the stars of the 1980s was the blue-roan Sh.Ch. Cilleine Echelon. This dog soon won thirty-six CCs, and was a dominant sire whose services were sought into old age. He continued to be a regular on the show scene, often winning Veteran classes. He was line-bred to Ch. Scolys Starduster, and to Sh.Ch. Courtdale Flag Lieutenant through his Styvechale dam. His maternal grandsire Styvechale Stormcloud was by Sh.Ch. Normanview Thundercloud, who came from a base comprising, in the third generation, Ch. Ouainé Chieftain, Sh.Ch. Wells Fargo of Weirdene and Sh.Ch. Weirdene Questing Strathspey.

Following the evergreen Echelon came the black-and-white dog Sh.Ch. Matterhorn Montana, who was home-bred in Wales by Howard Jones. He was by Sh.Ch. Matterhorn Mick The Miller, who was by Coltrim Confederate of Craigleith, a Wells Fargo grandson. Montana was Best of Breed at Crufts and Cocker of the Year in 1985 before being exported and gaining his American title.

The acquisition from Scotland by Mr and Mrs E. W. Darby of the blue-roan Normanview Midnight Runner of Classicway (who

Normanview Midnight Runner of Classicway. (Anne Roslin-Williams.)

descends several times over from Sh.Ch. Normanview Thunder-cloud) has provided the breed with an immensely popular stud who has sired a number of title holders at home and abroad. With the help of this dog and of Sh.Ch. Cilleine Echelon and other notable studs, the Darbys have produced a series of recent winners, including Sh.Ch. Classicway Concorde, who later became an Australian Champion, and Sh.Ch. Classicway Cutty Sark, Cocker of the Year 1989.

Another breeder to have turned out several show champions of late is Mrs A. Hackett whose Sh.Ch. Lindridge Gypsy Girl was Cocker of the Year in 1984. Gypsy Girl's son Sh.Ch. Lindridge Venture, whose pedigree appears in Appendix 3, page 251, is one of the top sires of today.

Success of the Solids

Meanwhile, particolours were not having things all their own way. As has been said, back at the time of Ch. Bournehouse Starshine, solids were playing a major role in the Cocker Spaniel scenario. They had long been worthy of attention in the big ring and had taken high honours (*see* Crufts, page 123). Many times, rivals to Starshine for Best of Breed awards were Sh.Ch. Lochranza Newsprint, a son of Butterprint of Broomleaf from a daughter of Sh.Ch. Lochranza Quettadene Marksman (a Dancing Master son), and then Newsprint's son, Sh.Ch. Newsreader of Lochranza. Newsreader was line-bred to Marksman, his maternal grandsire Sh.Ch. Kavora Merrymaker being a Marksman son. Between 1972 and 1976 Newsprint won sixteen CCs and Newsreader won twenty-two.

Hot on their heels came Sh.Ch. Lochranza Man of Fashion, who took twenty-three CCs all with Best of Breed. He was Cocker of the Year in 1978 and 1979 and had eight Group wins. Like many of the Lochranzas, he was owned and bred by Miss Macmillan and her partner Mrs Jean Gillespie. The Lochranzas were frequently piloted to their top awards by Jean's husband John. Man of Fashion, by a son of Sh.Ch. Janeacre Nightskipper of Helenwood, out of a bitch by Sh.Ch. Lochranza Newsprint, spent some time in Scandinavia where he became a Norwegian champion before returning to his old home at Lochranza.

The breeder of Newsreader, Miss Pam Trotman, has had a long association with the breed. She has bred one successful Cocker

Sh.Ch. Lochranza Dancing Master, grandson of Ch. Lochranza Latchkey. (Fall.)

Sh.Ch. Newsreader of Lochranza. (Anne Roslin-Williams.)

after another and her Kavora affix has become internationally famous. Her Sh.Ch. Kavora Merryborne Sweet Martini won nineteen CCs and was the dam of Sh.Ch. Kavora Merrymaker.

The previously mentioned Cornbow Manfred (*see* page 34) was mated to Quettadene Bernadette, a bitch by Sh.Ch. Glencora Black Ace, and from them Mr and Mrs J. Smith bred the golden dog Sunglint of Sorbrook. In the same litter, born in 1968, was the black bitch Sh.Ch. Amanda Jane of Sorbrook who was the first of many show champions produced by the Smiths. As for Sunglint himself, he became probably the most prepotent stud force of his generation and his descendants can be found in many parts of the world. Several of his progeny gained their titles, including Nightskipper.

Sunglint of Sorbrook was also responsible for Sh.Ch. Valsissimo of Misbourne of Wittersham who had an unusual show career. This black dog was bred by Miss Hahn from a granddaughter of Sh.Ch. Valjoker of Misbourne, and was campaigned to his show champion title by Mrs P. Price (Sandover) before being exported to Singapore. Eugene Phoa made him a champion there and in Canada where the Wittersham kennel later settled.

It sometimes happens that a chance opportunity provides a lucky acquisition, as was the case with Sh.Ch. Janeacre Nightskipper of Helenwood. Mrs Jackie Marris-Bray saw an advertisement for some solid puppies, and realizing his potential she decided on the black dog Nightskipper. He turned out to be a success in the ring, winning eight CCs and Best of Breed at Crufts in 1974. He was a dominant sire and from him Mrs Marris-Bray has developed a sound line of solids consistently taking top awards both at home and abroad. One son of Nightskipper, Sh.Ch. Helenwood Checkmate, went Best in Show at Bournemouth Championship Show before being exported to South America. Nightskipper's red daughter Sh.Ch. Helenwood Capelle proved her worth as a brood, and in turn her son, the black Sh.Ch. Helenwood Avalaf (by Sh.Ch. Broomleaf Bright Memory), has become a stud force of the present day.

Other people too have benefited from Nightskipper's influence. He sired many winners for Miss Trotman, including Sh.Ch. Kavora Nightlight. There was, too, Kavora Nightstar of Olanza who became a show champion for the kennel of Miss Poppy Becker. Miss Becker also now has the guardianship of the Broomleaf dynasty which has been so influential since the days of Bonny Lad. From Nightstar and Bright Memory came Olanza Princess Gem, who in turn became the dam of Sh.Ch. Olanza Poachers Moon and Sh.Ch. Olanza Promise

Me. Bright Memory and his grandsire Butterprint were products of many generations of successful Broomleaf breeding.

From a long and successful Quettadene line, Mrs P. M. Lester, who inherited the care of the strain, produced Quettadene Fascination; this black-and-tan bitch was sired by Lochranza Go For Gold, a Sh.Ch. Lochranza Newsprint grandson who later became an Australian champion. Mrs Lester mated Fascination to Sh.Ch. Sorbrook Christmas Knight, a black dog line-bred to Sunglint of Sorbrook, most prominently through his grandam Sh.Ch. Burnished Gold of Bryansbrook (a Sunglint daughter). From this union was produced the black Sh.Ch. Quettadene Emblem, who was the next vital step in the solid chain. In his highly successful show career, he notched up twenty-seven CCs and his winning progeny abounded. These included Sh.Ch. Canigou Mr Happy (fifteen CCs), who took Cocker of the Year over his sire in 1986, Sh.Ch. Olanza Poachers Moon (fifteen CCs), top Cocker in 1987 and 1988, Sh.Ch. Canyonn Cassandra (eleven CCs), Sh.Ch. Asquanne's Ghia (thirteen CCs) and Sh.Ch. Roanwood Flint (Crufts Best of Breed 1989), all blacks. Incidentally, Flint's dam, Roanwood Isadora, also produced the top-winning Sh.Ch. Roanwood Ripple for her owners D. R. Clarke (originally with the Cornbow partnership) and his wife Shirley. Ripple herself gained twenty-five CCs.

Sh.Ch. Charbonnel Fair Cher. (David Bull.)

Sh.Ch. Charbonnel Fair Cher, a black granddaughter of Sh.Ch. Quettadene Emblem, jumped to stardom in 1990, then capped her Cocker of the Year award by going Best of Breed at Crufts early in 1991. A year later she had twenty-one CCs to her credit.

Mixing Colours

Once the reds had been brought up to the level where they could compete on equal terms with the other colours, little cross-breeding of the colours took place. Since the Second World War, solid has been bred to solid, more or less to the exclusion of particolours, and particolours have gone their own way.

Sh.Ch. Broomleaf Black and Tan was an example of solid to particolour breeding, but there have been few breeders of more modern days who mix marriages. The chief exponent of this before and after the war was probably Mrs K. J. Gold. Her Oxshott Cockers resulted from a combination mainly of blacks and blue roans. Ch. Oxshott Marxedes, though mainly particolour bred, had a solid line through his maternal grandsire Oxshott Padgett (black) whose red dam, Red Rougette of Oxshott, was by the black Valclipse of Misbourne, a close relation of Bazel Otto, Dominorum D'Arcy and (through his sire Golfhill Eclipse) Treetops Treasure Trove.

It is interesting that at a later time a knowledgeable breeder would occasionally introduce a particolour dog into a solid line. One example which springs to mind occurs in the pedigree of Sh.Ch. Lochranza Man of Fashion, whose great-grandsire was the parti-colour Lochranza Barsac Farrier, by Sh.Ch. Wells Fargo of Weirdene. As a result of Farrier's union with Lochranza Tan Slippers came a black-and-tan bitch Painted Doll of Lochranza. Black and tan can result from a solid to particolour mating, though in this case the dam herself was black and tan. There are some solids, too, such as Sh.Ch. Quettadene Emblem in recent times, who have the propensity for producing black and tans to solid-colour bitches.

Brown Dogs in the Ring

The liver colour and its variations go back deep into the history of the Cocker Spaniel, but since the establishment of the blue roans, livers seem from time to time to have dropped out of favour. There

Treetops Tortoiseshell. (Fall.)

were, however, many liver roans (which were sometimes termed red roans) being shown in the 1920s. Several of them won CCs, as did the liver, white and tan bitch Falconers Clove in 1931. In 1946, Mrs de Casembroot was winning with a liver-roan-and-tan dog called Treetops Tortoiseshell. He was of Deepdene breeding and a descendant of Manxman and Sir Galahad of Ware, and was the sire of the aforementioned Bumble of Broomleaf, his name also appearing in some of the Merryworth pedigrees. My own liver, white and tan bitch Bronze Coat of Ware was also in the ring at around this time. Although livers were not uncommon in the field trial world, they were infrequently seen in the show ring for many years, but they were certainly not non-existent. Sh.Ch. Weirdene Questing Strathspey, in the 1960s, sired several liver roans, including Sorncroft Suntan (a Best in Show winner) and Witch Broom of Weirdene, the grandam of Waylight of Weirdene who joined the Cahills' Yardew kennel. Miss P. Bartlett's Humbar Cocker Spaniels, who incorporated Chayn (Falconers based), Ch. Domino of Ide and Bandleader of Broomleaf breeding, often produced them as well as solid liver. So did the Coritans who were sometimes bred to them. Sh.Ch. Blueprint of Broomleaf, interestingly a descendant of Sh.Ch. Broomleaf Black and Tan, also sired the liver colour. These three

47

Olanza Sweet Story, who was exported to South America, and her sire Sh.Ch. Blueprint of Broomleaf.

dogs – Strathspey, Blueprint and Bandleader – can all claim Treetops Tortoiseshell as an ancestor.

In the last decade, there has been a revival of interest in the liver-roan colour, popularly termed chocolate roan. Oldberrow Scorched Earth of Coppynook, born in 1981, made something of an impact, doing well in the ring and being much used as a sire. He was by Yardew Wild Venture out of an Oldberrow bitch, Normanview-bred. It seems that many dogs of the colour can be traced back to Sh.Ch. Weirdene Questing Strathspey, especially through the blue-roan Wild Venture and the Normanviews. Further interest has been created by Oldberrow Chocolate Sundae of Sprogmore winning a CC in 1987, and by her son Sh.Ch. Sprogmore Sachmo who was made up in 1991.

Through using Miss K. I. Stirling's solid-liver Ashwell Galena, who is Humbar-bred, Mrs P. Walker of the Cardamine Cocker Spaniels has had some interesting results.

The Emerald Isle

There has long been a movement of Cocker Spaniels and people to and from Ireland to shows and field trials, and because of an exchange of dogs for breeding stock, many good Cockers have been bred in Ireland. In the 1920s, Dr W. J. Dawson was running his Cocker Spaniels at field trials, and had several who became field trial champions. His Fews kennel became a force to be reckoned with and was an important part of field trial history. Amongst those he bred was John Kent's great F.T.Ch. Pat of Chrishall.

Miss D. M. Fagan, who was for many years secretary of the Cocker Spaniel Club of Ireland, was interested in workers and show dogs, and her Lick Bla kennels have produced field trial as well as show winners. One of the workers was Barney of Ware, born in 1928, who became an international field trial champion by winning in England and India. Thirty years later she bred the orange-roan Lick Bla Berenice who became a full champion in the UK for Mrs I. M. G. Agnew, a Northern Ireland resident. Arbury Squib, a liver son of Lick Bla Buster, was one of that rare kind, a dual champion, taking titles in both show and field in America. The Lick Bla affix, including Irish champions such as Lick Bla Brand, is still familiar in the pedigrees of show-bred dogs.

In the 1930s, regulars to shows on both sides of the Irish Sea included Mrs Agnew and W. McCausland (Melfort), both of whom became Championship Show judges, while the Meröks were becoming established before eventually settling in South Africa.

There seems to have been a good deal of Irish interest in Cocker Spaniels in the last forty years, and several kennels have had a long and successful association with the breed. At the Cocker Spaniel Club Show of 1946, the first Championship Show after the war, the bitch CC went to a Belfast-owned blue roan, Mrs F. E. McGladdery's Harmac Hycilla, under no less an authority than Mrs Jamieson Higgens. Hycilla subsequently gained two further tickets for her show title. John Lee did some winning with Sh.Ch. Golden Valerie of Durban who, it is recorded, also had a best all breeds win at a Championship Show.

At Crufts Show in 1950, J. C. Spiller from Eire had a day to remember when he won the Reserve Challenge Certificate (RCC) with his blue-roan Diana of Akron, whose grandsire was Ir. Ch. Maxim of Akron; but this was not all, for he had also bred the dog CC winner, Sh.Ch. Marcus of Akron of Ware. About this time W. D. Smyth's blacks, Ir. Ch. Harley Presentation and Ir. Ch. Presentation Saucy Sue, were well known. Winning affixes included Waterfall, Hy-Niall, Barbary, Fasseroe, Marvin, Copperally and Mulgeeth.

Another Belfast breeder, J. Duncan, had some successes with his Ormeau Cocker Spaniels, and bred my own tricolour bitch Sh.Ch. Silver Cloud of Ormeau of Ware who won fourteen CCs. Among regular exhibitors were T. Forster (Ashuex) and T. Cardy, the latter being a frequent visitor to Great Britain to show his Reaghbels. He also bred Sh.Ch. Aberthaw Commander of Reaghbel for the Scottish owner, John Thaw. Mr Cardy has for many years been secretary of the Ulster Cocker Spaniel Club.

Another outstanding field trial success was Speckle of Ardoon, who became a field trial champion in 1970. She was owned and bred by W. C. Sloan and, interestingly, was from show and field trial stock, her sire being Tireragh Silver Starlight who was by Sh.Ch. Sixshot Otto the Owl, and her dam was an Elan bitch from two field trial champions.

It must be realized that while the British Kennel Club allocates CCs to shows in Northern Ireland, the Southern Irish activities come under the rules of the Irish Kennel Club (IKC) where Green Stars are awarded. Irish exhibitors have tended to travel around and gain awards under both rules. From time to time, exhibitors from Britain make forays to Ireland and often meet with much success. Ch. Ouainé Chieftain gained his Irish title thus claiming international champion status. Mrs M. Snary was a frequent visitor to both Northern Ireland and Eire with her Platonstown solids (several of them show champions here) and won many Green Stars, as well as the CC and Best in Show all breeds at Belfast in 1984 with Sh.Ch. Platonstown Scooby Doo. Mrs Kay Creamer, the Dublin-based breeder of the Cretoka kennels, which have been very successful over the years, did things in reverse: she campaigned her Cretoka Alfredo at shows in the UK as well as at home, gained his qualifier in the field and made him a champion in both countries. Local exhibitors are often hard pressed by the showgoers who travel over to the Northern Irish Championship Shows and take away the top awards. However, one of the recent English successes, Sh.Ch. Asquanne's Grainne (thirty-one CCs), has Irish influence from Faymyr and Lowacre breeding.

Although dogs are normally allowed freedom of movement to or from Ireland, it is wise to check on current regulations before arrival at the port of entry. When there have been outbreaks of foot-and-mouth disease, for instance, passage has been restricted.

There are three specialist breed clubs in Eire, and Cocker Spaniel lover Tom Creamer is currently chairman of the Irish Kennel Club.

3

The Breed Standards

The Standard Explained

The Breed Standard is the blueprint against which a breed is judged; it is a guide to the level of excellence or quality for which breeders should aim.

The Cocker Spaniel Club had adopted the Breed Standard at its formation in 1902 and sixty or so years later instigated a revision. By 1969, the Scale of Points, considered irrelevant, had been dropped and, after due debates at home and abroad, some alterations were agreed and approved. These were to clarify certain details and remove unnecessary wording – certainly not to change the breed in any way. Approximate heights were introduced as guidelines, not as strict limits. Despite amended wording calling for a moderate neck, exaggerated necks became a fetish, perhaps at the expense of other points.

Some years later, the Kennel Club decided to standardize all its breed descriptions so that all Standards now follow the same format. These have been brought together in one volume known as *The Kennel Club's Illustrated Breed Standards*, which was first published in 1989. The Kennel Club recognizes over 180 different breeds, divided into six groups: Hound, Gundog, Terrier, Utility, Working and Toy. Breed Standards by group are available in booklet form as well as a Glossary of Canine Terms.

The Cocker Spaniel is officially termed Spaniel (Cocker) and, because of its sporting origins, the breed comes within the Gundog group, whether or not an individual dog has ever seen a rabbit or heard a gun. Other spaniels classified as Gundogs and currently on the Kennel Club list of registrations are: American Cocker, Clumber, English Springer, Field, Irish Water, Sussex, and Welsh Springer.

When the under-25lb weight limit was abolished at the turn of the century, the way was open for sportsmen to develop the breed on larger lines and with greater freedom of action. They were looking for something slightly taller on the leg, which could range further afield: a dual-purpose dog who could hunt and find game in the thickest undergrowth, and of sufficient size to retrieve it as well. It needed stamina to be able to work all day, courage to face thick cover, and scenting power to find the game, all combined with the intelligence to put its abilities to good effect. A merry, sturdy, sporting dog was developed, well balanced and compact. In the years between the wars, the Cocker Spaniel became popular as a family and show dog, but in assessing the breed one must never lose sight of its original purpose and the needs for which it was developed.

The UK Breed Standard

(Reproduced by courtesy of the Kennel Club)

General Appearance

Merry, sturdy, sporting; well balanced; compact; measuring approximately same from withers to ground as from withers to root of tail.

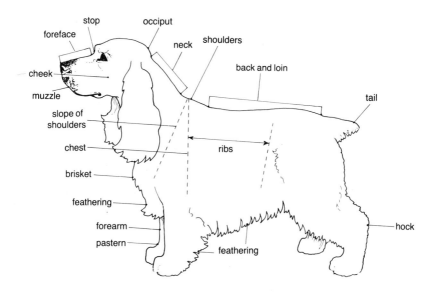

Points of the dog.

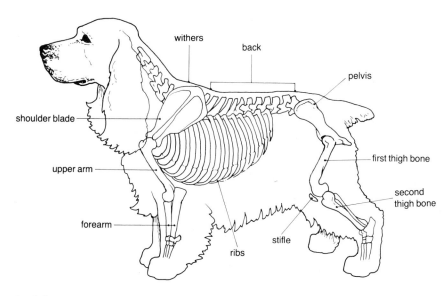

The skeleton.

Characteristics

Merry nature with ever-wagging tail, shows a typical bustling movement, particularly when following scent, fearless of heavy cover.

Temperament

Gentle and affectionate, yet full of life and exuberance.

Head and Skull

Square muzzle, with distinct stop set midway between tip of nose and occiput. Skull well developed, cleanly chiselled, neither too fine nor too coarse. Cheek bones not prominent. Nose sufficiently wide for acute scenting power.

Eyes

Full, but not prominent. Dark brown or brown, never light, but in the case of liver, liver roan, and liver and white, dark hazel to

53

harmonise with coat; with expression of intelligence and gentleness but wide awake, bright and merry; rims tight.

Ears

Lobular, set low on a level with eyes. Fine leathers extending to nose tip. Well clothed with long straight silky hair.

Mouth

Jaws strong with a perfect, regular and complete scissor bite, i.e. upper teeth closely overlapping lower teeth and set square to the jaws.

Neck

Moderate in length, muscular. Set neatly into fine sloping shoulders. Clean throat.

Forequarters

Shoulders sloping and fine. Legs well boned, straight, sufficiently short for concentrated power. Not too short to interfere with tremendous exertions expected from this grand, sporting dog.

Body

Strong, compact. Chest well developed and brisket deep; neither too wide nor too narrow in front. Ribs well sprung. Loin short, wide with firm, level topline gently sloping downwards to tail from end of loin to set on of tail.

Hindquarters

Wide, well rounded, very muscular. Legs well boned, good bend of stifle, short below hock allowing for plenty of drive.

Feet

Firm, thickly padded, cat-like.

Tail

Set on slightly lower than line of back. Must be merry in action and carried level, never cocked up. Customarily docked but never too short to hide, nor too long to interfere with the incessant merry action when working.

Gait/Movement

True through action with great drive covering ground well.

Coat

Flat, silky in texture, never wiry or wavy, not too profuse and never curly. Well feathered forelegs, body and hindlegs above hocks.

Colour

Various. In self colours no white allowed except on chest.

Size

Height approximately: Dogs 39–41cm (15½–16in); Bitches 38–39cm (15–15½in). Weight approximately: 12.75–14.5kg (28–32lb).

Faults

Any departure from the foregoing points should be considered a fault and the seriousness with which the fault should be regarded should be in exact proportion to its degree.

Note

Male animals should have two apparently normal testicles fully descended into the scrotum.

Interpretation

General Appearance

Balance should be the watchword for the breed. The Cocker Spaniel should be balanced both in looks and character, and there should be no exaggerations. He is a compact, sturdy dog. He should have a squarely proportioned body, and should measure roughly the same from the withers (the top of the shoulder) to the ground as from the withers to the root of the tail. The depth of body should appear proportionate to the length of leg. He should not appear low on the leg, nor long in the back. The head and neck should be in correct relationship to the size of the body.

Overall, the Cocker Spaniel should give the impression of being a strong dog in a small frame, with an aristocratic demeanour and a happy disposition. He should be a heavy little dog, built more on the lines of a hunter, which has the stamina to go all day at a moderate pace, rather than the lines of a racehorse or Greyhound, which are built for speed. But with his gently curving lines, silky

The Cocker Spaniel is a compact, sturdy dog.

coat and feathering, there is also something glamorous about a Cocker Spaniel.

Characteristics and Temperament

One of the most attractive features of the Cocker Spaniel is his temperament. He should be a happy, friendly dog with an equable temperament. He is intelligent and can be trained for a variety of tasks; he is adaptable and will usually fit into any situation. Many are successfully trained to the gun and the majority make devoted companions. He is known as 'the merry Cocker' and displays a typical bustling movement, particularly when following a scent, not only in the shooting field but also when out for a walk. While most are responsive to training, they can be self-willed and some require a firm hand.

Head

The head is an important feature of the Cocker Spaniel. A really beautiful head is most appealing, and is one of the great attractions of the breed. The head should have a slightly domed appearance, and the skull should be an oval shape. The stop, which is the point between the eyes, midway between the nose and the occiput, is an obvious indentation but should not be exaggerated. The occiput, the bony ridge at the back of the skull, is also obvious, but should not be as prominent as it is on an Irish Setter. The skull should have clean lines and not be rounded or fleshy, nor too bony. A rather ugly feature has crept into the breed in recent years: the eyebrows and front of the skull are very raised, in extreme cases giving the appearance of a unicorn! It is quite alien to a well-bred Cocker Spaniel, where one expects to see the lovely gentle expression so characteristic of the breed. The skull should allow for brain room, and the muzzle should be of suitable strength and size to be able to carry game; the skull and muzzle should be balanced with each other. The whole head should be in keeping with the rest of the body.

One can tell a great deal from the eyes. The expression should be one of openness and frankness, indicating an honest character. The eyes should be slightly oval but not too full. A full eye would be in danger of damage by brambles. An almond eye, or one that is very narrow or slitty, is undesirable, the latter giving an indication of

Craigleith The Boy Friend.
(Fall.)

rather sly temperament. Another unwanted feature seen in spaniel breeds is the 'hooded' eye, where there is too much loose skin falling over it. This gives a rather shifty expression and must make vision difficult. One looks for fairly tight rims to the eyes. A loose eye would permit seeds and dust to become troublesome when the dog is hunting, and a loose red rim, or one showing the haw, is very unsightly. Sometimes a dog will have a white or flesh-coloured third eyelid, perhaps only in one eye, with the third lid of the other eye being dark. Provided the rims are not loose, it is not a point to worry over too much. Some judges and breeders are fanatical that both third lids should be dark and rims very tight, but others feel that light third lids give a soft expression.

Eye colour is another point to consider. Dark brown or brown is required by the Breed Standard; eyes should never be light. The colour should blend with the main colour of the coat. This is sometimes well exemplified in a deep orange-roan or orange-and-white dog where the harmonizing eyes are a rich dark-chestnut colour. A difficulty occurs with dogs of any of the liver colourings, where a rather yellow or 'gooseberry' eye is sometimes present. Apart from looking very unpleasant, many will argue that it is an indication of a doubtful temperament. Breeders should strive for a darker eye, though with dogs of liver colouring, eyes will be a little lighter than in the blue roan, for instance. The Standard allows for this.

The ears of a Cocker Spaniel hang low and are designed for protection when the dog is out working in the field. Dogs will lift the ears to hear various noises, though the set of the ears is about level with the eye. By the time the dog is adult, the ears will be covered with long silky hair, forming fringes which extend below the leather or skinny part. Nevertheless the hair should not be excessive, or it will become tangled and matted. The ear colour should match the solid colour of the markings. For example, on a blue roan or blue roan and tan, the ears should be black; on an orange and white, the ears should be orange. To have a white streak or half-white ear is undesirable for exhibition. On a tricolour, the ears very often have tan on the underside like a lining to a cloak.

The teeth should be set in regular alignment and the upper teeth should closely overlap the lower teeth. This is known as a scissor bite. It is incorrect for the upper teeth to protrude, which is termed overshot, or for the lower jaw to extend beyond the upper (termed undershot). An undershot jaw might present difficulties for a bitch when whelping as she may not easily bite the cord, and it is undesirable for the working dog who may not be able to perform his task effectively. A Cocker Spaniel is expected to have a 'soft' mouth and be able to carry game firmly but gently without damaging it. Some very small Cocker Spaniels are being shown nowadays, usually bitches, and with their tiny heads and muzzles it would be surprising if they were able to pick up a rabbit, or even a dummy.

The nose should be as dark as possible, in most cases black. However, in the liver and orange colours it is often brown, but the darker the better. In some instances it will change colour with the seasons of the year. A 'butterfly' nose, one which is marked with pink (or is partly unpigmented), can occur in dogs who have a good deal of white in their colouring. It is undesirable, and it is better to breed from stock that produces stronger pigment.

Neck and Forequarters

The Standard states that the neck should be moderate in length: the neck should be sufficiently long for the dog to pick up his quarry efficiently, and strong enough for him to be able to carry it some distance, perhaps over fences or through water. It should be long enough to hold the head elegantly, but the current fashion for a 'giraffe' neck is unnecessary and merely puts the dog out of balance. To hold the head elegantly, an obvious crest from the base of the skull is required. In this way, the head can be held high, and with the nose pointing downwards the beautiful dome of the skull can be viewed. The skin of the throat should not be loose and sagging. One is looking for clean lines in profile.

The neck should fit into neat sloping shoulders. There should be a small gap between the withers so they do not rub in movement. Too wide a gap would create too wide a front, while close withers and upright shoulders would make the front too narrow. Viewed from above, the shoulder blades should gradually slope outwards neatly and without being lumpy. It must be borne in mind that they need to be of sufficient width to balance the big ribs behind. When viewed from the side, the shoulder blade should be set at a distinct angle to the upper arm, as can be seen in the skeleton diagram (*see* page 53). The lay of shoulder, therefore, permits length of neck. The positioning of the upper arm in relation to the forearm allows for good length of stride, so that the dog can cover the ground well. If he were able to take only quick short strides, he would soon tire. With a good layback of shoulder, a dog should automatically have a good forechest. Or, to look at it conversely, a fairly prominent breastbone will help to give a good layback of shoulder. The length of the bones of the shoulder blade, upper arm and forearm also need to be balanced to give a good stride. A short upper arm would shorten the stride.

The legs should be straight, with the hair on the front smooth and with feathering at the back. A Cocker Spaniel's limbs should be strong and substantial in order to carry his big-ribbed body and enable him to work all day. The bone should not be fine or spindly. The dog should not be high on the leg. His original task was to work under cover, rather than over the heather and moors which was a setter's or pointer's job, so a small strong dog was required.

Body

The body should be of compact appearance, short and deep. At the same time, the bone formation must be correctly constructed in

Correct front.

order to make a framework for the body. To give plenty of space for the heart and lungs of an active dog, a well-developed chest, deep brisket and well-sprung ribs are required. The chest should be deep and the brisket, or lower part of the body below the chest wall and between the forelegs, deep and moderately wide. If the legs are too wide apart, energy will be used up with extravagant action, and if set too close together, there will be a lack of freedom and insufficient room for the rib cage.

On viewing the dog from the side, you should see a slight drop over the withers, the virtually level back then rising almost imperceptibly over the loin. The ribs should run well back and the loin should be short. From the end of the loin, the topline slopes gently to the tail, but the croup must not be too short, which gives a stilted action, nor too long and steep, which gives cramped movement. Both of these faults are frequently seen within the breed. Viewed from above, the body should be slightly narrower behind the withers before the ribs widen to more or less a barrel shape, decreasing to a waistline at the loin.

Good hindquarters.

Hindquarters

As with the forequarters, the hindquarters should be well angulated. With a good bend of stifle and a good angle at the hock, the Cocker Spaniel should be able to crouch down and creep through the undergrowth to seek game. The hindquarters, as in the case of the forequarters, are made up of three principal sections, each at a distinct angle to the next. The thigh bone is connected to the second thigh at the stifle joint, and the second thigh to the lower part of the leg at the hock. It is noteworthy that the hock is a joint, and as such should not be described as long or short. Shortness below the hock is advocated by the Breed Standard, but as with all points concerning the breed, this should not be exaggerated to unbalance the structure. The Cocker Spaniel should be wide through the thighs with a nicely rounded rear end, the hocks standing well apart. The hind legs should be well muscled as it is from here that the propulsion comes.

Tracey Witch of Ware, from a painting by F.T. Daws, 1951.

Feet

The feet of a Cocker Spaniel should be neat, tight and thickly padded. Contrary to popular belief, they should not be large and flat. In fact, with a well-boned animal, the foot should be almost a continuation of the leg.

Tail

The tail, which should be set on slightly lower than the back but carried more or less parallel to it, is another indicator of character. The Cocker Spaniel should be a happy dog with an ever-wagging tail, which, if frequently cocked up or carried high, may indicate a rather bossy temperament, and if always carried low could indicate a shy and timid animal. The tail of the working dog would have been docked so that it did not become entangled in the briars or matted with mud. Enough tail would have been left so that the

63

handler could keep track of the dog when he was working in the distance.

Movement

The movement of the Cocker Spaniel is not generally referred to as 'gait', but the term is used in the Standard to conform with Kennel Club style. When moving, the dog's legs should move straight forward, turning neither in nor out, and not too close together. The hind legs should work with great power and flexion, bending easily in low undergrowth.

Coat

The coat should be flat, and soft to the touch, but fairly thick and weather resistant. It should be of a texture to repel the wet and cold, but not so profuse as to become a hindrance to the dog when working in the field. The longer hair or feathering is carried on the front below the breastbone, at the back of the forelegs, under the body and on the hind legs above the hocks. Over the years, the quantity of coat carried by the Cocker Spaniel has considerably increased, and in some cases it could be described as excessive.

Colour

The many variations in colour of Cocker Spaniels make breeding most interesting. In the solid colours – liver (or chocolate), black, and red or golden – no white is permitted except a little on the chest, perhaps more clearly described as 'down the front'. The particolours can be liver and white; liver roan; liver, white and tan; liver roan and tan; black and white; blue roan; black, white and tan; blue roan and tan; lemon and white; lemon roan; orange and white; or orange roan. If it is difficult to ascertain whether a dog is black and white or blue roan, it may be termed 'black and white ticked'. The same could apply to orange and white or liver and white. Opinions differ as to whether liver and tan, and black and tan, should be termed solid or particolour.

Size

The height and weight measurements are not intended as precise limits; they are given as a rough guide for breeders to aim for. Even so, there would seem to be too great a departure from these guidelines within the breed today, and Cocker Spaniels vary considerably in weight and height from the stated dimensions. One often sees a tiny Cocker Spaniel, usually a bitch, being carried in the arms of her owner, and one wonders what such a young puppy is doing at a show, only to find that she is being exhibited, perhaps even in a senior class.

Entirety

The male dog must be 'entire', that is have two testicles descended into the scrotum. A dog with only one testicle descended is described as a monorchid, and with neither descended as a cryptorchid. A male dog who is not entire will be penalized in the ring.

Comment

The Cocker Spaniel should be a short-backed, compact dog, and it is unfortunate that breeders' efforts in this regard have resulted in many short-bodied dogs lacking in angulation who are therefore unable to stride out and cover the ground. As W. Calvert says in the book *The Sporting Spaniel*, 'A body can be so short as to leave insufficient freedom between back ribs and stifles, and thus retard movement'. In the aim for shortness, the shoulder has become upright and the forechest lost in some dogs. The breastbone, which is perhaps more easily visible with the larger dimensions of the setter breeds, should be obvious and project a little. Uprightness at the front end inevitably causes lack of angulation at the rear. The pelvis tends to be short and steep, and rear angles have become straight. Other proportions have also altered and therefore many dogs appear overlong from hip to stifle, with elongated second thighs and exaggerated shortness below the hock. In the quest to shorten the whole dog, an animal has emerged with front and back legs too close together, giving the impression of being about to sit down. As a result, rear action has become stilted and the narrow A-line hindquarters, as viewed from the rear, go forward with a straddling movement.

Perhaps the breed has suffered from show breeders having no interest in the working dog, for working owners can appreciate the purpose of a dog being built in a certain way. Some breeds, like the

The tricolour Craigleith The Great Waltz (a descendent of The Boy Friend and Sweet Charity) appears in many pedigrees of today.

Continental hunt, point and retrieve breeds, are more dual-purpose than the Cocker Spaniel, and a slight tapering of the ribs and a moderate tuck-up allow room for the dog to bend the stifle and bring his hocks up under him for proper propelling movement. This is not so emphasized in a Cocker Spaniel; the scale is different and he was originally used for a different purpose, but the principle is similar. So long as judges give top prizes to poorly constructed specimens, the breed will suffer.

The American Breed Standard calls for a slightly larger dog of different proportions, with a few further variations, and it gives a fuller explanation of what is required than the UK Breed Standard does. It is worth comparing them; and aspiring judges may find that comparison helps towards a greater understanding of breed requirements. Note that, in America, the breed is called English Cocker Spaniel and is included in the Sporting group.

The American Breed Standard

(Reproduced by courtesy of the American Kennel Club)

General Appearance

The English Cocker Spaniel is an active, merry sporting dog, standing well up at the withers and compactly built. He is alive with energy; his gait is powerful and frictionless, capable both of covering ground effortlessly and penetrating dense cover to flush and retrieve game. His enthusiasm in the field and the incessant action of his tail while at work indicate how much he enjoys the hunting for which he was bred. His head is especially characteristic. He is, above all, a dog of balance, both standing and moving, without exaggeration in any part, the whole worth more than the sum of its parts.

Size, Proportion, Substance

Size Height at withers: males 16 to 17 inches; females 15 to 16 inches. Deviations to be penalized. The most desirable weights: males, 28 to 34 pounds; females, 26 to 32 pounds. Proper conformation and substance should be considered more important than weight alone. **Proportion** Compactly built and short-coupled, with height at withers slightly greater than the distance from withers to set-on of tail. **Substance** The English Cocker is a solidly built dog with as much bone and substance as is possible without becoming cloddy or coarse.

Head

General appearance: strong, yet free from coarseness, softly contoured, without sharp angles. Taken as a whole, the parts combine to produce the expression distinctive of the breed. **Expression** Soft, melting, yet dignified, alert, and intelligent. **Eyes** The eyes are essential to the desired expression. They are medium in size, full and slightly oval; set wide apart; lids tight. Haws are inconspicuous; may be pigmented or unpigmented. Eye color dark brown, except in livers and liver parti-colors where hazel is permitted, but the darker the hazel the better. **Ears** Set low, lying close to the head; leather fine, extending to the nose, well covered with long, silky, straight or slightly wavy hair. **Skull** Arched and slightly flattened when seen both from the side and from the front. Viewed in profile, the brow appears not appreciably higher than the backskull. Viewed from above, the sides of the skull are in planes roughly parallel to those of the muzzle. Stop definite, but moderate, and slightly grooved. **Muzzle** Equal in length to skull; well cushioned; only as much narrower than the skull as is consistent with a full eye placement; cleanly chiselled under the eyes. Jaws strong, capable of carrying game. Nostrils wide for proper development of scenting ability; color black, except in livers and parti-colors of that shade where they will be brown; reds and parti-colors of that shade may be brown, but black is preferred. Lips square, but not pendulous or showing prominent flews. **Bite** Scissors. A level bite is not preferred. Overshot or undershot to be severely penalized.

Neck, Topline and Body

Neck Graceful and muscular, arched toward the head and blending cleanly, without throatiness, into sloping shoulders; moderate in length and in balance with the length and height of the dog. **Topline** The line of the neck blends into the shoulder and backline in a smooth curve. The backline slopes very slightly toward a gently rounded croup, and is free from sagging or rumpiness. **Body** Compact and well-knit, giving the impression of strength without heaviness. Chest deep; not so wide as to interfere with action of forelegs, nor so narrow as to allow the front to appear narrow or pinched. Forechest well developed, prosternum projecting moderately beyond shoulder points. Brisket reaches to the elbow and slopes gradually to a moderate tuck-up. Ribs well sprung and springing gradually to mid-body, tapering to back ribs which are of good depth and extend well back. Back short and strong. Loin short, broad and very slightly arched, but not enough to affect the topline appreciably. Croup gently rounded, without any tendency to fall away sharply. **Tail** Docked. Set on to conform to croup. Ideally, the tail is carried horizontally and is in constant motion while the dog is in action. Under excitement, the dog may carry his tail somewhat higher, but not cocked up.

Forequarters

The English Cocker is moderately angulated. Shoulders are sloping, the blade flat and smoothly fitting. Shoulder blade and upper arm are approximately equal in length. Upper arm set well back, joining the shoulder with sufficient angulation to place the elbow beneath the highest point of the shoulder blade when the dog is standing naturally. **Forelegs** Straight, with bone nearly uniform in size from elbow to heel; elbows set close to the body; pasterns nearly straight, with some flexibility. **Feet** Proportionate in size to the legs, firm, round and catlike; toes arched and tight; pads thick.

Hindquarters

Angulation moderate and, most importantly, in balance with that of the forequarters. Hips relatively broad and well rounded. Upper thighs broad, thick and muscular, providing plenty of propelling power. Second thighs well muscled and approximately equal in length to the upper. Stifle strong and well bent. Hock to pad short. Feet as in front.

Coat

On head, short and fine; of medium length on body; flat or slightly wavy; silky in texture. The English Cocker is well-feathered, but not so profusely as to interfere with field work. Trimming is permitted to remove overabundant hair and to enhance the dog's true lines. It should be done so as to appear as natural as possible.

Color

Various. Parti-colors are either clearly marked, ticked or roaned, the white appearing in combination with black, liver or shades of red. In parti-colors it is preferable that solid markings be broken on the body and more or less evenly distributed; absence of body markings is acceptable. Solid colors are black, liver or shades of red. White feet on a solid are undesirable; a little white on throat is acceptable; but in neither case do these white markings make the dog a parti-color. Tan markings, clearly defined and of rich shade, may appear in conjunction with black, livers and parti-color combinations of those colors. Black and tans and liver and tans are considered solid colors.

Am. Ch. Olde Spice Sailors Beware and Miss Vicky Spice; the judge is Dr Arthur B. Ferguson. (John L. Ashbey.)

Gait

The English Cocker is capable of hunting in dense cover and upland terrain. His gait is accordingly characterized more by drive and the appearance of power than by great speed. He covers ground effortlessly and with extension both in front and in rear, appropriate to his angulation. In the ring, he carries his head proudly and is able to keep much the same topline while in action as when standing for examination. Going and coming, he moves in a straight line without crabbing or rolling, and with width between both front and rear legs appropriate to his build and gait.

Temperament

The English Cocker is merry and affectionate, of equable disposition, neither sluggish nor hyperactive, a willing worker and a faithful and engaging companion.

Approved October 1988

4

Selection and Purchase

Because of their looks and character, Cocker Spaniels have a general appeal. They are good natured and very affectionate, and they always give you a big welcome when you return from going out. They are very expressive and you can 'read' their feelings, from the intense expression in their eyes to their quivering rear ends and wagging tails. They are full of fun and, whether kept in the house or a kennel, they like to retrieve a ball or stick and to play with their owner or each other. The soft mouth, which is a feature of the breed, is not only a point in their favour as a gundog, but also indicative of a gentle nature. They should give up game willingly to hand, as well as bones or toys. The size of a Cocker Spaniel, too, commends him to many and, given the time and attention he deserves, he will become a devoted companion and a joy to own.

A Pet Cocker

As a pet, the Cocker Spaniel would suit most households, be they large or small. He is a sensible enough size for the master of the house not to feel embarrassed when taking him for a walk! And he is not too big and strong to be managed, after appropriate instruction, by children, or to be a companion for the elderly. He will not take up too much room even in a small house or car. A Cocker Spaniel is quite adaptable and whether his life is to be spent in kennels with other dogs or on his own in the house, he will usually fit in very well. He is quite at home curled up by the fireside with grandma and even likes to be a lap dog. He will enjoy playing with the children in the garden, but if the family want to walk by the seaside or go on a long country ramble, he will keep going all day. He should be even-tempered, both with other dogs and with people; he should not be expected to be a guard dog, but he will protect his own territory as a watchdog. In the home, he will usually give

71

warning of strangers and bark at unusual sounds, though he should not be aggressive.

Although a Cocker will usually fit in well with a family's arrangements, time must be set aside to devote to the dog. When he is still a puppy, someone should be in attendance most of the day and, even when adult, a dog should not be left for more than a few hours at a time. As a puppy he will need time for playing and for training, and when mature for exercise. Owners should be prepared to give the dog frequent grooming, which will not only be good for the dog but will help to prevent loose hairs spreading around the house.

If there are children in the household, you should consider whether they are old enough to respect an animal who is to become part of the family. While the dog should be loving and playful with the children, he should not have to tolerate torment of any kind. Particolours are usually recommended as having a more reliable temperament. Although reds and goldens are very attractive, and many have delightful personalities, some are prone to jealousy. (*See* page 169).

If you are an elderly person on your own contemplating dog ownership, you must ask yourself whether you are active enough to exercise the dog daily, not only now but in a few years' time. If you take on a puppy, consider that in five or six years you may not feel like, or indeed be capable of, going out in all weathers – wet, snow or ice – to walk the dog, who will still be in his prime. You may have a good neighbour who would take on this duty for you, but it would need to be a reliable, regular and possibly long-term undertaking.

It is sensible to ensure that all members of the family are in agreement about owning a dog. In particular, the mother should be happy about the situation, as it is usually on her shoulders that the main responsibility and care of the animal falls. It is also wise to think about any other animals already in the home, and whether a dog is a suitable and compatible addition. A prospective buyer should also look into the cost of purchase, feeding and care bills before deciding whether he can afford to own a dog. Most pet dogs live indoors, so it is necessary to set aside a suitable small area for the dog's sleeping quarters.

A Dog for Show

Cocker Spaniels are very popular in the show world so it should not be difficult to find them scheduled at events within a reasonable distance of your home. Because of their numbers, there is of course much competition in the breed. Beginners can usually get a lot of fun at the small or Open Shows, but Championship Shows draw entries from experienced exhibitors and top-winning dogs from all over the country. In time, of course, you may feel you have a dog good enough to join their ranks.

If you intend to go in for showing, it is essential that you learn to prepare your dog's coat yourself. A Cocker Spaniel with his aristocratic bearing can look very glamorous parading in the show ring with the sun shining on his gleaming coat and silky feathering, but it takes an enormous amount of time and patience to achieve this standard.

Showing dogs is a costly business. Apart from the outlay on the dog himself, his feeding and the grooming equipment, there are show entries and petrol expenses to be paid for. With a few exceptions, prize money is minimal or nil. The rewards are in showing a good dog, the pleasure of meeting other like-minded people, the opportunity to learn and have a nice day out. If your dog wins a card or a rosette, it is a bonus.

Choosing the Right Dog

Having looked at the environment into which the dog must fit, considered the purposes for which he is required and concluded that a Cocker Spaniel is the dog for you, your next step is to endeavour to select the right one to fit the role.

Whether you are looking for a dog for show purposes or as a family pet, you must consider the questions of sex, age and colour. As to the latter point, it is probably best to decide on either solid or particolour beforehand, and then make some enquiries about availability before being too specific in your demands. You will find that the majority of breeders specialize in either solid or particolours; not so many keep both.

Dog or Bitch?

This is an important question. It is often felt that a bitch makes a more loving companion, but in the spaniel breeds a male, particularly one brought up as a pet from an early age, can be equally

Appealing puppies. (Tracy Morgan.)

affectionate and quite satisfactory. If there are small children in the family, the decision would probably fall in favour of a bitch. But you must remember that a bitch comes into season twice a year, and at the vital time may make attempts to seek a mate. Unless she keeps herself very clean she may leave spots of blood around, so it may be necessary to confine her to one part of the house for the duration of the season. For these reasons, members of the family must be extra vigilant about closing doors and gates at this time. You would need to consider whether any male dogs living nearby would give unwelcome attention to your bitch when in season, and whether you have access to a suitable exercise area for her for these few weeks. Your own garden, with regular playtime with a ball, may be sufficient. If you have an open-plan front garden, you may find that any Romeos in the district will beat a path to your door.

If you habitually look after a friend's or relative's dog when they go away, or if you regularly visit another dog owner, you would probably decide on the sex to coincide.

Your puppy could, of course, be neutered at a suitable age, but there are disadvantages to spaying a bitch. She may tend to put on weight and grow a thick, coarse coat difficult to deal with. Spaying is a major operation and thought should be given to any side-effects.

Male Cocker Spaniels generally make satisfactory pets and it is not usually found necessary to neuter. However, if yours proves to be the exception then castration should be considered.

Points such as these should be discussed with your veterinary surgeon or a breeder, before making a decision about the sex to choose. If you are a garden lover, you may not relish the brown patches which a bitch's urine will leave on the lawn, and a male should be prevented from cocking his leg on the cabbages!

Some people feel they would like to have two dogs in the home, and in general two Cocker Spaniels of the same sex get on very well together. There is an opinion that if two are chosen from the same litter, one will always be dominant, but dogs who live together will usually establish a pecking order whether they are related or not.

In order to keep a dog and bitch together in one household, it would be necessary to neuter one or the other for the sake of peace and quiet. Although people say they can shut them in separate rooms when the bitch is in season, it is very frustrating for a dog to know there is a bitch in that condition nearby.

Adult or Puppy?

If you decide that it is a puppy you want, you will make some enquiries as to sources of supply. Prospective purchasers should go to a reputable breeder, rather than a dealer. You will also find that a breeder will be willing to give an 'after-sales' advice service, and will take an interest in the puppy's progress. After all it is to their benefit to receive information as to the satisfactoriness or otherwise of their stock.

While personal recommendation is one of the best ways of locating a breeder, you could also obtain from the Kennel Club the address of the secretary of your local breed club or canine society. He in turn should be able to put you in touch with breeders in your area. The Kennel Club could also forward you the list of advertisers whose names appear in the Kennel Index section of *The Kennel Gazette*. Advertisements also appear in the weekly dog papers, *Our Dogs* and *Dog World*, obtainable from newsagents, and of course in various national or local papers and sporting and other journals. Your veterinary surgeon could be approached for local information.

You may be obtaining your first dog or looking for a successor to one you have just lost. Whichever it is, it is a good idea to give the breeder as much information as possible about your home situation so that he can try to match you up with a puppy to suit your circumstances. Some prospective buyers feel they must have a different colour or sex from the last dog; others would like to replace the old one with the same again. But it is a mistake to believe that you can wholly replace a beloved old friend. Much as the owner may wish it, the new dog will neither look nor act exactly like the old one. Even litter-brothers brought up as a pair will display separate personalities, reactions and behaviour. Hereditary characteristics may prevail, but personalities are individual.

Timing is another factor which must be taken into consideration. Do not be surprised if there are no puppies available at the precise moment you have decided to buy one; you cannot order things when dealing with nature. You must also consider whether you are going to be at home for the few months following the purchase. You do not want to disrupt the puppy's house-training, or upset his routine, by asking someone else to look after him. Many boarding kennels will not accept young stock and it may not be sensible to take a youngster away with you.

An adult dog may be the choice of an older person who may not want to cope with the problems of house-training, or who may be wary of a playful puppy tripping them up. Breeders sometimes have available mature stock for whom they would like to find a good home. A dog who has spent a few years in kennels deserves to be somebody's special favourite and companion, and is usually only too delighted to become a house dog. There are many good reasons why an older dog may be available. It could be one that has not made the grade for showing, or a bitch who has reared a couple of litters and retired from maternal duties. Sometimes a breeder will run on two puppies, being company for each other, and after a few months select the one that shows the greater show potential; the other then becomes available for a new home. He may not be house-trained but he would not need to make puddles so frequently as a small puppy and, if the kennel is run to a good routine, he will probably already have learned to be clean indoors. A problem could be that the youngster has had little discipline or lead-training and may be rather boisterous. Here again the prospective purchasers should put their circumstances before the seller and seek his advice as to the suitability of the animal. However, they should not expect

'That's my dad!' (Tracy Morgan.)

to find a dog ready-made and must be prepared to put in some effort themselves.

A retired brood-bitch should present no difficulty in settling into a domestic situation. More often than not, a breeder will have a bitch in the house for whelping and a few weeks afterwards, so that she will already have some knowledge of home life.

An older male dog who has been used at stud could be more difficult to adapt. It could be that he would cock his leg against the furniture, attempt to wander in search of a female, or pester visiting dog owners by scenting their clothing. For similar reasons, it is unwise to consider using a pet dog at stud if all is happy and stable in his life. If you are considering having a retired stud, discuss the matter fully with his present owner, who should be able to describe to you the nature of the dog so that you have an idea whether you could cope. Not all, by any means, will present such difficulties. It is fair to say that there are numerous such dogs who have quickly learned the house rules and proved a delight to their new owners.

The other category of adult with which a breeder may part is a young dog or bitch who has been shown, but has not achieved the success at first hoped for. Such a youngster could be quite a find if you are looking for a mature dog. He will have been well-handled, lead-trained, be used to travelling and meeting people and accustomed to serious trimming. How often pet owners say their dog will not stand still or does not like being groomed!

Apart from a breeder, another source of supply, especially of adult dogs, is a rescue organization. The Cocker Spaniel Club runs a rescue scheme which organizes the care of Cockers who for one reason or another are forced to leave their present home. It puts those seeking a dog in touch with those parting with one and efforts are made to match dog to prospective owner. The scheme was masterminded by Mrs Olive Norfolk (Tarling), for whom the task became her life for fourteen years, but there is now a network of contacts in different regions. Enquiries can alternatively be made at general rescue or charitable organizations to find out whether these have a suitable Cocker Spaniel needing a home. No pedigree papers are given as the dog is not purchased, but you would be expected to make a suitable donation to the fund.

Whether you are buying a puppy or an older dog, you should look for a happy healthy animal. He should be clear-eyed and friendly, and the coat should be in good condition. A staring coat, a bony back and pot belly would probably indicate a wormy animal. Puppies should be alert and not nervous, but a very young litter will be less responsive to sounds and movements than one of a couple of months old. This is one reason why there is little point in viewing puppies when only a few days or weeks of age. Puppies will run around and play, eat a meal, then sleep for a couple of hours. If the puppies are sleepy at the time you visit, it may be nothing to worry about but just their natural resting period. Also, it may be difficult for a novice to visualize the eventual colouring. A blue roan, for instance, is born black and white.

Initially, an owner may prefer that you do not touch the puppies at all for fear of bringing in any infection. Never pick up a puppy without first asking permission. In any case, a puppy could feel insecure in inexperienced or unfamiliar hands, and after a number of years one tends to forget how lively a puppy can be! If children are allowed to handle the litter, it is better for them to sit down before holding a puppy, so there is no danger of his falling. Puppies often wriggle about when being held, and the owner will show you how to hold them confidently.

If you are choosing a puppy as a pet, the matter of looks is a personal choice. The pedigree can give a lot of information to an experienced person but, more often than not, it means nothing to the pet buyer. In all probability you would see the dam or other relatives to give you an idea of how the puppy should grow on and an indication of his nature. But if the litter is very young or the bitch is a house dog, do not be surprised if she is slow to make friends with you as it is natural for her to be protective towards her progeny. Choose the puppy who first of all attracts you. There is little point in analysing them all inch by inch, for it is usually the character which settles the matter. Children generally find it easy to make a choice and quickly pick out the one that appeals to them.

Many people are reluctant to consider 'the last puppy left in the litter'. Sometimes they are not prepared even to see him, presumably on the assumption that he is inferior. This is a misconception. Although there may be a runt in some litters, in many cases there is nothing to choose between the puppies. In any case, previous purchasers' personal preferences will not be the same as yours. The runt, if such there be, will in all probability have learned to stand up for himself against his bigger siblings, and he may already have been chosen on account of his cheeky character. The 'pick of the litter' may up until then have been kept back for possible retention by the breeder or a hoped-for enquiry for a show dog. The last one could in fact be the best. One simple reason for a puppy being 'left' is that there have been, say, only four purchasers for five puppies. If the rest of the litter has not already gone to new homes you will probably be able to see them for comparison.

One point worth mentioning is that buyers should not automatically assume that vendors will sell puppies to any enquirers. They will need to satisfy themselves as to the suitability of the future home and lifestyle for their puppy.

While one would expect to buy a sound, healthy animal, there is no guarantee in nature. Whatever one is buying, whether it be livestock or plants, one has to take a chance on its future.

If you have made enquiries at two or three sources, you will have ascertained the going rate for a pet puppy; or you could consult the breed club when making your initial enquiries. Older stock is a different matter, and prices will vary. A youngster should already have had vaccinations and the cost of these will be added to the price. But the older the dog is, the lower the price tends to be, unless he is a show prospect.

When you buy a puppy you can expect to receive a feeding guide and pedigree. The dog should have been registered at the Kennel Club and the vendor should pass on the registration with the transfer section duly signed. You should subsequently submit it to the Kennel Club who will in due course supply a certificate confirming you to be the rightful owner. All is then in order when the time comes for your dog to be bred from or to take part in shows or competitions. A small puppy may not have received his vaccinations before purchase, but where this has been done, and for older dogs, the relevant certificate should be provided.

Show Potential

There are probably as many good specimens sold to pet owners as ever reach the show ring, but if you are hoping to take up showing, you would no doubt go out in search of something with show potential. If you are looking for a show prospect for the first time, you will need to seek advice. Attend a few shows, talk to exhibitors and breeders, and perhaps join one of the breed clubs or local canine societies. Having acquired all the information you can, decide on the colour, type and strain you like. Then approach the owner of that strain. He should be able to help you select a promising puppy, or point you in the right direction.

Many good pups are excellently reared in pet homes, but it would be rather hit-and-miss to select a puppy from such a source if neither you nor the owner of the litter were sufficiently qualified to assess the quality of a particular puppy. Most aspiring showgoers would be advised to make their first purchase from, or at least on the advice of, a well-known, reliable breeder or exhibitor.

At an early stage, it cannot always be ascertained whether a male puppy is entire, and this is one of the points you would expect your adviser to check. If you were keen to show, it would be a great risk buying a puppy who was not entire, though the testicles can descend even as late as ten months of age.

Unless your circumstances do not permit it, you will probably decide in favour of a bitch as your first show dog. There is not usually a great demand for the services of a stud-dog unless he is a top winner or champion or belongs to an established kennel.

You should also read the Breed Standard and have it firmly established in your mind, together with a mental picture of the ideal. It is best to select a puppy whose overall form approximates to your requirements, rather than be too analytical. A study of the Standard, however, will have indicated any major faults to be avoided. Minor faults will have to be accepted as the perfect dog has yet to be found. But you should try to obtain the best you can, and keep in mind that you may be able to breed on and produce something better.

You will probably view the puppies running around in a pen, or preferably out in the garden or yard. There may be one that stands out from the rest; one that catches the eye will look good in the show ring. Do not decide on a shy one, for the puppy who hangs back will not make the most of himself. You should see them individually standing on a table and hope they will, with a restraining hand, stand still long enough for you to go over them. The coat of a young puppy can be rather difficult to assess, but as the puppy grows, the texture becomes more obvious. A very thick woolly coat could be rather difficult for a beginner to manage. A well-reared puppy will feel heavy for his size when you pick him up. Remember that a Cocker Spaniel is a lot of dog within a small compass.

You cannot expect to buy a top winner at your first attempt. You will have a great deal to learn. Winning prizes is not just a matter of owning a good dog – he must also be reared and trained correctly and presented to best advantage in the ring. Your purchase will be the means of your learning how to do this. At the same time, it is hoped that the two of you will give friendship and pleasure to each other.

Eight weeks is a good age to judge small puppies. They should be firmly on their feet, and the proportions should be similar then to those of the fully grown animal. The muzzle, for instance, is rather short at birth but the puppy will be more balanced overall by eight weeks. After that age they suddenly shoot up. They will go through various growing stages and appear to be 'all legs and wings' and as different puppies grow at different rates, it is not easy to assess a growing youngster.

You must expect to pay a higher price for a pup with show potential, although many breeders do not differentiate between show and pet with a small puppy.

5

Management and Training

Puppy Care

Before taking your puppy home, you will need to make proper arrangements to receive him. You will need not only to obtain suitable foods and bowls, but also to plan sleeping quarters and an exercise area.

Initially, a cardboard box, preferably raised off the ground an inch to enable the air to circulate, with a small section cut from the front for access, should be adequate for a bed. Puppies can be quite destructive and there is little point in paying out for something fancy until they have outgrown the chewing stage. A suitable blanket should be used as bedding, not one of the loose-knit type in which a puppy could easily get his teeth or toes tangled. The bed should be placed in a draught-free corner, where the puppy can sleep undisturbed. The room should not be cold and the floor should be easy to clean after mishaps. You should ensure that the fencing round your garden is intact, for a puppy will enlarge the tiniest hole by chewing or by digging if he wants to find a way out.

A cardboard box can also be used to bring the puppy home. You need one with fairly high sides, so the little fellow cannot clamber out, which can be wedged between the seats of a car. Use small pieces of blanket that can be thrown away if the pup is travel sick. Cocker Spaniels usually travel well, but a puppy may cry or be distressed the first time, and may then prefer to sleep on the lap of a passenger. If the journey is a long one, or the day is hot, offer the puppy drinks of water. It is preferable for him to be without food while travelling unless the journey is of many hours. Although a puppy that has not yet completed his inoculations should not be put down in a strange area, it is as well to have a slip lead or little lead and collar with you in case of emergencies. In any case, puppies can be very quick and slip out of inexperienced or unfamiliar hands, but

82

watch that the puppy does not chew the lead. If you are travelling by public transport, you might be able to borrow a small dog-carrying crate or cat basket so that you know the puppy is secure.

When you arrive home, allow the puppy to familiarize himself only with his own area of house and garden. Introduce him to a small family circle; the rest of the house, friends and neighbours can be met with later. Take things slowly at first; there are many changes in his life to cope with. Offer a light meal and, if all is well, proceed according to the diet sheet for the next allotted dish. But do not be surprised if he does not eat well for the first day or so. Make sure that fresh water is always available.

Electric flexes can be a danger to a puppy, who may chew or pull them, so ensure that they are out of reach. Some owners find it necessary to provide a receptacle for mail deliveries so that communications are not shredded!

At Night

Although his mother may not have slept with the litter during the last couple of weeks, the puppy will miss her being around and will certainly miss the warmth and companionship of his litter-mates. A hot-water bottle or ticking clock, well wrapped up in a blanket so the puppy is not tempted to chew at it, can be placed in the bed to simulate the presence of the dam or siblings. Even a lump of wood in a cosy wrap is something to cuddle up to.

If possible, partition off a small area round the puppy's bed. He cannot then follow you when you say goodnight, and lie against a draughty door or get lost in a large unfamiliar room. Puppies do not usually soil their bed, so put newspaper down on the floor near it and he will use this if he needs to in the night.

Many owners have found a crate method very satisfactory. A large box, such as a tea-chest, is used for the sleeping bed and if a wire-mesh door is attached, the puppy can be shut in just for the night hours. Puppies usually feel very secure in the enclosed space, so if he cries in the night, it is likely that he wants only to go out to relieve himself. You must ensure that there is ample ventilation by drilling holes in the sides of the box to allow circulation of air. Otherwise, in a warm house, the puppy could become overheated. Puppies usually love their box, and use it as a retreat until they have outgrown it. Cages of the folding type are now available and are most useful as they can double as travel crates.

If the puppy cries at night, never be tempted to take him to your room, or it will become a habit; start as you mean to go on. A small cuddly puppy is one thing but it is quite another having an adult dog with muddy paws or a bitch in season sharing your duvet, so never let the situation arise. It will probably take three or four nights before the puppy sleeps right through, and you should not go to him every time he cries, or he will learn that this is a way of getting attention.

You should prepare for night-time almost as soon as you get the puppy home, and for this reason it is better to fetch him as early in the day as possible. Do not take the puppy round the house with you all day, then suddenly abandon him at bedtime. Put him in his sleeping quarters for intervals of, say, about ten minutes at a time during the day, and leave the room. If he is good, fuss him; if he cries, soothe him, but if he persists tell him severely 'No!', giving him a gentle shake by the scruff. Have a rolled-up newspaper to hand, and use it to tap the puppy's rear end as a correction which will not physically harm him. Always be firm in your commands and always give plenty of praise when the dog behaves well.

House-Training

House-training can begin at once. The puppy will want to pass water or faeces very frequently while he is awake. You will soon learn to recognize the signs that he is preparing to do this, for he will sniff the ground and turn round in circles. A puppy should also be put outside as soon as he wakes up, whether after a night's sleep or just a nap, immediately after food and last thing at night. He should be taken to the place in the garden that you wish him to use. For hygiene reasons, you may want this area not to be adjacent to the house, or, although dogs usually prefer grass, you may like to train him to use a paved area which can easily be washed down. It should, however, not be too far from the house, because you will find that while he is small he will need to go out numerous times.

It is important always to clear up after your dog. One modern aid for disposal is a specially designed plastic container which is buried in the ground, into which you dispose of your dog's waste. The addition of chemicals or environmentally safe powder speeds the dissolution of the excrement. This may be adequate for the house dog, but may not be ideal for the kennel.

On the first occasions, carry the puppy to the spot and wait. You

An adventurous puppy. (Tracy Morgan.)

must devise a short order to indicate that you want him to go out to be clean and repeat it every time, so that eventually he will do it on command. Gradually you must try to send the puppy on his own; you may find that he will not perform while you are watching, so you will have to leave him for a few minutes.

Never leave the puppy out for long periods unattended. For one thing he may try to find an escape route from the garden, or otherwise get up to mischief. Remember that you cannot correct him for wrongdoing unless you catch him in the act. You may prefer to fence temporarily a corner of the garden which you want the dog to use as a toilet area, or around the vegetable patch for instance to prevent him entering.

Do not leave your puppy or dog out in the wet, and do not leave him out on a hot sunny day unless he can get to shade and water. During the winter months, the difference in temperature between a centrally heated house and the outside can be considerable, so again the dog should not be left out for long. However, Cocker Spaniels are a hardy breed, and provided he is on the move, for instance going for a walk or actively playing, your dog should come to no harm. If your dog gets a little wet when at exercise, stand him on newspaper, then rub him down with an old towel or chamois leather. Attention must be prompt and thorough.

Many owners cannot understand why a puppy who is allowed to roam around the house and with free access to the outdoors will suddenly spend a penny on the sitting-room carpet. This is because the situation is confused and there is no distinction between right and wrong. The puppy should thoroughly understand house-training rules before he is allowed this type of freedom. He will then automatically take himself off to the designated area, or will go to the door and make his desires known. Until such time, he should be restricted to one room, and only allowed in the sitting room or elsewhere when socializing and under supervision.

It is essential that all members of the family support the rules laid down for the dog. A dog should not be given food from the table, or he will continually pester for it, which is not good for him and can be a nuisance or embarrassment for visitors. Every person in the family must ignore the dog at table. When there are young children about, leave the dog in a separate room at mealtimes.

When introducing your puppy to children, it should be done in a quiet manner. Puppies and children will usually play happily together but, although puppies are quite resilient, accidents have been known to happen so playtime should always be supervised. Puppies also need plenty of sleep; they should be allowed their own space, and the opportunity to retreat to it undisturbed.

Children should get a good deal of fun from owning a dog, whilst at the same time learning about caring and responsibility. They should not be allowed to walk the dog on their own on the public highway until they are of a responsible age, and until they can manage the dog who should by then be lead- and road-trained. To teach a small child to handle a dog, use two leads: one for the child to hold, the other for the adult who can then exert ultimate control.

If you have other pets, supervise their initial meeting. Older dogs should be treated with respect by the puppy. Cats can learn to get on with dogs, but it is important to be watchful until you are certain they have accepted each other.

Feeding

A Cocker Spaniel's dominant interest is his food and although he will eat almost anything, it is a wise owner who controls the diet. Quantity and quality must be taken into consideration. As well as protein, carbohydrates and fats, the diet will need to supply vitamins and minerals.

When a puppy goes into a new home from his breeder, he will almost certainly be accompanied by a diet sheet, and in the early days this should be closely followed. The change of surroundings and handling, the transfer of associations from his own family group to the human family, will be sufficient stress without a change of diet as well.

Puppies have small stomachs and should be fed little and often. An eight- or nine-week-old puppy will probably be fed four times a day, with two milky and two meaty feeds. From this first stage of feeding, he will progress over the next few months through two more stages before reaching the goal of one main meal per day (or two small ones), plus dry biscuits, for an adult dog. The puppy's meals should be suitably spaced throughout the day. Breakfast might consist of a porridge or basic wheat cereal with warm milk. Flakes or cereals that have been sugared, flavoured or aerated in order to make them attractive to children are too light and are unsuitable for a puppy. Cow's milk should be slightly diluted, with a teaspoon of glucose added. It is a better idea to start with to use a powdered milk which can be reconstituted with water. Dried milks are generally available at pet shops and are specially formulated to suit the digestive systems of young puppies and provide essential vitamins and minerals. The tips of the puppy's ears should be wiped with a damp cloth after milky foods.

Raw meat, cut up finely or minced, or minced tripe, could be fed at midday with a puppy-grade biscuit meal previously soaked with hot water or stock. It should not be fed sloppy. Fish or chicken, with bones removed, can be given for a change. A calcium and mineral supplement, again obtainable from pet shops, should be given during the growing stages. Many people prefer to use canned meat with the biscuit meal, in which case information on the can should be read carefully. Usually all nutrients have been included in the manufacture and there may be no need for further additives. In fact, such additions could upset the balance of the product.

Care, however, should be taken with the quantity of canned meat used. Sometimes manufacturers' instructions advise a generous amount! Some varieties appear to be rather rich and overfeeding canned meat can result in an upset tummy. If the puppy has previously been accustomed to fresh meat, but you wish to use canned meat, you should make the change gradually.

At teatime, a similar meal to the midday feed should be given, and in the evening, about an hour before bedtime, repeat breakfast. Rice pudding, scrambled egg or egg custard can be given sometimes as the milk feed. Eggs should not be given more than two or three times a week and should not be fed raw.

Small biscuits, such as tiny bone-shaped ones suitable for puppies, are obtainable. As the puppy grows, and needs a harder biscuit when teething, he can progress to something a little more substantial. Biscuits of appropriate size should be given throughout life as they are beneficial to the teeth. Give a few at bedtime, or as a reward, but numbers should be limited to complement the overall diet.

It is very difficult to give a guide on quantities of food, as each animal's needs are different. An energetic, lively puppy may require more food than the more placid one who already looks solid and well fed. One with a big frame will probably have a bigger appetite than a small lightly boned puppy. Puppies will grow at different rates and meals should be increased, or even decreased, according to the needs and development of the puppy. As a very rough guide, 2–3oz (60–85g) of meat should be given with three heaped tablespoons of puppy meal at each of the main meals and up to half a pint (60 ml) of milk daily. You will soon discover the needs of your own pet and make adjustments accordingly. You should test the temperature of the food with your finger before offering it to the puppy, and remember to wash your hands before and afterwards. If the puppy bolts his food and looks for more, you should increase the quantity at the next meal, but you must remember that Cocker Spaniels are generally greedy animals and may merely be making an appeal to your generosity. You will have a better guide over a few days as to whether you are giving the puppy sufficient. He will soon appear thin and restless if he is hungry. If the puppy leaves any of his dinner, reduce the quantity at the next meal. A puppy who appears 'blown out' and uncomfortable after his dinner, or has to struggle to finish it, has also been overfed.

In rare cases, leaving of food could be the sign of a faddy feeder. You must not encourage his fussiness or feeding him will become a difficulty. Never leave food down, as it will become stale. Give him a reasonable time, say ten minutes, and if he does not clear it up, remove it and let him wait until the next meal. He will eat when he is hungry. If he still will not eat, consult your vet as there may be a medical reason for his reluctance. A puppy with a normally good appetite will sometimes play around with food and leave some owing to soreness of gums when teething.

Upset Stomach

It is not unusual for a new puppy to have an attack of diarrhoea. There could be several causes. The first and most immediate one may be the journey home, but it may simply be the change of environment from living in security with his litter-mates to the unfamiliarity of a new home. It could be over-excitement, perhaps from too much play with the family or visitors, or it could be the heat, from the weather or from a centrally heated house to which he is not accustomed. Small puppies, like babies, are easily upset by a change of diet. Over-indulgence could be responsible as new owners tend to overfeed. Puppies put things, anything, in their mouths, and something which they have chewed could make them sick. Another cause of sickness and diarrhoea is worms, but in these days most breeders are aware of the necessity for regular worming, and the new owner should continue a routine worming programme. If the puppy has loose motions or is a little sick, but is lively and not obviously ill, starve him for at least two meals. Keep him quiet and warm, and put down a bowl of cooled boiled water. A dose of a teaspoon of whisky in two teaspoons of milk with half a teaspoon of glucose is a good old remedy. If he is soon crying anxiously for food there is probably not much wrong with him, but feed a light invalid diet of a little fish or scrambled egg for the next twenty-four hours, and if he is all right after that, return to the normal food. If, however, the puppy is not active at any time and is sitting moping in his bed, the diarrhoea continues, or you suspect that he has swallowed a foreign body, such as a button or an earring, you should consult your vet immediately. A sick puppy with diarrhoea can quickly go downhill.

Three Months to Adult

Feeding

At about twelve to fourteen weeks, one of the milk feeds can be omitted. Indeed, puppies will very often decide that milk is no longer to their liking and prefer the milky food only at breakfast. At five to six months, the teatime meal should consist of meat with a few crunchy biscuits, omitting the soaked meal. At about this time, you can gradually start to introduce the puppy to a coarser biscuit meal by replacing some of the puppy meal with the larger-sized terrier meal. This is the type that is generally available in pet stores and supermarkets. If the puppy easily accepts it and does well on it, he can soon have the terrier meal entirely. By the time he is eight to nine months of age, he should be on two meals, the breakfast having been dropped.

As well as kibbled biscuit meals, which are intended to be dampened and mixed with meat, there are other mixer biscuits on the market which can be fed dry with the meat. There are also complete foods which are a modern way to feed dogs. They come in various forms, such as flakes, nuggets or pellets or a mixture, some to be fed dry, others moist. Another form of complete diet is a semi-moist food, rather like minced beef in appearance and available in portion-size packs. These are all scientifically formulated to supply the entire nutritional needs of the dog and are intended as the sole food source. No other feeding is necessary.

Complete foods are a very convenient way of feeding as the product keeps well and does not quickly deteriorate, unlike fresh meat or an opened can, but many people still have reservations about the method, especially with a small puppy. Clean water must, without fail, always be available as this type of feeding can give the animal a great thirst. Some owners feel that this could be a strain on the kidneys of a young puppy. They also feel that they prefer to be more 'in control' of the diet. They like to provide a change, such as tripe, fish, milk, eggs, and so on, and feel that the food would not be so tasty without the addition of some form of meat. A few brands make allowance for the fact that owners will be tempted to add to the diet, but the maker's instructions must be strictly followed or using this type of food is pointless and could be harmful.

The type of diet will not only depend on the owner's choice, but also on cost and, most important, what suits the puppy. Puppies are not all the same, and not all their needs are the same. When trying out new types or brands, it is best to buy only a small quantity at a time until you are sure it is acceptable to him, and the puppy must thrive, develop and maintain good condition on it.

Unfortunately, far too many pet Cocker Spaniels are overweight.

Owners are doing their dogs no favours by succumbing to the appeals for titbits and more food, and should be cautious with recommended quantities. It is far more pleasurable to own a Cocker Spaniel who is fit and sleek and able to exercise without becoming short of breath than one who pants at the least exertion and has a back like a table top!

Do not give the dog his main exercise of the day immediately on top of his main meal. If you feed an evening meal, but find the dog needs to relieve himself during the night, it might suit him better to eat at midday. Once you have established a pattern, stay with it. The dog will in any case expect to have his meal at a regular time, and his inner clock will tell him when that is.

At a year old the dog should be accustomed to one main meal per day, be it midday or early evening (or two small ones). The meal could consist of meat, fresh or canned, and a terrier-grade biscuit meal, moist or dry, or other mixer; the food should be fed crumbly and not wet. One cannot be precise over quantities, as to what is right for your dog. You should provide sufficient good-quality food to maintain good condition and to keep him happy and healthy. A dog who has reached maximum growth will probably not require more than 6oz (170g) of meat per day and about the same quantity of meal. A dog who is still maturing, has a large frame, or is in other ways using up energy, will probably require more. It would not harm a mature house dog, who takes only modest exercise, to receive a smaller quantity as his daily ration, and all dogs should enjoy a few dry biscuits.

Puppies and dogs should always have access to clean drinking water. They should have their own bowls, and drinking and feeding bowls should be washed up after each use with a brush kept especially for the purpose. All utensils should be kept separate from those used by the family. A small dish is all that is required initially, shallow enough for the puppy to reach the food easily, but he grows very quickly and during the growing months consumes quite large meals, so a feeding bowl should be provided that is large enough and deep enough for the food not to scatter when a hungry youngster dives in!

Feeding dishes and bowls come in various materials, shapes and sizes. For a house dog, an earthenware bowl makes a good container for water and keeps it cool. The disadvantages of plastic dishes are that they are light and slide around the floor. Alas a puppy, or sometimes even an older one, may chew it, and if pieces of plastic are swallowed they can do internal damage. Stainless steel is probably the most satisfactory material for feeding bowls. Those with sloping sides are more steady in use and are not easily tipped over. Steep-sided bowls are available which are intended for spaniels, so their ears fall over the rim. However, these can be narrow, so make sure that the bowl is large enough for the dog to enjoy his food comfortably.

Bedding

The dog should have his own bed and never be allowed on yours. Types of bed vary from the cardboard box to the sophisticated, machine-washable, purpose-made bed. Wicker baskets or fibreglass beds are also available and reasonably priced. Bean bags are popular and usually have separate, washable covers. All bedding should be regularly shaken out and washed; even a well-kept dog will shed a certain amount of hair and dust. Cocker Spaniels can be trained not to sit on the furniture, although some owners allow the dog his own special chair.

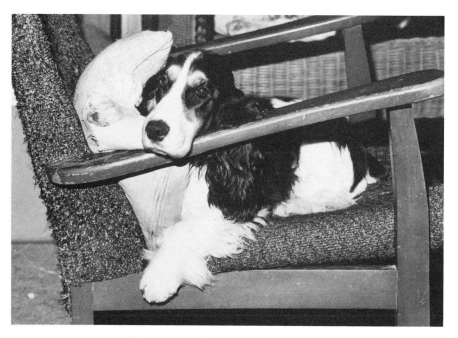

'So what? Mum's busy!' (Tracy Morgan.)

Holidays

Many owners very happily take their pet away on holiday with them, but it must be ascertained beforehand that pets are allowed. You must remember to make provision for the dog's needs just as you would at home and that you cannot completely relax until you are sure the dog is secure and happy. A travelling cage is very useful for short rest periods but it must be ensured that wherever it is placed the dog has protection from wind, rain and sun, and yet has sufficient ventilation.

If the dog is not to accompany you, he must be put in the charge of a responsible person or taken to boarding kennels. Most dogs settle into kennels quite well after a day or two, and come to enjoy their holiday too. Seek out a kennel where the owner and staff seem understanding and the dogs are happy. Enquiries should be made well in advance as good kennels become fully booked up at popular holiday times.

When you go abroad, you must of course leave the dog behind, for he cannot re-enter the UK without undergoing a six-month period in quarantine kennels.

The Law

All dogs in public places must wear a collar with a tag bearing the name and address of the owner, and it is an offence for owners to allow their dogs to become a noise nuisance. Owners must keep their dogs under control in the countryside. There are serious consequences for a dog found worrying sheep and measures may be taken against dogs loose in a field with livestock. Owners are also liable if a dog does serious damage or causes an accident, so it is wise to insure.

Insurance

Owners should cover for third-party liability, though it is worth checking whether this is already covered by the household insurance.

Unexpected veterinary fees can come as a shock, so health insurance might also be considered. There are companies that specialize in animal or pet insurance, and have a wide choice of policies on offer.

Training

While heredity has an influence on the dog's character, environment also plays a significant part in its formation. The way you treat and train your dog therefore has a great bearing on his development into a well-adjusted and acceptable member of society and your household.

You must accept at the outset that discipline is needed to produce a well-behaved animal. Firmness must be tempered with kindness and patience, and you must never lose your temper with a dog. For instance, if after calling him for ten minutes in a field, he returns to you in his own time, you must not smack him or shout, however angry and frustrated you may be. You must praise him, or he will associate coming back to you with your displeasure.

The serious training should be carried out by one person, but the ground rules must be followed by all members of the family. Be consistent in the use of commands and use short words. Give commands in a clear, firm voice, but reserve the shout for emergency.

Training sessions should be regular and kept short. While repetition is important, do not allow the session to become boring, and take a break between exercises. Always make training sessions fun, and try to end with a game.

Training is a matter of anticipation rather than correction. House-training, for instance, is successful more as a result of your alertness and foresight than it is of the puppy learning the rules by repeatedly making mistakes. If you are watchful and catch the puppy before he makes a mistake in the house, and quickly put him outside, he will soon associate being outside with the action of relieving himself. In the same way, if you expect your dog to be fearful of some situation, you will transmit that fear to him and cause his anxiety. Many a sensible dog has been ruined by an over-protective owner. If you introduce your dog to new situations gradually and with common sense, and do not expect him to be nervous, he will accept them as a matter of course.

From the first days in his new home, the puppy will be learning the word, 'No!', firmly spoken. There are many lessons that a puppy has to learn, and a puppy's lively ways will often need controlling if they are of the kind that could become a serious problem. A puppy is never too young to be told right from wrong, and the earlier it is done the better. It is easier to teach a young puppy with gentle firmness, than to correct an adolescent when a bad habit has formed. For instance, a puppy who nips the fingers, perhaps only in play, should be corrected promptly. The puppy must always understand who is master, as such behaviour could lead to unwelcome aggression in the future.

Similar rules will apply over toys. Puppies love to have their own playthings and owners like to provide items which their puppy can enjoy and which will also keep him occupied. Simple things can give as much pleasure as doggie toys bought from the shop. However, if such items as an old slipper are provided, the puppy will have to learn to distinguish between his plaything and your footwear. The golden rule, of course, is not to leave anything you value within reach of the puppy until he has passed the chewing stage. An empty carton or cardboard roll can provide amusement, but care must be taken that all toys are made of a material that will do him no harm if he chews it. Toys can sometimes be taken away, and given back later or different ones provided, in order to make a change, but do not tease him over it. Balls should be large enough not to be swallowed, and should be hard enough not to be easily chewed up. Games of tug-of-war should not be indulged in as, again, this could lead to a situation of aggression, besides pulling the dog's teeth out of alignment. If the slightest possessiveness is shown over toys, it must be checked immediately.

Puppies or adult dogs will enjoy an occasional bone. Only large marrow bones should be given. Never offer chicken or chop bones. Dog chews are available on the pet market. Chewing bones is good exercise for the jaw and helps clean the teeth, as well as being beneficial to puppies at time of teething.

Commands

A well-behaved dog is a pleasure to own and it is worth while spending time teaching him to be obedient. As well as the word, 'No!', there are two further instructions which every family dog should be taught: one is to come to his name, and the other is to sit on command. The puppy can start learning them from a very early age. The puppy's name will have been used from his arrival into the house and, if used frequently, he will soon learn to respond. When the puppy comes to command he should always be greeted with pleasure. To correct wrongdoing, go to the dog; never call him for chastisement or he will cease to come willingly. Coming to call

95

when off the lead and away from home territory is another matter and can be learned as an extension to lead-training.

Meanwhile, the puppy can be taught to sit. Place one hand under the head and with the other, push his rear end into a sitting position, at the same time telling him, 'Sit'. Even if he sits only momentarily when you remove your hand, praise him. A small puppy will not readily wish to stay still but, with perseverance and repetition, he will gradually understand the lesson. In training, it is important to keep the lessons short, probably not more than about five minutes at a time. A small puppy only has a short concentration span. It is also important to repeat the lessons frequently, at least daily, until they have been thoroughly learned. As soon as the puppy makes the required response, make much fuss of him by patting and using a praising tone of voice. Small titbits can be given as a reward, but should not be used extensively or the dog could become demanding.

Although a dog should always be on a lead in traffic, it is helpful as a point of safety if he will sit at the kerb. Equally, he should sit or wait for instructions before jumping out of the car. But a word of counsel here if you contemplate showing your dog. It is better to teach him to wait or stay in the standing position rather than the easier sit, as you will not want the dog sitting every time you stop in the ring, and exhibits are expected to stand for long periods while the judge makes his deliberations.

The command, 'Leave!' is another very useful instruction for a puppy to learn as there are often times when you would like the dog to ignore something, such as food that is not intended for him or items found during a walk. Such lessons can be taught in the general upbringing by repetition, firmness, consistency, and praise when the instruction has been obeyed.

Lead-Training

A puppy should not be expected to walk on the road until he is four or five months old, and certainly not before he is fully inoculated. A youngster's bone formation can be damaged if walked on hard pavements before being sufficiently developed, and an untrained puppy can also spoil his shoulders and front by pulling on the lead. Therefore lead-training the puppy at home is a preliminary to his entry to the big wide world. A small soft collar can be put on the puppy for short periods so that he gets used to wearing one. The collar should be loose enough to insert two fingers, but tight enough so that it will not slip over the dog's head. It should never be so loose that the dog's lower jaw could be caught in it. Many owners like to leave a collar on the house dog permanently, as it is an easy restraint, and if the dog gets out he may more quickly be recovered by the help of an identification disc. Unfortunately, a permanent collar will interfere with the lie of the hair on the neck, so particular care must be taken with potential show dogs.

After the puppy has worn a collar a few times, take him into the garden and put the lead on too. If the puppy wishes to walk round and investigate, go with him leaving the lead slack. Then encourage the puppy to come to you, gently pulling the lead towards you. Do not drag him but, talking to him all the time, try to persuade him to move. If the puppy rears up on his hind legs, you must be very patient and, with kind words and coaxing, encourage him to walk towards you instead of fighting against the lead. It may take several lessons before the puppy will walk round the garden with you. Titbits can be used here to encourage the puppy to walk with you.

So that the outside world should not be too awesome when the time comes, the puppy should become accustomed to new sights and sounds. While he is still small, gradually introduce him to traffic and people by carrying him about with you when appropriate. Caution, however, must be exercised so that he does not come into contact with other dogs, where they have been, or the people handling them until his vaccinations are complete.

Having learned to walk nicely on the lead at home, the puppy can then be taken out for short walks on the road. In his excitement, he may pull. He should be firmly jerked back by a sharp pull on the lead. The severity of the correction will depend very much on the response and sensitivity of the dog. A strong self-willed six-month-old may require a really hard check, but a gentle sensitive puppy may respond to a slight pull on the lead and the command, 'Heel' or 'Walk'.

Your Cocker Spaniel should have his own collar and lead in leather or nylon, the collar being of a suitable size for him, and bearing an identification disc. Check- or slip-collars or chains are not usually necessary for a Cocker Spaniel, but if one is used for a particularly boisterous dog, it is *absolutely essential* that it is fitted and used correctly. It must automatically slacken from around the dog's neck when the handler releases tension.

It is wise to seek the advice of a more experienced person when fitting a check- or slip-collar for the first time, as they can be dangerous when used improperly. They should never be worn around the house, or at any time when the dog is not on a lead. If you wish your dog to wear a collar all the time, use the fixed leather or nylon one, reserving the check-chain for training or road work when its use can be supervised.

The basic principle of recall will have been picked up at home, when you have attracted his attention by calling his name, then followed this with the command, 'Come!'. However, before letting the puppy loose in the public park, you will need to give him some further lessons. Other dogs, new smells and people will distract his attention from you, and you must be sure that you can regain that attention before allowing him any freedom from the lead.

Take him to the park or open space with a long line or extending lead attached to his collar. Let him walk around at the full length of the lead, then after a few minutes call him back to you. If he does not respond, you will be able to tug on the line to initiate a response, at the same time pulling him back towards you and coaxing him by repeating his name and the command, 'Come!' He must then be rewarded and the exercise repeated. It is a lesson which must be thoroughly learned before you risk letting the dog off the lead. An extending lead is a useful aid to training for a difficult dog, or in a strange area or in the countryside where it is not wise to let a dog run free, but it should not be used near roads. If at any time a loose dog fails to return to you when called, do not run towards him as this will only encourage him to run away from you. Attract his attention by calling him sharply, then turn and walk away, encouraging him to follow. Most dogs will, as they may think you are going to leave them behind.

Retrieving

Cocker Spaniels have a natural instinct to retrieve. Some will bring a thrown article back without much training, but for those more stubborn who would rather keep the object to themselves, the handler must resort to the long line or extending lead, as used in the recall. From the start, encourage the puppy to bring the retrieved article right up to hand. Dropping it at your feet is a habit hard to correct and is not acceptable for serious training.

Retrieving is good exercise for dogs and a pastime they enjoy. It can be performed in the garden or the park or, to make it more interesting, in the woods, or over common land, where the natural instinct to scent will also be practised. However, for some dogs, retrieving can become an obsession, so it is probably wise to reserve it for recreation times.

Cars

Get your dog accustomed to the car early and you are unlikely to have problems. Aids, such as adjustable dog guards and purpose-built cages, will keep the dog secure, both for his own safety and so that he does not interfere with the driver. When purchasing a cage for a puppy, it is sensible to obtain one that he will be able to use when adult or he will have little benefit from it. If using a travel box, care must be taken to ensure that ventilation holes are not obstructed.

It is perhaps opportune here to stress the necessity for providing ventilation at all times when in the car, and the importance of removing the dog from a stationary car in hot weather. *Never* leave a dog in a car in summer, and at other times ensure that the car is parked in a shady position, as even a little sunshine can make the interior temperature rise very fast. It is like leaving the dog in an oven, and it is unfortunate that dogs have been known to die from the heat when left unattended in parked cars. At most summer shows, exhibitors are forbidden to leave any dogs in a parked car.

One difficulty that arises when conveying a caged youngster by car is that should he object to being confined, the driver is virtually helpless to control him; you can only correct him by the tone of your voice. It is therefore advisable to train the dog at home first. Do this by making a bed for the dog in the back of the car, and leave him for about ten minutes. Do this several times before actually driving him out for a ride. If he is quiet, praise him at the end of the session, but if he makes a fuss, go back and chastise him. It is helpful to have an assistant in case the dog is noisy or distressed when travelling for the first time. Most dogs soon love the car and will not miss an opportunity of going in it.

As a rule, Cocker Spaniels are excellent travellers, but odd ones will suffer from travel sickness. It is better for the dog, even a puppy, if going on a long journey, to travel on an empty stomach, and to be fed at an interval after arrival. It does a dog no harm to miss a meal on the odd occasion. If sickness is a problem, obtain some tablets from your pet store or consult your vet, but usually the

S. Afr. Ch. and Sh.Ch. Craigleith Sweet Charity. (Fall.)

dog will outgrow it, particularly if you train him to travel in a calm and quiet manner.

Classes

Owners find it very useful to attend training classes, where both dog and handler can learn the elements of basic obedience. It is sometimes surprising how a dog who ignores your instructions at home will submit to the authority of the trainer. Obedience classes are also a way of reinforcing the lessons learned at home. Very often a dog will behave perfectly in your own garden, but get him out in the company of other dogs and people and, in his excitement, he forgets his manners. The instructor will be able to iron out any difficulty an owner is having with the training of the dog.

When dog and handler have learned the basics, there may be no further need to continue; but if you make good progress and are both enjoying it, you may want to proceed to competition level. Because a Cocker Spaniel likes to use his initiative and has a natural instinct to take notice of what is happening, training to a high standard becomes a challenge.

Exercise

Having taken a dog into the family, it is your responsibility to give him adequate exercise. A puppy will obtain this by free running in your own garden, if only a small one, and by following you around the house; his exercise should be little and often. Formal walks should be limited until he is older. By all means take him to the park, but do not overtire him. The amount of exercise he is given should be gradually built up over the months until at about a year old he will be able to take all you care to give him.

The same applies if you are taking on an older dog, particularly if he is a little overweight. Do not expect him to walk ten miles if he is only accustomed to going round the block. It is kinder to give regular short walks, gradually increasing in length to improve his fitness. Nonetheless, all spaniels will appreciate some creative activity, such as retrieving exercises and search and discovery.

The adult Cocker Spaniel should have at least one daily walk, but preferably two. A short walk in the morning would suffice, but an owner must be prepared to devote something like an hour to the dog's recreation at a later time. Many people themselves enjoy a walk on the heath or through the woods, and this in the company of an active Cocker Spaniel can be even more pleasurable. The daily exercise can be taken in conjunction with family activities, such as meeting the children from school or a game in the park.

As a pet owner, you are also responsible for clearing up after your dog in public places. Try to train your dog to use an appointed area in the garden at home before he goes out for a walk and, in an emergency, let him use the gutter. Always take a hand-sized plastic bag with you: put your hand inside to pick up any faeces, reverse the bag, tie it up and drop it in the nearest litter bin.

Never allow your dog on to a sports field or children's playground. It is uncongenial and unhygienic to let him foul public areas, and indeed there are many places these days, such as some parks and beaches, where dogs are banned. In other places, it is becoming common for scoops and bins to be provided by the local authority for the disposal of dog waste. Byelaws in some localities make it an offence for a person to allow a dog to foul the footway.

101

It is wise to keep your dog on a lead in the countryside until you have ascertained that it is safe to let him free. He should always be on a lead where there are sheep and cattle in case he is tempted to chase them; farmers are within their rights to shoot at a dog who is seen worrying sheep. Cultivated and fenced land usually belongs to a farmer, so respect his property: keep to footpaths and keep the dog on a lead. Public access is also restricted over areas where shooting takes place. There are, however, many areas – riverside walks, common land and parts of national parks – where dogs and walkers are welcome, but you must be able to exert complete control in order to prevent his becoming a nuisance to others.

Kennels

If you have two or more dogs for showing or work, or intend to breed a litter from time to time, you may decide that an outside kennel is desirable. It is often satisfactory to convert an existing building, provided the construction, dimensions and situation are suitable. A kennel needs to be light, airy and draught-free; something like a stable or workshop is probably ideal for conversion.

As a general rule, adult Cocker Spaniels do not need heating when suitable sleeping quarters and regular exercise are provided. In some cases, as with a young litter or in severe conditions, extra warmth is required and, for the short days of winter and for emergency night attention, electric light certainly helps. Installation must of course be completely safe, with cable and switches out of reach of the inmates. Water should be available and initially an outside tap may suffice for replenishing bowls.

Although, for the sake of hygiene, some people may prefer kennels not to be near the house, there are advantages to such a position. Puppies need frequent attention, and it is more convenient to have them near at hand; but dogs this close will be alert to activities such as food preparation, and may thus present a nuisance.

If your kennel has a wooden floor, it should not be placed directly on the ground but raised a few inches and the space below closed off. Sleeping beds in a kennel on a concrete base should be placed on a low platform, off the cold floor, but with ease of access for the dog. You do not want your young show prospect spoiling his front by constantly jumping up and down from a high bench. A kennel for two Cocker Spaniels should have a minimum floor space of about 6ft × 4ft (2m × 1.2m) and it is convenient if it is high enough for the attendant to be able to stand upright. Window shutters can be an asset for extra warmth and to prevent the light streaming in to wake up your litter in the early hours of a summer morning.

Wooden panels of a few feet high make an adequate pen for the occasional litter of puppies or quiet dogs not inclined to chew, but if a run were to be used long-term, steel mesh panels or a sturdy chain-link fence would be more suitable, as they admit light and air. The height of the fence should be at least 4ft (1.2m), as it is not unknown for Cocker Spaniels to escape by jumping or climbing.

A small run should not be left to grass, as it will quickly deteriorate to a mud patch with the constant walking up and down of dogs and people. The area should be concreted or paved, with some thought given to the gradient so that puddles do not form after rain, and for ease of washing down.

If you intend to keep a number of dogs in kennels, there are various considerations which must be taken into account, not least the laws on keeping dogs and local authority regulations within your area. It is often felt that legislation is hitting the wrong people, but the law that a breeder who has more than two bitches of breeding age must obtain a breeder's licence was aimed to control the puppy farmer who overbreeds and rears stock in poor conditions. In some countries, owners are restricted to a certain number of dogs, even if they are only pets, if the garden is less than a stipulated acreage. Proximity to neighbours must also be considered. It is your responsibility to take the utmost care over hygiene and to control barking dogs.

Thorough cleanliness must be observed at all times to keep dogs fit and healthy. It is a good idea to have shovel, broom and covered bucket handy, so that excrement can be collected almost as soon as it is deposited. A watering can of a mild disinfectant solution also at hand means that patches of ground can be sprayed or washed down, but the disinfectant or cleaner used must be recommended as suitable for use with dogs. Collected waste should be disposed of hygienically and frequently. Incineration is widely recommended, but before installing elaborate equipment check with your local authority on building regulations, the Clean Air Act, fire precautions and health hazards.

Plastic and fibreglass beds are sometimes used, and are easy to clean, but if young dogs chew them they can be hazardous. Zinc edging gives wooden boxes a longer life.

103

It is most important to check each night that the bedding is quite dry. Blankets do not make very satisfactory bedding as they retain moisture. Clean straw is very good; some will get eaten but it seems to do the dogs no harm. If it gets a little damp from wet feet, it can be shaken out and soon dries off. It should, of course, be changed at regular intervals and the beds lightly sprinkled with louse powder. Dry sawdust of a medium grain is a good covering for the floor of the kennel: not only does it absorb moisture from wet feet, but also absorbs any urine and can be easily swept up and disposed of with the excrement. Shavings seem to tangle the coat. Many people use newspaper on the floor, and this is probably the best material for small puppies. Paper shreddings could also be used for bedding.

The kennel should occasionally be thoroughly washed down using a suitable bleach or household soda crystals dissolved in water, and the floor scrubbed. This is necessary not only to remove any grease and grime which may have collected, but because fleas and the like lay their eggs in cracks and crevices. Ideally the dogs, too, should be bathed and dried before returning. Other maintenance work must be carried out regularly to ensure that buildings and equipment are safe. Always make sure that there are no places where a dog can damage himself. Prevent accidents.

If you are kennelling a lot of dogs, you will need to buy food in bulk. A separate freezer for the dogs' meat is ideal, but if you use the household freezer, ensure that the meat is contained separately from the family's food. Biscuit and other foods must be stored in a dry place, in corn bins or rubbish bins with tightly fitting lids. Any small spillages must be cleared up immediately to avoid attracting vermin.

A kennel routine for feeding, exercising and grooming will soon develop, according to the requirements and the number of dogs housed, and this routine should be adhered to as strictly as possible. Kennelled dogs need as much care and attention in the form of recreation and grooming as the house dog. They cannot be constantly restricted to one small area, but must be taken out regularly for exercise and a change of environment. Feeding times must be supervised to ensure that each dog gets his share, and each should have his own food bowl and access to fresh water. They must be let out frequently to relieve themselves and their health and condition should be checked daily. Smoking should be prohibited at all times and fire-fighting equipment must be available.

6

Grooming

A well-groomed Cocker Spaniel is a pleasure to behold and is something which should be the aim of every owner. It requires only a little effort to make your dog a credit to you and to make him feel more comfortable. Whether it is through laziness or lack of control over the dog, it is surprising how few pet owners will undertake the simple task of keeping their dog tidy. All that is needed is the willingness to learn, and once you have mastered the technique, you will find it quite easy. Grooming need not take more than a few minutes if carried out daily. You can of course take the dog every few months to a grooming parlour, but you must nonetheless undertake basic, regular grooming inbetween visits to keep the dog in good health and a desirable member of the family. This is one of the responsibilities you accept when you bring a Cocker Spaniel into your household.

Many owners rely solely upon the occasional visit to a professional groomer, and do not carry out basic care between times. As a result, the dog becomes so matted that the groomer has no option but to clip off the entire coat in order to remove the mats. This is a long process and leaves the dog looking most uncharacteristic in appearance. So, to avoid such drastic action, groom your Cocker Spaniel regularly, making sure that you groom right down to the skin, disentangling all the knots before they become a problem.

Equipment

In addition to the main equipment listed below, you will need cotton wool, a rubber mat, petroleum jelly, a soft toothbrush and towels.

Bristle or dandy brush This should be a stiff brush of a reasonable size to be effective on a dog as substantial as an adult Cocker

Grooming equipment.

Spaniel. At the same time it must, as with all equipment, be comfortable for you to handle. The brush is used to untangle the hair and brush out loose hairs and dirt. A small dandy brush as used for horses is ideal.

Wide-toothed comb The local pet shop usually has a selection of metal combs available, with or without handles. Some have a combination of coarse and finer teeth. Such a comb is used to work through the long hair to free it of knots after preliminary brushing.

No. 76 comb This is known all over the world as the Spaniel Comb. It was originally designed as the Spratt's No. 6 and is commonly called by that name today. It is a fine-toothed comb and is an essential piece of equipment. If your pet shop cannot supply it, do not be palmed off with any other – no other will do. It can be obtained by mail order from one of the many suppliers of equipment, with whom your dog's breeder or local canine society could put you in touch.

Body brush Again, this is of the type used for horses, but slightly smaller. It has soft bristles and a canvas band to put the hand through, and is used for polishing.

Hound glove This grooming glove can be all rubber, or canvas with closely set short bristles, and is also used for polishing.

Straight scissors Long, narrow, pointed scissors are usual, and are used to cut the hair from around and under the feet.

Thinning scissors Scissors with serrated edges are used to thin out thick growths of hair.

Finger cones Rubber thimbles, or finger stalls of the medical variety, are useful for gripping the hair when plucking. A rubber glove or the fingers cut from one could be used instead.

Chalk block Small blocks of white chalk are available which are useful as a trimming aid. It is a Kennel Club rule, however, that any such substance must be well brushed out and removed from the coat before a dog is shown.

Benzyl benzoate This is a white lotion, available from dispensing chemists, and should be diluted two parts lotion to one part water. It can be used for cleaning ears, and can also be applied to small areas of the skin in cases of lice, harvest mite or scurf. It should be used sparingly and must not be used near the eyes, genitalia or on nursing bitches. A spirit substance is appropriate for use in the ear; an oil will leave the ear damp thereby making an attractive situation for bacteria.

Nail clippers These are also required. They come in different types and it is probably best to seek advice before purchase.

Puppies and Juveniles

Discipline must be exercised, for grooming is impossible unless the subject keeps still. Start right from the beginning with a small puppy, teaching him to behave while having his daily groom. You must not be afraid to assert your authority over your young charge, who may in the early stages fight against your control. The easiest way with a puppy is to sit down and hold him on your lap. If he tries to bite or chew your fingers or the equipment, he must be scolded with a firm 'No!' and a tap on the nose.

Using a small bristle brush, start at the head and ears and work towards the tail. Then comb the puppy all over with the No. 76 comb. You must ensure that there is no food or other dirt dried on the tips of the ears, and anything which does not comb out fairly easily must be washed. You can dip the tips of the ears only, in a cup or small bowl of warm soapy water, working with your fingers, and then rinse and rub dry. Turn the puppy over and, carefully holding him between your legs, check the tummy for dirt or tangles.

The eyes should be wiped with cotton wool dampened with clean water and then dried. A spaniel's eyes are usually a little moist, but if your puppy's eyes seem weepy or droopy, rub some zinc and castor oil cream around – but not in – the eye two or three times a week. A smear of petroleum jelly can be used when the skin surrounding the eye seems dry. Any condition which persists should be referred to a veterinary surgeon.

While brushing, you can gently brush the hair on the back against its growth to ensure there is no dandruff. Check for fleas by combing with the lie of the hair and keeping the comb almost flat. If one or two are combed out, drop them in a bowl of water. Skin parasites must be got rid of by using insecticidal powder or spray, or bathing the puppy in a special shampoo; take care to ensure that the product is suitable for use on a young puppy. Ozone-friendly sprays are available.

About once a week use ear drops, or apply a cleaner such as benzyl benzoate on a little cotton wool to the inside of the ear, taking care to clean only the area you can see and not to poke into the ear channel. Look inside the puppy's mouth to ensure that gums are not unduly sore from teething. A simple mouth ulcer ointment may give relief. A puppy's teeth will begin to work loose any time from twelve weeks of age. It is not normally obvious that the teeth are falling out, though occasionally a dropped one will be found on the carpet! You will just see reddened gums and the second teeth erupting. It is as well to keep an eye on things as sometimes an adult tooth will grow alongside a milk tooth which, if stubborn, will have to be removed. Teething takes place until the pup is about six months old. The jaw goes on developing for even longer, so it is not necessarily a cause for concern if a show prospect appears a little overshot during these stages.

From time to time, a dog's nails will need shortening. A small puppy's nails become long and sharp and they should be blunted, using ordinary nail scissors. As the puppy grows and the nails become coarser, special clippers should be used. Ask the veterinary surgeon to trim them when you are on a routine visit, or consult the breeder or the grooming parlour. A dog can grow very long nails, which can get caught up in things or grow back into the foot if neglected, particularly dew-claws (those on the insides of the fore-legs) if they have not been removed at birth. Plenty of exercise on hard roads or pavements may help to keep the toe nails of an adult dog under control.

When each aspect has been dealt with, finish off with a brushing to make sure the hair is in place. Then praise the puppy and put him down outside as he will probably want to relieve himself.

As the puppy grows, you must train him to stand on a table or other sturdy structure for grooming. A blanket or a rubber mat should be placed on it if the surface is at all slippery. This will make the dog feel secure and he will relax. If an assistant can steady the youngster's head and put a hand underneath to prevent him sitting down, it will greatly help matters until the pup learns what is expected. The dog can, however, sit while the head and ears are groomed.

If the hair on the feet of the puppy is kept tidy, he will not bring too much wet and dirt into the house and it will be more comfort-able for him. Lift the paw and using the straight scissors, cut the hair on top of the foot downwards level with the foot. Turn the foot back and cut the hair flat across the pads. This will ensure the foot does not become matted or too caked in mud. The Cocker Spaniel's foot needs protection, so do not cut the hair out from between toes or pads. Check for grass seeds or thorns, particularly at times of risk.

Cut the hair from under the tail: hold the tail up and use the thinning scissors, pointing them away from the dog's body. A dog will usually clean himself up around the anus and genital areas, but the hair there should be kept short to prevent soiling.

To a greater or lesser degree, all Cocker Spaniels grow a top-knot or tuft of hair on top of their heads. As this is mostly dead hair, comb it out with the No. 76, using it flat against the head, combing towards the occiput and with the forefinger laid across the teeth of the comb. To get a finer result, hold a small bunch of hairs firmly between thumb and forefinger of the left hand; then taking only a few hairs at a time between thumb and side of the first knuckle of the forefinger of the right hand, pluck them out in the direction in which the hair grows. Many people use finger stalls to get a better grip, and rubbing the hair with chalk also helps.

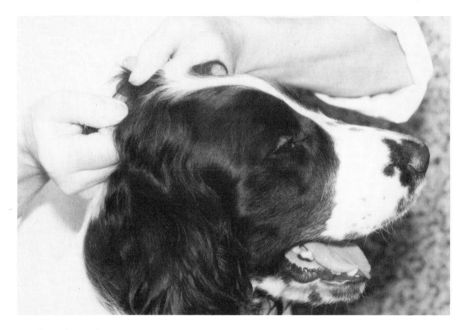

Plucking the top-knot.

As the puppy gets older his coat will grow longer and thicker, and you will find that you need to use the stiff bristle brush. After brushing through the coat with it, the wide-toothed comb should be used to comb out any tangles, particularly in the feathering on the back of the legs. Then comb all over with the No. 76 to remove loose and dead hair. The comb can be used on the body in the same manner as it is on the head. Tuck the puppy's head under your left arm, and comb along the back towards the tail. Also comb down the outside of the legs. Then turn the puppy round and, holding the comb almost flat to the body with your thumb along the teeth, comb towards the tail and yourself.

Many Cockers grow a very fluffy or dense puppy coat which is quite soft, and the inexperienced owner may be very shocked to find his smooth Cocker Spaniel baby gradually turning into an Afghan! The feathering and fluffiness of a golden will be much lighter in colour than the body coat at this stage. The puppy coat will not be ready to come out until the pup is about eight to nine months of age. The grooming procedure as described should be carried out until that time, but no serious trimming should be done

Using the No. 76 comb.

until the coat is ready to 'give' as more harm than good can be done. When the time is right, you should be able to exert some pressure when using the No. 76, and you will be surprised at the amount of hair that can be removed by simple combing.

It is essential that the first major trim or removal of the puppy coat should be expertly done. You should, if possible, consult the vendor of the puppy. Most welcome the opportunity to see their puppies again and are pleased to give some guidance.

The puppy coat should be removed carefully by combing and plucking and without in any way cutting the hair on the head or back, or the coat will grow through thick and wavy. A terrier or stripping comb should not be used on these parts. You may find that with some advice you are able to do the job yourself. It is, in any case, better to take the hair out over a period of time and easier on the animal to have it done in short sessions. The coats of Cocker Spaniels vary very much; some, such as solid colours and dark-blue roans, may be very heavy.

If you are doubtful of your own ability, try to locate a professional groomer in the area who specializes in spaniels. Try to discuss your

111

Mrs V. Hillary's six-month-old Bidston Final Flutter in puppy coat.
(Alan Carey.)

requirements with the groomer beforehand, and ask for hand-stripping. If the growth of coat is very dense and you have neg-lected it, there may be no alternative to clipping; but if you have endeavoured to keep it under control groomers will be sympathetic and do their best.

In keeping the coat free of mats you may find it helpful to use the slicker brush as described on page 116. The dog who is unaccus-tomed to much grooming sometimes tolerates this, when used gently, better than the comb and although it really gives only a superficial result, some pet owners get on quite well with it.

When your Cocker Spaniel has his full set of teeth, they should be cleaned once a week. Obtain some canine toothpaste or powder from your pet shop or vet and apply it with an ordinary soft toothbrush. Your dog may struggle against it the first few times, but will soon accept this attention as a matter of course. Tooth scalers can be used on any build-up of tartar, but a visit to the vet might be more advisable as the dog can then also be checked for diseased teeth or gums. A good diet, crunching hard biscuits and gnawing bones help to keep the teeth and gums in good order. Before completing a weekly check, rub a little petroleum jelly into the dog's nose to prevent it becoming dry and crusty.

Bathing

From time to time, your Cocker Spaniel will need a bath, and it is as well to get him accustomed to this while he is still young. Providing you give proper attention to his general grooming, and the cleanliness of the bedding and sleeping area, a bath every few months should be sufficient.

He can be bathed in the kitchen sink or in the family bath, using a rubber mat to prevent slipping. On a warm and sunny day, he could be bathed outside, using an old enamel or tin tub or a discarded baby bath. Use a shower attachment or plastic cup and sponges to wet the hair. The water should be lukewarm. It is best to purchase a shampoo formulated for use on dogs and to follow the instructions carefully. Before putting the dog in the bath, brush and comb him, as water cannot penetrate to the skin through knots of hair. Rub a little petroleum jelly round the eyes and be careful not to splash them with shampoo. The ears can be plugged with a little cotton wool, but do not forget to remove it afterwards. After the dog has been shampooed and rinsed thoroughly, remove him from the bath and towel-dry. A chamois leather frequently squeezed out is very useful. Comb the coat through to ensure it is lying correctly. A hairdrier helps speed the drying process, but the dog will be nervous of it on the first occasion, so run it on a low setting and switch it off at intervals. Be particularly careful around the ears. Comb through again, and keep the dog in a warm airy room.

Grooming the Adult

Theoretically, the adult Cocker Spaniel will moult twice a year, in the spring and autumn. Many male dogs do not shed very much, but bitches often lose their coats a couple of months after their season, which is the time they would have had pups had they been mated. The body coat becomes quite thin and the feathering on the legs and tummy gradually falls out. Indeed, some bitches appear almost naked!

Grooming and bathing the adult is much the same as for the puppy and juvenile, and the same procedure should be followed. However, the adult grows more hair, so more trimming or hair removal is necessary. Only work on a thoroughly dry coat.

You will find there are places apart from the top of the head and the feet that need tidying up. With a little patience, and a firm hand on the dog, you may find that you can undertake much of this yourself, carrying out a trim of this sort every three to four weeks depending on hair type and growth. It is now that you will find the thinning scissors coming in handy, but if you want to keep your dog's coat looking as sleek as possible, the thinners should be used only on the underparts.

It is a common belief that spaniels have problems with their ears, but this is a misinterpretation of the situation. Because they are a drop-eared breed, the air does not easily reach the ears and bacteria builds up; but if the ears are properly looked after and cleaned regularly there should be few problems. It is important, therefore, to keep the hair under the ears short. Some Cockers grow thick tufts of hair under the ear and this, and the hair at the back of the ear, should be reduced with the thinning scissors. You should be most careful when using scissors near dogs' ears, as this of course is a very sensitive area. Do this somewhere near the middle of the grooming session when the dog has relaxed into the routine, and before he becomes bored and fidgety.

Many Cocker Spaniels, particularly the heavily coated ones, grow thick hair or an Elizabethan ruff around the throat, and this too can be lessened by using the scissors. Cut against the lie of the hair, but not across it, and keep combing out the trimmings.

One must be very careful to comb thoroughly under the elbows. The hair in this area seems to tangle very easily and mats soon form. It is a good idea to cut away some of the hair there too. The dog can be taught to lie on his side while some of the grooming tasks are performed. It is then easier to see what you are doing and more restful for the dog.

Another place where the thinners can be used is around the tail and below it where the hair sometimes seems quite bushy. It is also a matter of good hygiene that there should not be excessive furnishing in this area. The dog does not need to carry fluffy hair on the back of the hind legs from the hock to the ground. It is in order for a pet dog to have this trimmed down with the straight scissors. The long hair on the lower part of the front legs up to the pasterns can become muddy and tangled, and this should be cut back, taking care to avoid the carpal pad situated behind the knee (or wrist). Any excessive feathering on a heavily coated dog can be reduced by the use of the thinning scissors. On a lighter-coated animal, it may be necessary to shorten overlong fringes but otherwise a good combing to remove loose hairs is all that is required.

Some owners like to cut back the dog's whiskers which, while not absolutely necessary, gives a smarter appearance. There are, too, usually a few stray whiskers in the eyebrows and under the chin.

Plucking from the top of the head should be continued, and if some hair is plucked from the top of the ears it will give the head a more aristocratic appearance. Although the hair on the muzzle should be smooth, it seems to grow thickly on some Cocker Spaniels, giving an unkempt appearance. It should be gently but firmly plucked, particularly from in front of the eyes. Otherwise the dog is continually peering through hair, which cannot help the eyesight. Likewise, the front of the legs should be smooth, but with some colours and the heavier coats this will need plucking out. Tufts on the side of the elbows and the side of the hind legs should also be plucked or thinned to give a neater appearance.

To finish off, give the coat a polish with the body brush or hound glove. A good bloom to the coat can equally be achieved with a piece of velvet, towelling or soft cloth.

With a little practice you can become quite skilled at trimming your pet. The important thing is for him to be clean and comfortable, and if at the same time you can keep him looking like a respectable and typical specimen of the breed, it will be worth while. With regular attention you should be able to keep the coat under control, and if in the summer your dog is not panting under a heavy coat, he will appreciate it.

Trimming for Show

The basic equipment needed to prepare a Cocker Spaniel for show has not changed over the years. But there have been many developments in this field and there is now a plethora of equipment and accessories available. The choice is truly bewildering.

However, the aim of trimming a Cocker Spaniel is to emphasize his better points, minimize his faults, and to present him looking as natural as possible with curving lines, no sharp angles and a good

A respectable and typical specimen of the breed. (Alan Carey.)

bloom to a smooth coat. Providing you have good-quality tools, an excellent result can certainly be achieved using the equipment already described for trimming the pet Cocker Spaniel. The techniques simply need to be refined. However, some additional pieces of equipment could be mentioned here.

Slicker   This is a brush-type implement made up of steel pins, usually bent at the ends. It is used to ensure the coat is lying in place before entry into the ring, and most exhibitors seem to regard it as a must.

Wire glove   This has a similar effect to the slicker but the pins, not being hooked, make it less severe on the dog. If the coat is fine, the slicker is hardly necessary; a soft hound glove is more appropriate.

At the general Championship Shows there are usually avenues of trade stands selling all manner of doggie requirements. Here is the best hunting ground for your grooming needs, as there will be a large selection of specialist goods at competitive prices. Some stalls will usually be found at the smaller shows as well, and many of the larger concerns will supply by mail order. You can often leave your scissors for sharpening with appropriate traders at shows.

The preparation of a Cocker Spaniel's coat for show cannot take place overnight, but has to be built up over weeks. You must ensure that the dog is clean and free of skin parasites. If he scratches, a red or orange discoloration to the hair will be visible and will not wash clean. You have to wait for it to grow out. An area typically prone to this is the armpit, clearly seen when a dog is moving towards you and most unsightly.

The process of trimming should be spread over several sessions. Put the dog down from the table at intervals and allow a little exercise and fun. This also affords you the opportunity to check your progress. Try to have the table situated so that you can walk all round it. A large mirror on the wall helps you to view the dog from various angles.

There are tables on the market especially designed for dog grooming with built-in non-slip matting. Some of these are portable and are very useful to take to shows, though any small folding table might be suitable. Gangways at show venues must be kept clear in case of emergency, so compactness and portability are important. Grooming posts, to tether the dog to while he is being worked on, are also available but *never* go out of the room and leave the dog unattended whilst tied up like this. He could try to struggle free and injure himself, or fall off the table and be strangled.

Start each session by giving the dog a good brushing with the dandy brush. Providing the dog is housed in clean quarters, a regular brushing is as good as anything to keep him clean. It also frees the feathering of tangles, stimulates hair growth, tones up the skin and is good for the circulation of both dog and groomer. The slicker brush does not have the same effect at all, and is too harsh for this purpose while only surface-brushing the feathering. It is important to keep the grooming equipment clean.

Assuming that the thorough grooming procedure has been carried out as previously detailed, you will need to increase the amount of trimming to emphasize certain features. Parts of the dog, like under the ears and the throat, are too tender for plucking so the thinning scissors should be used. The hair on the throat should be thinned out so as to give a clean line, but this does not mean that it has to be shaved right down to the skin. The hair should be thinned as far as the breastbone to show the length of neck. A small frill should be left on below the breastbone, but should not be exaggerated. The art of using the thinners is to reduce the amount of hair with as natural a look as possible. The operator must learn not to leave jagged or straight lines. You will learn by experience and by experimenting with different ways. Watch other people do it. Some use thinning scissors with one serrated and one plain blade; others prefer those that are serrated on both blades and with fewer teeth to give a more natural and less harsh finish. The thinners should be used under the ear, taking away sufficient hair to leave the ear lying as flat as possible against the head. Remove some hair from the back of the elbow as excess here can make the dog appear to be throwing his elbows out. The same applies to the feathering on the front legs. Get a friend to move the dog for you, and if the hair is flapping, reduce it.

The head and the top third of the ears must be plucked. It is in fact the easiest part to hand-trim and the soft lines of the Cocker Spaniel's head are part of his appeal. A shaven head has a harsh appearance, which is quite distasteful. The ears should be set low and it is a frequent mistake with novice owners that they do not trim sufficiently far down the ear. Hair must also be removed from the back of the skull working downwards, blending into a nice crest, and down the top and side of the neck. The neck and shoulders are a very difficult part to do. The hair here often seems to be stubborn. But it is essential in most cases for it to be reduced or the dog will appear heavy on the shoulder. After you have worked at it with the No. 76, with forefinger or thumb along the teeth, you will probably still need to pluck it by hand. Rub the chalk block on a patch of hair before plucking as this will help to give a grip. In some cases cautious use of the thinners may be necessary. If you are working on the right side of the dog and you are right-handed, you may find it easier to stand on the left of the dog and work from over the top. It certainly helps to do parts of the ears and neck in this way. Then move round to the other side to complete it.

Any excess hair on the back and flanks must be trimmed out by finger and thumb, having first worked at it with the No. 76 comb. Quite a lot of pressure can be employed, but the comb must be slanted to avoid damaging the skin, and care should be taken over the backbone itself. Many owners make the mistake of leaving long hair or make-believe feathering from somewhere half-way down the ribs, presumably to disguise the fact that the dog has no real feathering falling from under the body. The hair hangs in a curtain from a distinct line across the ribs. It is particularly ugly in colours such as golden and liver roan, where the 'dead' or excess hair is a lighter colour than the body coat. In such cases, it can present a problem to the groomer, but often dogs in the ring carry far too much hair anyway, and removal of some of it would present a far better picture. Whatever the colour, hair on the sides must be blended into the feathering so there is no obvious line.

Contrary to popular belief, Cocker Spaniels should not carry long hair on the outside of the stifle. This should be trimmed back to the short coat. Some hair falls from the inside of the stifle but this should not be excessive. The hind leg from the crook, in front of the hock, to the foot, should be covered with smooth hair. Any long or flapping strands should be removed to give a clean line when moving. Many of the heavily coated ones grow thick wool on this part of the leg and some assistance is needed here to give a smoother appearance. If the hair is very thick, use the thinning scissors first (chopping at it does nothing to enhance it), then smooth it off by plucking. The back of the hind leg from the hock down can be done with scissors but be careful not to make too sharp a line, nor to crop it too close.

The thinning scissors can be used on and around the tail area, as the body coat grows rather thickly here. Many novices leave a bush of hair below the tail and this can be thinned back, so that the feathering is falling more or less between the legs, and the dog does not appear long. Some owners like to leave a small quiff of hair at the end of the tail, especially if the tail is on the short side, and the hair should not be trimmed right back almost to the skin. The tail, after all, is the part which is the indicator of the Cocker's character. Let us see it, wagging happily!

The feet of a Cocker Spaniel should be small and tight. When preparing for a show, try to make your dog's feet as neat as possible. When moving, the dog should appear to be up on his toes, not plodding along on plates. To achieve a neat foot, you must keep the nails under control. Only a fraction should be taken from the tip of the nail, as when cutting your own. If you take too much off, you will cut into the quick and cause bleeding, in which case quickly apply a styptic agent or potassium permanganate to stop it. A handy alternative is cornflour or custard powder. Dogs are very touchy about their feet, and if any harm is done they will always resent future sessions. If you are not very confident about clipping nails, consult a more experienced person, or your vet. For dogs who grow very thick hair on the feet it may be necessary to enlist the aid of the thinning scissors, but be gentle about combing the hair out from this sensitive area. Many Cocker Spaniels appear in the ring carrying great tufts of hair on the top of their feet; perhaps owners think they are disguising flat feet! When you have cut from the top and underneath of the foot, make the dog stand naturally and finish off with the straight scissors. Cut neatly round the foot and tidy up any stray pieces. For a show dog it is not usual to cut the hair back from behind the pastern as can be done with the pet.

Finish off by brushing with a body brush which, if used with some effort, is a form of massage that dogs enjoy. This softer-bristled brush, or the hound glove, helps to get a shine on the coat. The slicker brush could be used to ensure the hair is lying in place.

You may want to bath your dog before the show (*see* page 113). However, too-frequent bathing removes the natural oils from the coat, and if the dog is entered for a series of shows within a few weeks, it should not be necessary to bath before each one. A dog with predominantly white legs may require them to be shampooed again to bring up the sparkle. If you are bathing the dog, it is advisable to do this two or three days prior to the show, not late the night before. Bathing disturbs the coat, making it soft and fluffed up, and sometimes leaves bits of hair sticking out. The days between are therefore necessary for the coat to settle and for you to have a final tidy up.

After rinsing, rub down, but not excessively as too much rubbing will tangle the ears and feathering. Then comb through to lay the hair in place. Put a towel over the dog's back, pin (with nappy or blanket pins) under the head and under the tummy, being especially careful here with males. Many groomers use the footless leg of nylon tights around the body.

Transfer the dog to a warm airy room for drying. If you are using a hand-held drier, you will really need an assistant, especially until the dog is accustomed to the procedure. It is best not to start with the head as dogs are very sensitive about heat and noise around their ears. You must be careful not to have it too hot here. Start with the front legs, holding the leg up and slowly combing through the feathering, at the same time blowing with the drier. Then do the ears and chest. Proceed to the feathering on the hindquarters before removing the towel, which will by then have absorbed a good deal of moisture from the body. Slowly draw the comb through the body coat in the direction in which the hair grows, using the drier all the time, and make sure that the hair on neck and shoulders and the tummy feathering are lying as flat as possible. Ensure that the dog is thoroughly dry all over. The hair on the ears, particularly, takes a long time to dry; wipe the inside of the ear with cotton wool.

Few dog beauty salons have the specialist knowledge to prepare Cocker Spaniels for show, and a Cocker's coat can be ruined for life if it is treated wrongly. Perhaps because of his homely nature, the Cocker Spaniel is taken up by people who care for and enjoy their own dogs. As a breed, it is not often managed by professional handlers and it is essential, therefore, that if you intend showing your Cocker Spaniel you should learn to present him yourself. Opinions differ as to whether hand-trimming or cutting implements should be employed, but the methods described – using a combination of plucking for the top of the dog and thinning for the underparts – have stood the test of time. They do no harm to the coat. Clipping the coat shortens the show life of the dog, who will often go prematurely grey, whilst the texture becomes coarser and more difficult to handle, but a beautifully hand-trimmed Cocker Spaniel will always be much admired.

In America, trimming styles and methods of preparation are totally different. More emphasis is placed on conditioning and coat texture. Exhibitors are geared to achieving good presentation by installing their own trimming set-up. Use is made of clippers and stripping knife. The throat, top third of the ears and muzzle are clipped, but in *The English Cocker Spaniel Handbook* (ECSCA Inc.), English Cocker expert Anne Rogers Clark says, 'Do not clip the top of the head.' She advises use of the stripping knife or thinning scissors and explains, 'Nothing is more unattractive than the "shaved with a clipper" top skull in the English Cocker. It should be borne in mind that all trimming, when it is done perfectly, looks as though the coat grew that way and has never been assaulted with sharp instruments. Each area must flow into the next with no sharp edges, no clipper marks, nothing to mar the continuous smooth line of a perfectly presented Spaniel.'

American groomers tend to leave more hair on legs and chest, and many refrain from using clippers in certain areas. By frequent shampooing and careful use of the stripping knife, smooth body coats result, and the dogs are beautifully presented in the preferred style.

7

Showing

Showing dogs, for most an enjoyable hobby, can be a consuming passion or a passing phase. For some it has become a way of life, while others involve themselves for the show lifetime of just one or two dogs until another interest takes their fancy. In either case, it is an activity to which you must be committed in order to do justice both to yourself and your dog.

The Kennel Club is the governing body which has made the rules and regulations under which societies and clubs run their shows, field trials and other activities; it licenses over 7,000 competitions annually. Before a dog can compete, he must be registered with the Kennel Club under a chosen name (*see* page 170).

The General Committee has disciplinary powers under Rule 42 for dealing with complaints. Persons found to have acted in a manner 'discreditable or prejudicial to the interests of the canine world' can be suspended or disqualified from taking part in competitions or from registering dogs for a period of time, or for life, according to the seriousness of the complaint.

Crufts

At the mention of exhibiting pedigree dogs, most people will immediately think of Crufts. The show takes its name from Charles Cruft, the great entrepreneur who founded the event a hundred years ago. By 1936 the show was drawing over 10,000 entries and was then the biggest dog show that had ever taken place. In those times, the shows were held over two days, with dogs attending on both days and judging in breeds with enormous entries, like Cocker Spaniels, extending into the second day.

Charles Cruft died just before the Second World War and the Kennel Club took over the show. As entries increased it became necessary, through lack of space, to limit the number of dogs entering, and a qualifying system was introduced. Qualifications

Mrs J. Caddy with Int. Ch. Ouainé Chieftain.

vary from time to time but, broadly, a dog must win an award in specific classes at any Championship Show during the previous year, before being eligible for Crufts. Those who are already Champions or who have a place in the Kennel Club Stud Book are also eligible, as are those who have won a Green Star of a specific value under Irish Kennel Club Rules. So only those who have proved they can compete with the best around the country will be seen at Crufts. It is no longer possible for a breeder to hold back a top-quality youngster in order to 'bring him out at Crufts', and a restriction on those in the lower age bracket prevents some from being exhibited which might have been of interest to the overseas buyer.

Cocker Spaniels have long made their mark at Crufts. The breed has constantly been conspicuous for its large entries, achieving over 700 regularly in the 1930s and, on a later occasion, over 1,000. H. S. Lloyd's Cockers took the top spot on no fewer than six occasions and the breed appears on the Roll of Honour more than any other. Cockers have also taken Reserve Best in Show several times: H. S.

Lloyd's Whoopee of Ware as well as his Silver Templa of Ware, and Mrs J. Caddy's Int. Ch. Ouainé Chieftain (all blue roans), and A. W. Collins's Colinwood Black Eagle and Miss J. Macmillan's Sh.Ch. Lochranza Strollaway (both blacks). Amongst the Cocker Spaniels to have gone as far as Best Gundog in Show after the introduction of judging by groups were Ch. Colinwood Silver Lariot, Sh.Ch. Lochranza Quettadene Marksman, Ch. Bournehouse Starshine and Sh.Ch. Lochranza Man of Fashion.

Crufts Dog Show has a certain mystique. Its charisma pulls in an entry which has now reached over 25,000 from more than 170 breeds. It is every exhibitor's ambition to qualify his dog for Crufts, and his dream to win.

Types of Show

Championship Shows

Of the many types of show, the most important is the Championship Show, where the top-placed dog and bitch in a breed win a Kennel Club Challenge Certificate (commonly called a CC or ticket). This award counts towards the title of Champion. Most of the Cocker Spaniel breed clubs run Championship Shows and these attract something in the region of 300 dogs. Since many of these will be entered in more than one class, the number of entries could total 400 to 500. There are about thirty general (all breed) Championship Shows where CCs are on offer for Cocker Spaniels.

A range of classes taking into account various ages and previous show wins is usually provided. No dog under the age of six months is eligible, and age classes in stages may be scheduled, starting with Minor Puppy – up to nine months, Puppy – up to twelve months, and Junior – up to eighteen months on the day of the show. Sometimes there is a Yearling class for dogs up to twenty-four months. At the other end of the scale, there is sometimes a Veteran class, which is usually for dogs of seven years or over.

Other classes are defined by previous show wins, the lower band excluding dogs which have already won a CC. As the dog progresses through his career, the wins in the higher classes are those which count. A dog with one or two CCs can enter the Limit range of classes. All dogs are eligible for an Open class, but at a Championship Show this will inevitably contain exhibits already 'made

Seven-month-old potential champion, Sh.Ch. Lindridge Gypsy Girl.
(Roger Chambers.)

up', i.e. Champions or Show Champions, so it is inappropriate for a novice or immature dog. Title-holders are not withdrawn as in some countries, but remain in open contest, making competition very tough within the breed.

When adding up wins, exhibitors must count all previous wins in breed classes, whether they were restricted colour classes or not. A dog can win any number of Minor Puppy or Puppy classes without its affecting his eligibility for other classes. Prizes won in Variety classes are ignored when totalling for breed class eligibility.

Often a Beginners class will be scheduled, where the previous successes of owner and handler as well as dog are taken into consideration. There is also sometimes a Brace class, which is for two dogs belonging to the same owner. It is expected that they should be of the same colour and well matched, the latter a point which is harder to achieve with particolours than with solids.

Judging often commences at 10.00 a.m., and where there is a judge for each sex they will judge simultaneously in separate rings. When all the classes for one sex have been completed, it is custom-ary for all 'unbeaten' dogs (or bitches) to enter the ring. It is not

Example of a Cocker Spaniel Championship Show Classification

DOGS	BITCHES
Judge: Mrs D. Beverley	Judge: Mr A. Woodcock
Kennel Club Challenge Certificate – Dog	*Kennel Club Challenge Certificate – Bitch*

Referee: Miss J. Lutterworth

Any Other Colour than Black, Red or Golden
1. Novice
2. Graduate
3. Special Open

Black
4. Novice
5. Graduate
6. Special Open

Red or Golden
7. Novice
8. Graduate
9. Special Open

Any Colour
10. Minor Puppy
11. Puppy
12. Junior
13. Maiden
14. Tyro
15. Special Beginners
16. Post Graduate
17. Minor Limit
18. Limit
19. Open

Black
20. Novice
21. Graduate
22. Special Open

Red or Golden
23. Novice
24. Graduate
25. Special Open

Any Other Colour than Black, Red or Golden
26. Novice
27. Graduate
28. Special Open

Any Colour
29. Minor Puppy
30. Puppy
31. Junior
32. Maiden
33. Tyro
34. Special Beginners
35. Post Graduate
36. Minor Limit
37. Limit
38. Open

uncommon for exhibits to be shown in more than one class, so a winner of one class may be beaten when competing in another. The CC winner will be chosen from the exhibits in the ring. The dog who was placed second in a class to the CC winner has no automatic right to challenge for the Reserve Challenge Certificate, but only at the request of the judge.

When awarding the CC and Reserve, the judge must consider both exhibits to be worthy champions of the breed. This is a safeguard in case the winner should for some reason be disqualified, and the dog placed Reserve would then be eligible to receive the CC. If, however, the judge has doubts as to their quality, he can withhold both awards, but must make a Best of Sex award.

When the judging of both sexes is completed, both CC winners come before the two judges for the award of Best of Breed. At a breed club, single breed, show this will be Best Exhibit in Show. If the judges cannot agree, a referee will be called in to make the decision. The judges will have selected a Best Puppy in each sex, and these will come before both judges in the same way, after Best in Show, for the award of Best Puppy in Show.

General Championship Shows provide classes for the majority of breeds and usually take place over two, three or even four days, with different groups appearing on different days. At these shows, Cocker Spaniels do not always have two judges, but one who will judge the dogs first, followed by bitches in the same ring. Often all classes are for any colour and around 200 Cocker Spaniels could be present. The dog or bitch awarded Best of Breed will be expected to take part in the group judging in order to compete against the best of all the other breeds in the group. Although this means remaining at the show until other judging is completed, most winners consider it a great honour to represent the breed in the 'big ring'. The dog awarded Best of Group will be asked to return for Best in Show, the final judging, and this may entail journeying to the show on the last day if gundogs were judged on one of the previous days.

Open Shows

As the name implies, Open Shows are open to all exhibits with no restrictions. All the Cocker Spaniel breed clubs hold at least one Open Show during the year, usually with fifteen to twenty classes. The Open Shows of the Black Cocker Spaniel Society, the Parti Coloured Cocker Spaniel Club and the Red and Golden Cocker Spaniel Club are restricted to their respective colours only (although the Parti Coloured Club also holds a Championship Show for all colours).

Often there are one or two champions present, as well as several of the top winners of the day, but exhibitors will not travel from so far afield. Owners find these shows good training grounds for their inexperienced dogs, and the novice owner has the chance of putting his dog in a class which is graded by colour or previous wins, where he will not come up against such stiff opposition as he would at a

Championship Show. These shows can attract many entries from across the spectrum, so the new exhibitor will have the opportunity of making comparisons and gaining knowledge, by seeing a good number of dogs at close quarters and by talking to breeders. In fact, a hundred or more dogs could be seen at an Open breed show.

Open Shows run by general canine societies often schedule between four and eight classes for Cocker Spaniels. The entries received will vary very much from show to show and area to area, but between thirty and forty dogs could be expected. Again the Best of Breed winner should go forward to the Best in Show judging, usually under a different judge, and not always operated on the group system.

If there are no classes for Cocker Spaniels, you can enter your dog in those for Any Variety Not Separately Classified (AVNSC). There can also be classes available for Any Variety or all breeds together, whether classified at the show or not. However, if your breed is classified, you cannot by-pass the breed classes and enter only Varieties. Exceptions to this are dogs entered in a Veteran class or dogs entered in a Puppy class if no Puppy class for the breed is scheduled.

When calculating the number of prizes previously won, owners must take into consideration wins in Variety classes as well as Breed classes when entering Variety classes. Wins in Variety classes do not count when calculating for Breed classes.

Dogs competing for Best in Show must be unbeaten, and Best of Breed winners can be withdrawn from any subsequent classes in which they may have been entered in order to remain unbeaten. When the Best in Show winner has been selected, Reserve Best in Show must be chosen from the remaining unbeaten dogs. The Best in Show and Reserve Best in Show winners must then be with-drawn from any further competition, but dogs who failed to reach those heights can resume competition in any remaining classes in which they were entered. The same principles apply to the judging of Best Puppy in Show, which must take place after Best in Show.

Limited Shows

Dogs who have won CCs cannot be entered for Limited Shows, which are events run by clubs and societies solely for their own members or for a restricted area. The definitions of classes are different from those for Championship or Open shows.

Sanction Shows

These are also for club members only, and CC winners are again excluded from competition. Post Graduate is the highest class permitted.

Primary Shows

These are evening or weekend events and are confined to members of a society. Neither CC nor Reserve CC winners can compete, and entries can be taken on the day. No class higher than Maiden is allowed, so these shows are especially for the inexperienced dog and are a good place for a beginner handler to learn.

Matches

Many clubs and societies hold Matches for their own members. They are competitions, often held in the evening, between teams from different clubs, or between the members of one club. In a Match, one dog is judged against another in a series of eliminating rounds. It is a far less serious side of showing and many owners go along for the sociality of the occasion.

Exemption Shows

These are often held in conjunction with a village fête or some similar event, possibly to raise funds for a particular cause. Nobody worries whether dog or handler is familiar with ring procedure, and although up to five pedigree dog classes may be provided, it is not even essential for entrants to be Kennel Club registered. There is usually a series of fun classes such as 'The dog with the Waggiest Tail' or 'The Dog that looks Most Like his Owner', for both pedigree and non-pedigree dogs. The show will be licensed by the Kennel Club although exempt from some of its rules.

Schedules, Entries and Prizes

Advertisements for shows appear in the weekly canine press, and give the address of the organizer. If any seem of interest, apply for a schedule and entry form. Show secretaries always appreciate a large, stamped, addressed envelope. A list of show dates is also published in the *Kennel Gazette*.

The schedule will give all the advance information you need about the show: date, location of venue, names of judges, time of judging, classification and entry fees. The definitions of classes should be read carefully as they vary with the different types of show, and beware if the word 'special' is used as this will mean the society has adapted an accepted definition to one of its own choice. Rules appertaining to shows and behaviour are also printed in the schedule. You will no doubt initially select a minor show for you and your dog to make your début, and not jump in at the deep end by attempting a Championship event.

Entries must be made in advance and posted by a stipulated date. First prizes won up to a week before the closing date for entries must be counted, and there is no necessity to make your entries further in advance than this or you may find your dog is ineligible for the class you have entered. Wins after the appointed time but before the show, do not count.

All classes are numbered or coded and by reference to the schedule you will be able to select a class or classes for your dog. Often people are overambitious and enter their dog right through the classes in everything for which he is eligible. It is probably better to feel your way gradually and learn slowly, so that you can become selective in your choice. There are reasons for this as with all show-going idiosyncrasies, as you will learn.

The majority of general Championship Shows no longer give prize money through the classes. Sponsorship has, however, increased over the years, dog food manufacturers and canine journals generously sponsoring some of the major awards at the larger shows. Some societies give good prize money for Variety 'Stakes' classes, but prizes do not compare favourably with those offered in other competitive hobbies. The chances of the average exhibitor going home with more in his pocket than his outlay are remote indeed. As for winning the Challenge Certificate or Best of Breed, exhibitors are thrilled by the honour (and grateful for any contribution to the canine larder), but they realize that dog showing brings no financial gain. At Open and other shows, rosettes are awarded, sometimes for all placed in the class, and those for Best of Breed and the finals can be magnificent indeed. Some of the clubs and societies that have been in existence for a long time own a formidable array of cups and trophies, some of which are silver and very valuable.

Regulations

The regulations for shows and the other events are contained in the Kennel Club Year Book, which is regarded as the show secretary's bible. It is here we find, for instance, that a dog may not be exhibited under a judge who has owned him in the previous twelve months, nor boarded him, handled him or prepared him for exhibition. Any preparation which alters the natural colour of the coat may not be used, and dogs who have had operations which alter their natural conformation may not be exhibited, some exceptions being made, as for docking. A dog must be exhibited in all the classes for which he is entered. Otherwise he is liable to disqualification. If an exhibitor has entered a dog in a class for which the dog is ineligible, he can only be transferred to certain alternatives. A dog who has been entered in a Puppy class, but is in fact over twelve months of age, can be transferred to Junior. In Cocker Spaniels, it occasionally happens that an exhibitor makes an error on the entry form and puts a particolour in a class restricted to solids. In this case, the dog can be transferred to the equivalent class for his colour. In fact, in cases of error, the dog can be transferred to the equivalent class for the correct breed, colour or sex, but if there is no equivalent class, he must go into the Open class. If an exhibitor arrives late and misses the class for which the dog is entered, the dog may not be transferred to another class.

Ring Training

If you are thinking of showing a dog for the first time, it would be as well to find some ringcraft classes run by general canine societies or clubs especially for the purpose. Here you can learn how to handle your dog in the ring, and your dog will become accustomed to behaving well in the company of other breeds, as well as to standing still while being examined by a judge.

Experienced owners, too, find classes helpful when training a puppy or giving a refresher course to an older dog. As with all training, little and often is the rule, and do not let the dog get bored. He must be reasonably well lead-trained before expecting him to behave in front of others. Some shows are held indoors, and in echoing hall may be off-putting to an uneducated puppy, so much good can be done by acclimatizing him to the atmosphere at ringcraft.

Training should continue at home to complement the work done at classes. Take the dog to the lawn or a quiet corner of the park and, holding the lead in your left hand, give him a short command, 'Show'. The lead should be held at a length so that you can feel sufficient tension to be in command, and if you lower your hand, the dog can walk on a relaxed lead if he is going well and in unison with you. Walk in a large circle at a brisk pace as if walking round the show ring. The dog should move with a steady trotting rhythm, not a slow walk nor canter, nor a stiff-legged gait. When you have made a couple of circuits, stop and make the dog stand.

The Cocker Spaniel must be taught to stand in the ring to show his points to best advantage. His front legs should be side by side and, with the body comfortably at full length but not stretched, the hind legs should be placed wider apart than the front legs. The dog should hold his head high to show a good length of neck.

The method of handling a Cocker Spaniel by kneeling down or leaning over the dog, gripping his muzzle and propping up his tail ('topping and tailing'), has become universal practice in the show ring. It is the exception to see a Cocker Spaniel shown free-standing on a loose lead and permitted to display his merry tail action, but when executed in an accomplished way it is always the subject of admiration. The newcomer to the ring may feel out of place if attempting this method when all other handlers are crouching, so the dog could therefore be taught both ways of being shown.

Sh.Ch. Lochdene Pepper Pot.

Noble Art of Ware, shown free-standing by Paula Carey, great-granddaughter of Richard Lloyd. (Dave Freeman.)

Not all breeds are topped and tailed; many are invariably shown on a loose lead. It is certainly true that some Cocker Spaniels respond more easily to this method than others, and the dog who spends time with his handler and has a rapport with him, is more likely to respond well.

When training, walk the dog into a standing position, halt smartly, giving the command, 'Stand', at the same time controlling the dog gently with the lead and turning yourself to face the dog. The dog should still face the direction in which he was walking and, if in a ring, would be broadside on to the judge. With very gentle pressure on the lead, and handler still standing upright, the dog can be pressed back half a pace or encouraged to move fractionally forward, in order to get all legs correct. Once in position, the right hand of the handler can be stretched forward to alert the dog. A small bait can be used if the tail is not responding to your encouraging voice. After a few moments, the dog can relax and be praised, then the exercise repeated. Keep him standing a little longer each time, and always fuss him when he does well.

The handler must anticipate the dog's reactions when standing, and if the dog moves forward he can be checked back on the lead, or if he is going to sit down, be prevented from so doing by quickly stepping forward a pace. Even in the ring the dog can often be put into reverse a couple of paces and then walked forward into pose,

Successful junior handler Sarah Swigciski shows off Cosalta Corina to advantage. (B. Hickford.)

but sometimes it is necessary to turn the dog round in a circle in order to regain a position. A handler will learn the reactions of the dog, and judge when to use a titbit and when to put it in a pocket. If a dog should lift his ears, it is better to put the bait away.

The method of topping and tailing must also be practised, so the dog gets used to being held in one position for a long time. Even this way does not ensure that the dog is standing correctly; much depends on the skill of the handler, for it is up to him to get the best out of the dog. As with free-standing, the dog must stand four-square, or with 'one leg in each corner', and not appear to have been pushed in from behind. Pose in front of a mirror to view the result.

The free-standing method needs more room for manoeuvre, and in a crowded ring this is not always available. The skilful handler will use the method to suit the occasion, and assess the dog's behaviour on the day in order to show him to best advantage.

When you have practised standing the dog three or four times, you could then move him again, this time in a typical triangle pattern. In the ring this would be your chance to give your solo display. Still with the lead in your left hand, move away from the imaginary judge, tracing the outline of a triangle and using as much of the available 'ring space' as possible. Your route should return you to the judge's position, after which move the dog in a straight line away from that position and back again.

The dog must be taught to stand on a table in the same show pose as on the ground. At a show, the judge will want to examine the construction and coat of each exhibit, so the dog must be rock-steady while being handled. The set of the teeth, with jaws closed, will also be inspected. When a certain degree of stability has been achieved, ask friends and relatives to go over the dog as well. It matters not whether they know what to do, so long as the dog gets accustomed to being handled by different people.

The dog should also be taken to busy streets or a railway station to get him used to different sounds and acquaint him with crowds. This is especially useful if you cannot get to training classes. Many owners find visiting a pub a convivial way of socializing their dogs.

The Day of the Show

Having made the entries, groomed and trimmed the dog to show standard and rehearsed the ring technique, you should be ready for the big day. Final preparations will need some organization. You should take basic grooming equipment as well as a slicker brush or hound glove, a fine show lead (usually nylon) and a towel. Many exhibitors also use a coat spray, but beware that you do not contravene Kennel Club regulations. Also take food and water for the dog, and a bowl. If the show is benched, you will need a collar and chain to hitch up the dog, and a rug for him to sit on. The chain must be of sufficient length for the dog to turn round comfortably, and so arranged that the dog cannot fall off backwards and hang. That said, thousands of dogs sit safely on benches every week, and thoroughly enjoy the comfort and seclusion of their own little space. A watchful eye should be kept on the dog the first time he is benched, but most quickly settle. Polythene bags or cardboard scoops should also be included for clearing up after your dog. Many people take a folding table. If the show is not benched, it is more restful for the dog to be in a cage. If situated outside this will need some covering to protect from sun or breeze.

When going to a show, leave all other animals at home if possible, making satisfactory arrangements for someone else to look after them during the day. Plan your journey to arrive at the venue about an hour before judging.

Thoroughly groom the dog in good time before your class. He must be given a walk round beforehand to familiarize him with the atmosphere of showground or hall, and also encouraged to relieve himself. After that, he should be allowed to rest quietly. Shortly before your class is due in the ring, give him a quick brush and comb and finish with slicker, hound glove or polishing cloth. Arrive at the ringside calmly and with time to take stock before your class is called.

It is better for a newcomer not to stand first in the line, as you can then see what procedure the others follow, and it gives your dog a chance to settle down if two or three dogs go before him. All the dogs not seen in a previous class are usually asked to make a circuit of the ring in an anticlockwise direction and with the dog on the handler's left, i.e. nearest to the judge. Then the judge will assess the dogs individually on a table, then on the move. This is your big moment to show your dog off in his best light. You may not get a second chance, so do it right first time. At the end of this display, the handler will halt the dog before the judge momentarily, letting the dog stand naturally rather than setting him up. Dog and handler then return to their position in the line.

When the judge has seen all the individual displays, he will walk up and down the line of 'old' or 'seen' and 'new' dogs, and if there are certain points he wishes to check, may perhaps pick out one or two to move again before making any decisions. Occasionally the judge will request two dogs to move up the ring and back side by side. In this case the dogs should be in the middle with handlers on the outside of them, walking at the same pace. At the top of the ring, handlers change the dog to their other hand, and return with dogs side by side again.

A practice more frequently seen is for a single dog to move in a straight line, but the judge will move to the side so that he can see co-ordination of movement broadside on. In this case, the handler must ensure that he walks on the side of the dog away from the judge and not forget to change the dog into the other hand for the return.

After deliberation, the judge will pick out several dogs, who will line up in the centre. If it is a big class, he may choose eight or ten, and the steward will dismiss the rest from the ring. After further assessment, the judge will place five, though sometimes only four, dogs in order of preference. You must always watch carefully so that if you are selected, you know which position to take up. If two dogs have already been chosen, make sure you know which is first and which is second, for if you should stand at the head of the line, you may be accused of taking an advantage while the judge's attention is turned to the selection of the next placing!

If you have entered a Variety class under a different judge, the ring procedure will be similar, and yours will be regarded as a 'new' dog that has not previously been seen by that judge. If it is the same judge as for Cocker Spaniels, you will of course join the group of 'seen' dogs.

If the dog is not fed until after he has been exhibited, he will be more alert and 'on his toes' in the ring. He should also be taken to the exercise area at suitable intervals, care being taken not to get his feathering wet before competing. Some exhibitors put their dogs into trouser suits (a somewhat amusing sight).

Once you have your dog trimmed, trained and prepared for the show, it is worth entering several shows close in time. You will be learning as you go along, and the tip you picked up at one show, you will be able to put into practice at the next. Don't be in any hurry to bring out your baby puppy. Many Cockers are slow maturers and the one that looks rangy at seven months may take till he is eighteen months to drop and fill out, but the first impressions a dog gives to the ringsiders are often long lasting.

If the judging table is on slanting ground, you should stand the dog so that he does not appear to dip behind the shoulder, and if there is uneven ground in an outdoor ring, manoeuvre the dog to a more level spot. Do not keep fussing over your dog in the line. Overhandling is very irritating to a judge who would prefer to see the dog standing quietly and as naturally as possible. Whilst in the ring, always keep one eye on your dog – and the other on the judge!

Do not rush home the minute your class is over. Apart from the fact that there are sometimes stipulated times for leaving the show, you will not learn unless you watch. Try to sit at the ringside and see at least some of the classes being judged and watch the top handlers of the breed. It is becoming noticeable that unsuccessful exhibitors are leaving before the end of judging, even when there are only four breed classes at an Open Show! This seems like bad sportsmanship and gives the impression that such exhibitors come to a show only for what they can get. If you lose, lose gracefully, and think of another judge and another day.

Good manners are as important in the ring as out. Exhibitors do not always make best use of available ring space, so if your neighbour in the line has a cramped situation, move away a little and ask others to do so as well. When moving round the ring, do not walk on the heels of the dog in front of you. Exhibitors are not expected to hold a conversation with the judge, unless he asks you a question in which case you should answer briefly. Certainly, a judge does not expect to hear a potted biography of a dog's achievements, and it is quite unnecessary.

It is obviously inconsiderate to show a bitch in season, especially at a show where there are mixed classes as, naturally, the males will be distracted. When making entries, one must consider the likelihood of a bitch coming into season at the time of the show.

Titles

Show Champion

A dog of a gundog breed who wins three CCs under three different judges can be called a Show Champion (Sh.Ch.), provided one of the CCs was won when the dog was over twelve months of age. A certificate is forwarded to the owner when the award has been confirmed by the Kennel Club.

Champion

In addition to the three CCs mentioned above, a dog of a gundog breed must also win a prize for field work before he can be described as a Champion (Ch.). An award at a field trial, or the Show Gundog Working Certificate, won under Kennel Club Field Trial regulations or the Rules of the Irish Kennel Club, is needed to qualify.

Show Gundog Working Certificate

There are two ways in which a Cocker Spaniel can gain the Show Gundog Working Certificate under Kennel Club rules. A dog who has already won a CC can be assessed at a field trial meeting for the breed, provided the organizing society is recognized for the Field Trial Championships. If the dog fails, he can make another attempt in the same field trial season, but not more than three times in all.

The other way is to run at a special trial for show gundogs, where a dog who has won a first prize in a Cocker Spaniel class at a show where Challenge Certificates were available for the breed, can attempt the Working Certificate (*see* page 240).

Junior Warrant

A Junior Warrant is available to a dog who has won twenty-five points while between the ages of twelve and eighteen months. Three points are awarded for a first prize in a breed class at a show where CCs are offered for the breed, and one point for a first prize in a breed class at an Open Show. Breed wins at a Championship Show where CCs are not offered for the breed, count as an Open Show. Application must be made to the Kennel Club by the owner of the dog.

It was possible for wins attained any time up to eighteen months to count towards the Junior Warrant but the regulations were amended in 1990. This step was taken to protect young puppies from the stress of continuous campaigning, but now gives less time to achieve the objective! Not all owners strive for the award, but if it is earned in the course of the dog's career it is a welcome bonus.

Stewarding

Anyone can steward at a British dog show. You do not have to pass tests or be authorized as in some countries. Certain duties are attached to the job, and those taking it on are responsible to the society and the Kennel Club to ensure that correct procedures are carried out. One or more stewards are appointed as assistants to each judge at a show and must carry out the instructions of the judge. Their duties and responsibilities are numerous.

Before starting, it is usual for the steward to ensure that an announcement has been made on the public address, as well as around the ringside and benches, that judging is about to commence. After that, it is the exhibitors' own responsibility to ensure that dogs appear in the ring for their respective classes.

The steward must check that the dogs in the ring are in the catalogue or judging book as being entered in the class about to be judged, and that their handlers are wearing the correct number. The steward usually has a catalogue; the judge does not, but has the relevant numbers written in the judging book. The steward must place in order dogs coming forward from previous classes according to the wishes of the judge, and stand the unseen dogs separately. Apart from competitors, only judge and steward are allowed in the ring while judging is in progress, and stewards must withdraw to a corner of the ring while the judge makes his assessments. Photographers must not enter the ring during judging, but many judges are happy for photographs to be taken on completion of a class or other award.

One problem which arises with some breeds, but which fortunately rarely occurs in Cocker Spaniel circles is 'double-handling'. This involves a person from outside the ring attracting a particular exhibit's attention in order to get him to show better. This is against the rules, and stewards must see that it is not done.

At the completion of each class, the steward must hand to the judge the judging book, notebook, dictating machine or any requirements requested, and will himself note the winners in correct order. Usually a position will be chosen so that the exhibitors' numbers are visible to the majority of ringsiders. The steward will hand out prize cards and any rosettes, and usually call out the numbers for ringsiders to hear. Often organizers will provide a squared chart (or stewards should bring their own) with classes going down the page and placings across. If this is filled in after each class, it is easy to see at a glance which dogs have beaten which. This is especially important in Cocker Spaniel judging where there are separate colour classes, to ensure that dogs entering later classes are positioned in the right order. The steward must ensure that the judge signs all Challenge Certificates and other awards, that the judging book is correctly marked up, that the judge has signed all award slips and that they are displayed where relevant and sent to the show manager's office. He is also responsible for ring hygiene.

If a dog is entered in a class incorrectly, he can only be transferred to another class on the authority of the show manager. A steward does not have the right to disqualify a dog, even though he may be considered ineligible. Authority to disqualify rests solely with the Committee of the Kennel Club.

As one gains experience of shows and showing, one picks up knowledge of stewarding. There are openings for stewards at most shows, and societies are grateful for the services of willing helpers who give them voluntarily.

Junior Handler winner Susan Crummey with Starbourne Sailing Master. (Tracy Morgan.)

Shows in Ireland

Dogs to be entered at shows in Eire must first be registered at the Irish Kennel Club. Green Stars are awarded towards the title of Champion under IKC rules. They carry a number of points depending upon the entry in the breed. To become an Irish champion, a dog must win forty Green Star points and gain a qualifying certificate in the field. The total points must contain two Green Stars of ten points, or one ten-point plus two five-point Green Stars. Any dog can attempt the qualifying certificate – it does not require a show win to be eligible. The dog is tested in a similar way as under British Kennel Club rules, but a spaniel is expected to swim. Any dog who has the required number of points on the bench can be titled Show Champion.

Shows in North America

In the USA, championship titles are awarded on a points system and all regular shows offer championship points. In order to become a champion, a dog must gain fifteen points, including two wins of three, four or five points each, known as Majors, which must be gained under two different judges. The number of points from one to five given at each show is determined by the show's location and the number of dogs in competition. They are awarded to untitled exhibits, for once a dog is 'finished' or made up (becomes a champion), he is shown only in Best of Breed competition. The points are awarded to the winner of the Winners Class, contenders for which are dogs placed first in the scheduled classes. Should this dog also be awarded Best of Breed or even Best in Show, he may be eligible for further points, but no dog may earn more than five points at any one show. By winning three sets of five points, a dog could win a title at three consecutive shows within the same number of days – and it has happened! In 1980, a black-and-white bitch, Druid Little Miss Muffet, handled by Mark Threlfall, won at three five-point shows in three days, taking fifty hours to finish her championship.

Only the Open Class can be divided by colour, and only at specialty shows. Specialties are like breed club Championship Shows in the UK. At these shows, a judge may make a club award of Certificate of Honour to dogs he feels deserve special commendation.

At all-breed shows, group placings are particularly highly valued as this is where the dog comes up against breeds where competition may have been stronger than his own on that particular day. For a breed like English Cocker Spaniels, still considered something of a minority, it is a great achievement, and until fairly recently it was somewhat rare for one to go Best in Show.

When a dog has completed his championship, he may be campaigned in Best of Breed competition, or 'Specials' as it used to be called, with an eye to a group placing. At a breed specialty, to see a class of maybe fifty champions is a sight to remember. Over 170 champions were made up in one recent year.

In the ring, the emphasis is on showmanship. Ring presence is of great importance and goes down well with the judges, who are not always breed specialists. Some breeders are occupationally ineligible through being professional handlers but all judges must be approved by the American Kennel Club (AKC). English Cocker Spaniels often come under all-rounders or American Cocker judges who may be impressed by style and pace.

Showing is done to a strict schedule, with times of each breed's appearance in the ring printed in the catalogue. Timing is of particular importance to both handlers and judges, who each may have

Sh. Ch. Lockdene Flamingo of Cardamine, made up in 1988, exported to Canada. (Tracy Morgan.)

eight or ten breeds to cope with in the one day. Judges are not normally expected to write a critique, although this is becoming more usual after specialty shows.

The English Cocker Spaniel probably has a majority of owner-handlers, but professional handlers play a most important part on the show scene. Many dogs are left in the care of handlers throughout their show and active stud career. All this makes dog showing a very costly and serious business. Dogs, even when made up, seem to change hands quite often, probably to make different bloodlines available in other parts of this large country.

A far less serious affair is the sanctioned match, intended for the novice owner or as a training ground for the young exhibit. To this end, classes are included for three- to six-month-old puppies.

The show system is similar in Canada but ten points are required to become a champion and these can be won one at a time. It is quite common for dogs to be shown in both North American countries within days of each other without much adjustment. The judges,

143

too, are interchangeable. Good dogs from Canada often do battle in the States and sometimes achieve American titles too.

Shows in Europe

Shows in most European countries are held under the auspices of the FCI (Fédération Cynologique Internationale), and the system throughout is similar though there are regional differences. The usual classes put on are Junior (nine to eighteen months); Bred by Owner; Open (fifteen months and over); Field Trial; Champion. Dogs are entered in only one class.

The judge, when carrying out the individual assessment, must dictate to a ring secretary a report on each individual dog there and then. This may be written in triplicate so that copies cannot only be retained but also handed to the owner and the show organizer. Qualifications are awarded: Excellent, Very Good, Good or Moderate, so that the dogs are graded according to their merit. At the end of each class, four dogs are placed in the judge's order of preference.

The CAC (Certificat d'Aptitude au Championnat de Beauté) is awarded to the best of each sex, provided it has the qualification Excellent and has been placed first in its class. In some countries, the winner of the Junior class and dogs already champions are ineligible to compete for the CAC, and sometimes CACs are given even for each colour. The international certificate or CACIB (Certificat d'Aptitude au Championnat International de Beauté) can be awarded only to a dog who has won First Excellent in the Open, Field Trial or Champion class.

To become a champion in Holland, where there are about fifteen Championship Shows a year as well as one breed club specialty, a dog must win four CACs, one of which must have been awarded after the dog reached the age of twenty-seven months. However, the CAC at the Winners Show or at the breed club show has a value of two CACs. A dog can also become a champion from specified combinations of CAC and Reserve CAC wins. The awards must be made by at least two different judges on three different occasions. To become an international champion, a Cocker Spaniel must win two CACIBs and a prize at an international field trial.

The requirements for the national title of champion are similar in most continental countries, though in Germany a year must elapse between the first and fourth Certificates. In Belgium, France, Italy and Switzerland, a qualification for field work is also required, which is more demanding than the Show Gundog Working Certificate. There are also a few other titles, such as Winner, which is awarded to the best dog and bitch at the annual Winners Show in Amsterdam; Bundessieger, won by the best dog and bitch at the Bundessieger Show in Germany each year; and European Champion and World Champion, which are awarded yearly in different countries directly by the FCI. The World Show was held in Czechoslovakia in 1990, when 12,000 dogs were entered, and Germany became the host country for 1991.

Wins in classes for Pairs, Groups (of three or more) or Breeders' Groups are highly thought of by owners, especially as the winners go forward to compete against other breeds. The appearance in the big ring of groups from different breeds, with possibly six or seven dogs parading in any one group, can be quite a spectacle.

Provided appropriate vaccinations and necessary papers are in order, dogs can often travel outside their own country, and indeed become multi-titled. However, from time to time restrictions are put into force, depending, for instance, upon the restraints caused by conflict or precautions against the spread of rabies.

Shows in Australia

In Australia, each state has its own body to rule canine affairs, subject to the constitution of the Australian National Kennel Council. The Council has followed the traditions of the Kennel Club since its inception, but in 1991 the delegates voted it to become a full member of the FCI. Discussions on implementation will take place with member bodies over a five-year period.

The Cocker Spaniel Standard, as published by the British Kennel Club, is the accepted Standard in Australia, where the breed is well supported by an enthusiastic band of followers, and is one of the more numerous at shows. Despite this, and because of the vast distances involved, entries at an all-breed Championship Show sometimes compare only to an Open Show in the UK. Challenge points can be awarded with alacrity, for the pressures of the system are such as they are in America, that the judge, very often an all-rounder or group judge, must move on to the succeeding breeds on his list. However, at the shows of the breed clubs things are different, and at these and each state's Royal Shows numbers usually reach into the hundreds, with a home or overseas specialist more likely to be sitting in judgement.

There are five types of show: Sanction; Members' competitions and Parades, all for the novice dog and inexperienced judge, from which champions are debarred; Open, for which champions are eligible, but the judge is still not licensed; and Championship, where Challenges are offered and which are judged by a licensed judge. Once licensed, judges may officiate only at Championship Shows.

A typical show classification would include Baby Puppy 3–6 months; Minor Puppy 6–9 months; Puppy 6–12 months; Junior 6–18 months; Intermediate 18–36 months; Australian-Bred and Open. At breed club Championship shows, all these classes may be provided for both solid and for other colours. The colours would not compete against each other, therefore, until the Challenge, and then again for 'In Breed' awards. Exhibits are customarily entered in only one class, and ribbons are given to place-winners in the classes.

A dog requires 100 Challenge points before becoming a champion, and points are allocated according to the number of dogs present. After the completion of judging of both sexes, and when the Challenge winners and Reserves have been declared, the In Breed awards are made. The dog and bitch winner of each equivalent class will enter the ring and be judged against each other on a one-to-one basis, and so on through the whole range of classes. At an all-breed show, this will be repeated with each In Breed winner competing against the equivalent winner from every breed within the group. Much importance is put on these wins, for it can be seen that with sometimes small classes within a breed it is the In Group judging (where twenty-five points may be gained) where a dog will really meet up against competition. The whole process is of course repeated for In Show awards. By the end of the day, then, numerous awards will have been made, and at a grand prize-giving ceremony the winners will receive trophies or other prizes.

8

Judging

What the Judges are Looking For

There are many more factors to winning prizes at shows than simply acquiring a well-bred promising puppy from a top breeder. Many a newcomer showing a well-groomed and well-behaved dog, who they feel approximates to the required Standard for the breed, has been disappointed by the dog's lack of success. To go to the top in the ring, the dog must not only fit the Standard and be perfectly trimmed and trained, but have a little extra something – a charisma that will set him apart from the others. Cocker Spaniels should display an alertness and a certain liveliness, which a good handler will know how to bring out.

The judge in the ring will carry in his head the Breed Standard. He will assess the dogs on breed type, temperament, physical construction, soundness of movement and coat presentation. A good motto to keep in mind when judging Cocker Spaniels is 'moderation in all things'. As the dogs move round the ring in a group, the judge will begin to form an opinion of those who approach his mental picture of the ideal. A well-presented, free-moving dog with a good stride, who carries himself well with an aristocratic air, will stand out from the rest.

On the Table

Not all points are clearly visible from the centre of the ring, nor indeed from the view which the spectators get at the ringside, so the next step is for the judge to examine each exhibit on a table.

The judge will stand back and view the dog from the side. It is important for the handler to ensure that the dog is standing in a good pose and does not sit during examination. The judge will be looking for quality in head, a feature of the breed, and for a gentle expression in eyes of a dark shade.

If the support were removed, the dog would topple on to his nose.

The judge will check the teeth and put his hands over head and skull, ensuring that cheek-bones are not prominent; he will feel the ears and look for clean lines of the throat. Here the folds of the skin should not be excessively loose, and the hair should be tidied up to give a neat appearance.

If the front of the dog is lifted, the dog will fall back into his natural position, so the judge can see whether the dog is too wide in front or whether weak pasterns allow outward-turning feet. He will also put his hand between the legs to ensure the front is not too narrow, and that the rib cage is deep and wide enough.

The dog should hold his head with a nicely arched neck, which should be sufficiently long and elegant to carry the head with pride. The neck as often seen stretched out by handlers puts the dog out of balance and it would not be surprising, if the support were removed, for the dog to topple on his nose. In any case, an overlong

148

neck on a working dog would be less efficient. A moderate neck with more strength would have greater control over the task of carrying a heavy burden.

Sometimes dogs are too heavy on the shoulder. This detracts from the general elegance and can even make the dog broad in front. It is as much a fault of maintenance as of construction. An overfed dog can sometimes put on weight over the shoulder and once established, it is not easy to reduce.

The ribs should be well sprung and are sometimes described as barrel-like, in the sense of expanding. Flat or slab sides are not required and would not allow for the proper functioning of internal organs under the stress of a hard day's work. A judge will look for well-muscled hindquarters with width across the beam. A Cocker Spaniel's tail is normally docked, but it should be long enough for him to display his merry character.

The judge will also check that the dog is entire. With the relaxing of the Kennel Club's regulations on exhibiting neutered animals, more of these may appear in the ring. However, non-entirety will be seen as a fault by most judges. Many overseas countries do not permit the exhibition of neutered animals.

The author judging. (Tracy Morgan.)

The judge will probably run his hands down the legs to check on bone and feet. The feet should not be large or flat, and tufts of hair and nails should be trimmed. The judge may stand behind the dog from where he will be able to see clean lines of shoulder. He will probably run his hands down either side of the blades and ensure the elbows are tucked in. He may lift the hindquarters to make sure they drop back naturally to a good width, and that they are strong under pressure.

The judge will expect the dog's coat to be clean and well prepared, with sufficient but not excessive feathering. He will find a harsh finish if clippers have been used, but a Cocker's coat should have a good bloom on it and look as natural as possible. A spaniel should have soft curves and no sharp lines.

The judge will give another glance at the head and sideview and check on topline. 'The gentle slope to the tail begins at the pelvis, not at the withers. When a Cocker's topline slopes from the withers, he is off-type.' (*The Cocker Spaniel*, C. C. Jenkins, Australia, 1990). Consider the structure of the dog and, as Macdonald Daly would have said, 'Imagine being able to put a saddle on it.'

Watching the Action

The handler will then be asked to move the dog. To move well, a dog must be correctly constructed, and the broadside view is where construction is revealed. Judges with great experience will often ask exhibitors to keep their dogs on the move for a long time – there can then be no camouflage. The head carriage, construction of one part in relation to the next, and the way the dog strides are evident. When standing, a handler may try to give a false impression by posing the dog in a certain manner, but this is almost impossible when moving. The Cocker Spaniel should not move with stilted action or short strides, but should have steady free-flowing movement and cover the ground well. High-stepping hackney action is undesirable in front. The hind legs should be brought well up and the dog should move with purpose. A good mover could be described as 'going like a train'. The dog should move at a collected trotting pace but there is no need for the handler to run. When walking directly towards the judge, the dog should move with straight true action, not pinning, that is turning the toes in, nor turning them out, nor loose at the elbows. A narrow front and elbows 'tied' too closely could indicate flat weedy ribs.

Aust. Ch. Mighty Rare of Ware (74 CCs), owned by Miss C.C. Jenkins. (Fall.)

In order to assess construction as well as locomotion, the triangle pattern comes in useful, but unfortunately it frequently happens that rings are too narrow for this to be carried out. As it is essential for a judge to view the dog in action from the side, he must himself move to the side of the ring and watch the dog walk past. It is not necessary for a judge to keep handling a dog to see whether he is correctly constructed, for it will be obvious from his movement.

The dog should preferably be walked on a loose lead, that is the handler should have gentle contact with the dog and be able to restrain him quickly if necessary. The lead should not be so long that the dog can stray from appropriate closeness to the handler. Stringing up, moving the dog on a tight lead with head held high and feet barely touching the ground, spoils the natural action and can sometimes pull up the ears and create a frown. To 'fly the ears' in this manner is uncharacteristic in a Cocker Spaniel; this method of handling also pulls up the hair on the neck.

Picking Them Out

While seeing the dog move as well as examining him on the table, the judge will have been assessing temperament. Moving with a clamped tail could indicate nervousness, or a lack of confidence in an unfamiliar situation. A cocked tail may mean the dog is unduly proud of himself and has a bossy disposition. The Cocker Spaniel must, of course, show no shyness or aggression while being handled, and when on the ground the 'merry nature with ever-wagging tail' should be obvious. This most important of characteristics, however, is masked by the majority of handlers who kneel down or bend over their charge, the dog being expected to stand passively in a manner quite contrary to the descriptive particulars of the breed. The term 'to stack' is commonly used, but is a most unsuitable term in relation to Cocker Spaniels, for it implies a procedure that is too restrictive upon the cheerful disposition required of the breed.

Apart from individual analysis, point by point, a judge must also consider breed type, something rather difficult to define. For a Cocker Spaniel, compactness is important, and a balanced head and good spring of rib are essential to type. The dog must appear balanced throughout with component parts in proportion. A dog of correct type can be described as cobby and Cockery. Even if such a dog has a few moderate faults, he ought to do better in the ring than one who perhaps has a glamorous head, neck and shoulder but not much behind to commend it.

Having given each dog a separate examination, the judge will then cast his eye around the ring for an overall picture of the class, not forgetting the repeats, those who have already been seen in an earlier class. He will have made a mental note of those who pleased him on analysis, or any with major faults. He will select those who closely resemble the pattern in his mind's eye of the perfect Cocker Spaniel. As no dog is perfect, however, he will probably judge by the all-over impression of symmetry, type and quality, keeping in mind the individual appraisal. To judge by specific weights, measures and faults will create an unsatisfactory result. The judge must not lose sight of the whole dog and his virtues.

Some judges will look for a rather showy dog; others may prefer one who is more workmanlike, but a dog will nevertheless need quality to take him to the top. The possession of quality does not mean that a dog should be lacking in substance; quality describes the difference between one who is a little common or course and one who has a certain refinement. Natural showmanship is desirable and is a feature that will help to put a dog above the competition.

Once the dogs have been placed from left to right in order of preference, the judge will make a few notes on the winners so that he can later prepare a critique to be published in the canine press.

Preconceptions

Ringsiders have been heard to comment that a judge is only putting up well-known exhibitors, but it has been proved time and again when all the placings in a class go to top breeders, that they do in fact have the best dogs. That is why they have such a position in the breed, and a study of the dogs in the ring will confirm this.

It is sometimes opined that in a Variety Class a judge will favour an exhibit of his own breed, but the truth is invariably the opposite. He will often be harder on it because he is more familiar with the level of excellence within that breed.

All judges interpret the Standard of a breed in different ways. Some will lay emphasis on a particular point such as length of neck, while others will give priority perhaps to movement. Because of each person's interpretation, as well as different competition, each show will come up with different results. It is when a dog is a

Paula Carey's Waltz of the Flowers of Ware. (Tracy Morgan.)

consistent winner time after time under various judges and against changing opposition, that he can be classed as a cut above the rest.

In a breed such as Cocker Spaniels, the majority of Championship Show judges are breed specialists. Some exhibitors do not welcome non-breed judges, though they are qualified under Kennel Club requirements. But it can be refreshing to have another opinion, and an outsider's results could even point out a trend creeping unnoticed into a breed because other judges have tended to follow the fashion of one particular dog or his progeny. Many people, experienced in judging and knowledgeable of other breeds, particularly of the same group, are perfectly capable of making appropriate judgements.

Although the majority of judges honestly do their best to judge the dogs before them, there are a few who are criticized for giving prizes to the handler at the other end of the lead. They prefer to award prizes to friends or to those from whom a favour might be expected, rather than correctly assessing the dogs. Such judging makes a mockery of the whole concept of dog showing, wasting both the time and money of the ordinary exhibitor. However, these judges are easily spotted and just as easily boycotted at their next appointment.

A judge must be careful to review all exhibits equally and fairly. The exhibitors have all paid entry fees, travelled distances, and spent time and trouble preparing their dogs, and are therefore entitled to have the judge's undivided attention for their turn. As Kennel Club regulations permit a person to judge up to 250 dogs of one breed in one day at a Championship Show, the time each dog is seen individually by the judge may not amount to ninety seconds.

Although there are some judges who are so experienced that they need only a glance to know that they will not be requiring some dogs for the line-up, they should give that second look to avoid disgruntled exhibitors leaving the ring feeling that their dogs have been completely ignored.

It is also worth checking down the line to avoid overlooking a dog who should have been amongst the awards. A judge must always be alert to the repeat exhibits, and this is particularly important in Cocker Spaniels where dogs may previously have appeared in the split colour classes. Among the entrants in a Junior Any Colour class, for instance, there may be a dog who was placed third in Novice Black, one who was second in Novice Red or Golden, some unplaced in Graduate Any Other Colour, and the Reserve from

Puppy Any Colour. The steward may have put them in order so that the second winner stands above the third, the reserve next and those previously unplaced behind. It is essential in such cases for the judge to check the whole line, for no matter that some were previously placed in their respective lower classes, those that were unplaced in the Graduate class are possibly more mature and worthy of serious consideration. Judges must, therefore, be wary of preconceived results or 'steward's judging'.

The judge can, however, request the steward to assemble the previously seen dogs in whatever order he wishes. Often stewards will place all previous first-prize winners together, then all second-prize winners, and so on. This gives little indication of which dog has already beaten which, and some judges therefore prefer an alternative method where dogs who have already met, stand in the order in which they were placed in their class, those from another class standing in their own group, and so on.

There are judges who are partial to knocking champions and can be relied upon to create a new winner. The inexperienced exhibitor should be cautious of the judge who strives to be different. It must be a tremendous thrill for a novice owner to win his first ticket with a young dog, and if that dog really is outstanding and has potential, then that is fair judgement. But if the dog is not yet ready for high honours, the judge will have done that exhibitor no favours. One CC can be more of a hindrance than a help in the long run in that the novice exhibitor and the dog will be excluded from entering many classes, and indeed ineligible for the smaller shows and club matches at which they were together gaining experience. They will be denied the opportunity of working their way up through the classes, having fun and learning as they go.

Becoming a Judge

When you have been in the breed for a few years, you may be asked to judge. It is usual to start off by judging three or four classes of the breed at an Open Show or one of the smaller ones. A fellow exhibitor or a committee member may have put your name forward to a club as being a likely candidate. Experienced judges of high reputation can command a fee, but this would hardly be appropriate for beginners. Judging is often undertaken purely for the honour of the occasion.

Before accepting a judging invitation you should have a thorough knowledge of the breed and be familiar with the requirements of breed type, construction and movement. You must ask yourself whether you can stand in the ring and have the courage of your own convictions in the face of possible intimidation, the trends of fashion or other influences. A judge has to come to his own conclusions in an honest and forthright way on the material put before him on the day, not what it was last week or might be in the future. If approached afterwards, he should be able to give reasons for his judgement.

You need to gain experience by sitting at the ringside and watching judging in progress and by discussing the breed with others who are more knowledgeable. Lectures and seminars are from time to time publicized and people have benefited from attending them. Such discourse on your own or other breeds yields useful information and even the experienced find they provide food for thought. There is always something to be learned.

It sometimes happens that people judge when they have been involved in the breed for seemingly a very short time. It may be flattering to be asked but it is a mistake to judge too soon before one has the necessary experience – the winning of one red card does not constitute the making of an expert! For the sake of the breed, it is better to serve a form of apprenticeship, for harm can be done to a breed if judges merely follow one another in their decisions without a sound grounding in breed construction and characteristics.

Awarding Tickets

After you have been judging for a few years, you may be invited to judge a Championship Show, but in order to award CCs you first have to be approved by the Kennel Club. Initially, you will be asked to complete a questionnaire about your experience in dogs, and in particular in the breed concerned. Questions will be asked on the number of dogs you have bred or owned, the occasions on which you have judged the breed and the number of classes and dogs judged; a breed club Limited or Open Show helps your case. It is important from your début to keep an account of all your judging commitments, for giving false information can lead you into serious trouble with the Kennel Club.

An organizing society has to apply to the Kennel Club for approval of a judge to award CCs, whether or not he has previously given

Mr and Mrs R. Wyatt's Sh.Ch. Classicway Country Life of Kendalwood, Best of Breed at Crufts in 1992. (Ian Scott.)

CCs in the breed, and confirmation of the appointment cannot be made until that approval has been given. The Kennel Club invariably seeks the opinion of the Cocker Spaniel Club and the Breed Council on proposed new judges.

For those actively involved in the breed, the Council's criteria of sufficient experience to award CCs is to have been judging for five years and in that time to have judged two breed club shows of at least twelve classes, plus a further sixty classes of Cocker Spaniels. Show organizers often apply to breed clubs for lists of judges when selecting for their forthcoming shows.

Overseas Judges

Judges from overseas sometimes officiate at shows in the United Kingdom. Those who are invited to award CCs, and who are already approved by their national kennel club to judge a breed similar in number and quality will invariably be passed by the

H.S. Lloyd and Tracey Witch of Ware being visited by Prince Ahmed Husain, whose recent imports to India include Crufts 1987 Best of Breed, Sh.Ch. Courtmaster Abracadabra (bred by Doug and Sue Telford).

Kennel Club. Otherwise their names will need to go through the same procedure as British nationals.

Points to Remember

A judge should go to the show neatly and tidily dressed, wearing something appropriate for the weather. As the task requires a certain amount of bending down, some walking and a lot of standing, clothes and shoes should be comfortable. Flapping raincoats, big hats and jangling jewellery are out of place.

A judge should be methodical in note-taking as well as assessment of the dogs, and resolute in judgement. It is the judge who is in charge of the ring, and the steward is there to assist. It is sometimes necessary for a judge to assert his authority, especially with Cocker Spaniel exhibitors who are guilty of overhandling. Exhibitors are so anxious to grip the dog's muzzle and pull the neck out, that some have to be asked to release their grasp before the judge can view the head. The practice of leaning over the dog when standing him in show pose prevents the judge from handling him, and some exhibitors almost have to be head-butted away to allow the judge access to the dog.

A judge should always be consistent in his method of judging, and look at each dog in the same way. It is logical to 'read' the dog from left to right, starting at the head and working to the rear, even if this means asking the handler to turn the dog round. The handler of the first dog to be put on the table should be allowed time to loosen the lead and place the dog as he sees fit. Some judges approach the table almost before the dog has been lifted up. They may themselves be unaccustomed to taking a dog in the ring, but should be aware of the demands of handling as well as judging!

The markings of Cocker Spaniels should be of secondary importance, but sometimes specific marks can detract from the overall picture. The make and shape of the animal should take precedence, and it is only when there are two exhibits of equal merit that marking might be taken into consideration. Equal tan spots on the head of a tricolour, for instance, will be more pleasing visually than a black and white which has no black around one eye. A heavy black mark on an elbow can give a false indication of unsoundness, or a rather wide blaze on the head can give the impression of a broad skull.

All judges hope that at the end of the day they will have seen a good number of Cocker Spaniels approximating to the Standard, and where there are several of the highest merit, an element of personal preference may be the deciding factor. Certainly a quantity of mediocre ones presents a harder task to sift through than a class of good ones. A judge can only assess what is put before him, and if they do not come up to his expectations, he is quite at liberty to withhold awards. He must please himself about his winners, but by giving all a fair deal he will ensure that losers too are satisfied.

9

Breeding

The person who goes in for breeding must have unbounded optimism to stand up to the disappointments which inevitably occur, and enthusiasm to try again. It is not a path which is strewn with roses, for difficulties will be met along the way, but it is a fascinating and absorbing occupation which has brought pleasure to many.

No one should become involved in keeping dogs or breeding with a view to profit-making. In fact, breeders are often out of pocket after a litter when stud fee and travelling expenses, veterinary charges, cost of rearing and registration fees are all taken into consideration, especially if it was not a large litter and one or two pups are being retained for possible future showing. It is more enjoyable to regard the matter as a hobby – though one which involves a lot of time and hard work.

Breeding is a serious matter which should not be undertaken lightly but should be the subject of much study before advancing into it. The aim of a breeder should be to produce sound and healthy stock with the right temperament, and to have the good of the breed at heart. Many have struggled with generation after generation to produce that elusive concept – perfection. A very few have come somewhere near to it!

The novice may start by purchasing a well-bred puppy, although an older bitch or even one that has already had a litter, would be a better prospect but not at all easy to acquire.

Successful breeding is not a haphazard affair, particularly with the choice of stud. It is important to look around at the dogs being shown and see if the ones you like are stemming from a particular sire or grandsire. Look for prepotency, which is the ability of a sire or dam to stamp his or her own qualities on stock. From reading as much as you can and seeking out pedigrees, you will be able to see how the strains combine, and whether one particular dog or bitch has had an influence. The club year books can also be very helpful, especially when owners include pedigrees of their stock in their advertising. A pedigree will provide more useful information to present and future breeders than a list of a few odd achievements, and make it worth while for newcomers to collect old issues.

In connection with advertisements, it may help some readers to know the correct usage of the terms 'by' and 'ex', which are quite often misapplied. In canine circles, 'by' is followed by the name of a male to indicate the sire, or father, of a litter. The word 'ex' literally means 'out of' and is followed by the name of a female to indicate the dam, or mother, of a litter. The dog's name should be put first, followed by the bitch's name, for example, 'Pups by Bobbie Brown ex Amanda Jill'.

Some plans should be made on paper by writing out the bitch's pedigree and comparing it with that of the proposed stud. A pedigree is not just a string of names; it indicates the individuals coming from certain families. A pedigree 'as long as your arm' is no proof of aristocracy in the animal world. Even a mongrel has an ancestry which goes back into the mists of time! It is what is on the pedigree that is important and the more one studies a breed, the more one will be able to picture the significance of the names involved. Pedigrees can be written out in different ways, but normally the top half shows the matings which took place to produce the sire, while those which took place quite separately to produce the dam are given on the bottom half. Reading from left to right, it will give the names of parents, then grandparents, great grandparents, and possibly on to five generations altogether. It certainly is worth investigating the fifth generation of any animals from whom you intend breeding.

By studying the dogs in the ring, perhaps by visiting kennels, and talking to people more knowledgeable, you should be able to ascertain some of the good points and the bad points of particular dogs, and weigh these up before deciding on the mate for your bitch. It is also a good idea to see other members of his family too, for near relations resemble each other. The quality of your bitch must also be noted. It is important for a breeder to be critical of his own stock and not blind to their faults, for how else can improvement be made? 'Kennel blindness' will get you nowhere.

Breeders must take the Breed Standard as their basis and, just as the judge in the ring, have the ideal in their sights. That is the object for which they are striving when breeding the next generation. Character is the first essential which must be kept foremost in mind, combined with stamina. Good spring of ribs, a deep chest and heart

Ch. Bournehouse Starshine. (Anne Roslin-Williams.)

room are where stamina will come from. Breeding stock must be typical of the breed and be 100 per cent constitutionally sound, that is mentally stable as well as physically unimpaired.

Honestly assess the faults in your bitch and try to locate a dog who will help correct these in the offspring; but it is no use trying to amalgamate opposing points. If your bitch is high on the leg and is put to a short-legged dog, some of the resulting offspring may take after one and some after the other in this respect. Choose a dog who is balanced and without exaggerations. One with a few minor faults is better than one who has a major fault you do not want perpetuated. Too much emphasis, however, should not be laid on one particular point that might be detrimental to the overall balance. If your bitch comes from a good family, select a mate who comes from the same family, as in this way type will be maintained. The characteristics of a given strain should reveal themselves in succeeding generations, and a keen ringside observer will be able to recognize the family of a dog being exhibited even before referring to the catalogue for details. When one's own strain is recognized in the ring, and even by the man in the street, it is achievement indeed!

Inbreeding

Inbreeding is the mating of close relations, such as mother to son or brother to sister, in order to fix a characteristic. It is a practice that should not be carried out by the novice breeder, but strictly only by those who have experience and knowledge of the ancestry, and where the stamina and intelligence of both parents have been proved. Inbreeding to strength will tend to fix the strength, but there are dangers, for unwanted characteristics can also be brought to the fore and can lead to those becoming fixed.

The uninitiated sometimes allege that inbreeding has taken place when a kennel name, or 'affix' appears on a pedigree several times. This is not necessarily so. Matings may have taken place within a kennel having a number of dogs without recourse to outside studs of other affixes. It is the individual dogs that matter, and a careful look may reveal that nothing closer than the mating of a bitch to a dog sharing perhaps the same great grandfather has taken place.

Line-Breeding

Line-breeding is much more commonly practised by breeders. The dog and bitch are not so closely related, but are from the same family and share a common ancestor, for instance a grandfather. This method usually comes up with good results, but again a knowledge of the individual dogs and their background is important.

Outcrossing

From time to time, an outcross, a mate from a different family, may be used, perhaps to correct a fault. This must be done with great care, or some undesirable trait may be brought in too, and undesirable characteristics seem to become fixed more easily than desirable ones. After using an outcross, breeding back into the bitch's own strain is the next step. When planning any mating, try to select a sire who has already proved capable of transmitting his good points; discard animals with defects, as well as those with the propensity for reproducing them.

A top-class dog can come from a chance mating for whatever

reason it was done, but, without the required family background, the dog is unlikely to reproduce himself, so should not be taken into breeding calculations.

Misconceptions

Some people are under the misapprehension that if they put their bitch to a champion dog, they will produce a champion. This does not often happen. The bitch must also make a contribution, and if she and her lineage are not good enough, the results will only be poor. Sometimes a champion is not a great producer himself, but an untitled dog in the kennel may more readily impress family virtues on his stock. Winning dogs are always popular, but the novice owner should not rush out and use the stud of the day, even if he is 'siring winners in every litter', without some study first being given to both sides. It can happen that bloodlines do not 'nick', and disappointments can result. If a dog with a fault or undesirable trait turns up from a particular mating, it is wiser to cast out that particular animal from the breeding programme than to try to breed out the fault in later generations. A good breeder should look some generations ahead and, for his own good as well as the good of the breed, try to plan for posterity.

It is not always the breeder of a dog who deserves the highest praise. Often, it is the subsequent owner who first saw the animal's potential, did the hard work of producing him for the show ring, and might even over the years have been instrumental in developing the line from which the dog derived.

It is a mistake, when a fault emerges, automatically to attach blame to the sire. It must be remembered that the dam shares responsibility for the results. Likewise when praise is being meted out, due credit must go to the lady. When the results of a particular mating have turned out well, it is often worth repeating if it is possible to do so. If a breeder finds he has a bitch who reproduces her qualities to a marked degree, it is worth holding on to her for she will become an invaluable brood. Nonetheless, it is inadvisable to overbreed from her, or any bitch, one litter per year being the maximum. Indeed, the Kennel Club will not normally accept registrations where the bitch is over eight years old at the time of whelping, nor if she has already whelped six litters.

There are people who take pride in raising their litters, and breed

Success for the breeder: Craigleith pups. (Tracy Morgan.)

Cocker Spaniels for pure enjoyment. Others breed because they are striving after perfection for the show ring. The continued presence of an outstanding dog in the ring helps to maintain the standard of the breed, as it provides a living example of the level of excellence for which breeders should aim. In order to reach or surpass this they must go away and breed an equally good or better dog. This gives justification for the repeated exhibition of champions. Their withdrawal from competition simply leaves the way open for poorer specimens to gain awards which they do not really merit.

There is no room for sentimentality in breeding. A good breeder must have strength of will and be hard-hearted, for it is necessary to keep for the next generation only the most vigorous stock. There is much to be said for the old-fashioned doctrine of 'survival of the fittest' where a weakling died at birth and was not forced to survive. Never keep back for future breeding one who is a poor feeder. To produce sound pups and avoid heartache, it is best to apply the old principle of breeding only from robust stock with stamina. Some breeders wonder whether contemporary rearing methods, incorporating much dry food and early inoculations, may have some bearing on any misfortunes which come to light.

Breeders must be cautious and keep a sense of balance in their selection of breeding stock. There is a danger that in their desire to avoid a problem, they do not give sufficient regard to anatomical and temperamental features. This could change the shape and character of the breed. So it is important that in breeding no hasty steps or panic measures are taken. Problems should be faced calmly; answers are not immediately forthcoming, even from the experts.

Pet Bitches

Sometimes owners have a desire to breed a litter from a pet bitch. The reason may be that they want another dog, but there are plenty of Cocker Spaniels about and breeding is generally best left to the breeders. If, however, you are determined, you must go into the matter thoroughly, and consider first whether you have the time available to devote eight to twelve weeks to the rearing of the litter, and whether the family is prepared for the household to be disrupted for that time. It is important to seek advice as to the suitability of your bitch, and to approach a kennel or breeder in order to locate a mate.

A pet dog should not be used at stud; it may encourage him to roam or change his habits and become an unpleasant house companion. In any case, it is unlikely that either owner would have knowledge of the suitability of the bloodlines. It is unwise to breed without sufficient knowledge, for an uninformed move could do harm to a breed in future generations. It is far better to use a stud who knows his job, with an owner who knows how to handle the matter.

Do not be persuaded to breed from your bitch if you do not feel competent or if it would cause any hardship to her or your household. The bitch needs to be mentally and physically relaxed for happy motherhood, and any tensions felt by the owner will be transmitted to her.

Licensing

A breeding establishment that keeps more than two bitches for the purpose of breeding for sale has to be licensed under the Breeding of Dogs Act 1973. However, if the sale is purely the disposal of small numbers of stock not considered suitable for showing, the licence may not be required.

In some ways it is fortunate that the breed continues to be popular and there is a steady market for the excess stock or those pups not required for show. Not every pup in a litter will be potential show material, and the average pet owner will not mind if his dog is short in the neck or carries his tail too high, provided he is fit and healthy. However, breeders must always keep in mind the ever-present rescue problem and restrict their numbers so that there are no more puppies than the available suitable homes.

Colour

In the last forty or so years, as has been said, solid colours have remained more or less separated from the particolours. With a breed as numerically large as Cocker Spaniels, there has been an abundance of good dogs who have made their mark in the ring or for breeding. Because of the availability of suitable mates, breeders have tended to retain the colours within their respective environs. In general, the bloodlines of the two variations are now so far apart that it would be an unwise move for a novice to undertake cross-matings. Any reticence about mixing them may, these days, stem from reservations about introducing to one side a rare problem from the other. Although a broad-minded breeder may devise a mating irrespective of colour in order to make an improvement or strengthen a point, for more reasons than mismarking such breeding is best left to the experts.

Hereditary Problems

To lose a beloved puppy or have an adult dog affected with one of the hereditary diseases is very distressing for the owners. There are, however, many thousands of puppies bred each year who grow up to be strong and healthy, and the chances are slim of a buyer obtaining one who may subsequently succumb to such a disease. Anyone who has the misfortune to suffer in this way should inform the breeder or person from whom they obtained the puppy. It is important to give as much factual information as possible and essential to pass on a veterinary report.

Familial Nephropathy

This is a form of kidney failure which can affect young Cocker Spaniels from about the age of three months to two-and-a-half years. It is commonly referred to as FN or shrunken kidney disease. Typical symptoms are a loss of appetite, loss of weight and an increase in thirst and urine output. Dogs become very ill over a period of weeks and as there is no treatment, they have to be put to sleep.

In 1980, the Cocker Spaniel Club was sufficiently concerned over the matter to set up an investigation. A test-mating in due course took place between two carriers, that is a dog and bitch who had previously produced affected offspring (from unions to different mates). This was a father-to-daughter mating; the pups were hand-reared and five survived. A urine testing programme was set up and the pedigrees of known cases studied. Genetic analysis was carried out and it was determined that FN is inherited through a recessive gene. Therefore, both parents of an affected pup would be carriers. It is unlikely they would be affected themselves as the disease normally manifests itself before breeding age. Conclusions were reached when the clinical work finished; with the test-mated litter barely two years old, one was diagnosed as a positive case and the others were found homes.

This particular disease seems to be confined solely to Cocker Spaniels, though something similar has occurred in a few other breeds. The majority of the cases so far seen have been particolours, the problem being minimal in solids.

The Cocker Spaniel Club set up a control scheme in 1986 and appointed a co-ordinator who should be informed of any new cases. The disease has to be identified by one of a small group of specialists. Symptoms and pedigree only are insufficient evidence. Even if the symptoms and age are typical and the pedigree is suspicious, it is unwise to jump to conclusions before expert diagnosis. The cause of the illness could be confused with some other problem. Kidney tissue or urine must be examined for confirmation.

Urine screening is available, and although this can allay suspicions regarding the dog himself, it can give no indication as to whether the dog is a carrier. It is recommended by the Club that the parents of an affected animal should be withdrawn from further breeding, and it is pointed out that the problem lies with certain dogs and bitches, *not* with the line or strain. Breeders are recommended to keep records of litters and to make subsequent health checks. The Club provides members with a list, fortunately occasional and small, of new carrier dogs and bitches in order to provide information for breeders.

Progressive Retinal Atrophy

This is a degeneration of the light-sensitive tissue at the back of the eye. The dog has difficulty in seeing in dim light ('night blindness') and may become totally blind. The problem was noticed in the breed in the 1960s and the Cocker Spaniel Club undertook investigation into the matter. The British Veterinary Association and the Kennel Club then extended a scheme for testing for eye disease in various breeds to include PRA in Cocker Spaniels, and the Cocker Spaniel Club has subsequently maintained a list of dogs who have been examined under the scheme and found to be clear. This condition is also inherited through a recessive gene, so the parents of affected offspring are assumed to be affected or to be carriers.

Over the years, the problem became less serious, but unfortunately there are some signs of it recurring. Owners are advised to have their breeding stock tested regularly, as the onset of the disease can occur in young or mature dogs. The dog must be examined by a specialist from a stated panel of experts and if not affected, a certificate is subsequently issued. The dog can be examined privately or at a special clinic which a breed club may organize, sometimes in conjunction with a show. Although the examination cannot indicate whether the animal is a carrier, it means that breeders using certified animals are breeding from clinically clear stock.

Entropion

This condition is where the eyelids turn inwards, thus causing the lashes to irritate the eye itself. It is associated with breeds with loose folds of skin, and was one of the problems with red Cocker Spaniels prior to their improvement. Surgery can be performed for the comfort of the dog, but any dog who has suffered from the problem should certainly not be bred from.

Temperament

It has always been stressed to breeders that much importance must be laid on temperament as the first essential above all other, and a dog with any defect in this should not be bred from. Both heredity and environment play their part in the development of a dog's character, and responsibility must be shared by the owner as well as the breeder for producing a well-adjusted dog. The majority of Cocker Spaniels are affectionate dogs with a happy disposition. However, from time to time over many years, there has been seen the occasional streak of a possessive nature, this trait associated in many people's minds with a particular colour.

In the early 1980s the term 'rage syndrome' became attached to serious uncharacteristic behaviour, and following some sensational and uninformed reporting in the media, the Cocker Spaniel Council set up a committee to investigate the alleged temperament defects in the breed. The Committee has been helped in its research by an animal behaviourist, as well as veterinarians specializing in neurology and in epilepsy. Through the channels of breeders, owners and vets, a proportion of Cocker Spaniels were identified who had defects ranging from 'occasionally growling at other dogs' to 'attacking a human without provocation'. From first investigations it would appear that the underlying trend is that more problems are found in reds and goldens, particularly males, than in blacks or particolours. It is, however, accepted that reds and goldens are popular and probably the most numerous. There is an indication that a few cases have come from recognized breeders, but a large number of bad-tempered animals have rather obscure origins.

It had been hoped for some years to have actual cases clinically investigated but this seemed impossible until, in 1990, the Companion Animal Research Group at the University of Cambridge came forward with a proposal to include Cocker Spaniels in a research project into aggression and other behaviour problems. Interested parties are endeavouring to raise money to help fund the research.

Kennel Club Registration

Until recently, many a pedigree pup was sold unregistered, especially if the breeder, perhaps a pet owner, had no kennel name or affix. The new owner could undertake the registration of a dog at any time provided the breeder had handed over the official forms.

However, in 1989 a regulation was brought in that only the breeder can name and register a dog, and this to be undertaken for all puppies in a litter at one time within twelve months of birth. Any puppies omitted will not normally be considered at a later date. This step was deemed necessary to expose overbreeding and provide information to help in the control of hereditary diseases. The Kennel

Club publishes the *Breed Records Supplement*, in which details of all registrations appear, and which reveals the number and frequency of litters and number of puppies that any bitch has produced.

The breeder of a litter is the owner of the dam at the time of whelping, and if you are breeding from your own bitch you should ensure that the stud-dog owner signs the form for litter registration.

Do not rush off and register your puppies the moment they are born. There may be a weakling who does not survive more than a day or two, and, in any case, many breeders like to wait a few weeks to get an idea of personality and potential before choosing names. The character or colouring of a puppy will often bring a suitable name to mind, and with Cocker Spaniels it is not always easy for an inexperienced breeder to be precise over the colourings of newborn puppies. Blue roans are born black and white, and orange roans can be very pale, almost cream, even the ears showing little colour. It is difficult to say whether they will be roan or clear. Sometimes the tan on a tricolour is missed at first sight.

Affixes and Names

If you are seriously thinking of going in for breeding or showing, you may wish to have your own affix, that is, a name for your own kennel or strain. An affix is a word which is protected for your sole use and no one else will be able to use that word in naming their puppies. Application must be made to the Kennel Club with an initial fee, and then a subsequent annual maintenance fee. Certain affixes have become synonymous with good breeding and on looking at a pedigree one can tell whether a dog has come from a successful line. Puppies can, however, be registered without the use of an affix.

Some kennel names have traditionally been used as prefixes, others have followed the dog's name. However, there are now positional limitations to the use of an affix and one no longer has the choice of where to put it. It must appear as the first word in the name for each puppy. If you have no affix, you will not be allowed to repeat one particular word in naming all the puppies in a litter. The name of a dog must consist of more than one word but not more than twenty-four letters including the affix. A dog's name can be changed once, but only by the addition of an affix at the end. This will indicate that the dog has been acquired, but was not bred, by his owner.

Any person making a registration is bound by Kennel Club Rules and Regulations, which may be amended from time to time, and accepts the provisions of the *Kennel Club General Code of Ethics*.

Exporting

There has been a constant interest in the breed abroad for show, companionship or sport, and between 100 and 200 registered Cocker Spaniels are exported annually. The time may come when you have such an enquiry for your stock.

The regulations for different countries vary enormously, and you have to determine well in advance what these are. Initial enquiries can be made to the Ministry of Agriculture, Fisheries and Food (*see* Appendix 2), which should be able to advise you of the certificates and vaccinations required, and whether these must be obtained through a Ministry-approved vet. Most countries require a health certificate.

If you are handling the export yourself, enquiries will have to be made with regard to flight times, procedures and prices from the cargo section of an appropriate airline, checking also that livestock is accepted on the particular flight. Arrival at weekends or a local public holiday is best avoided, as any veterinary inspection at the port of entry could be delayed. Transit insurance can be arranged through one of the canine insurance companies.

An approved travelling crate must be obtained which for some destinations will incorporate a special drinking bowl. There are regulations concerning bedding, and it is useful to attach a lead and collar for emergency use. Alternatively, there are livestock shipping agents who specialize in export, and they could undertake the whole matter for you.

Any dog being sold abroad for the purpose of showing or breeding, must have an export pedigree issued by the Kennel Club, and at the same time be transferred to the ownership of the overseas consignee. There are more regulations which must be checked.

The cost of all these requirements is additional to the quoted price for the dog, and you may also need to charge for travelling expenses involved in obtaining certificates, as well as any consular fees. Also consider the cost of caring for the puppy while all these arrangements are made, and note that the client should pay you in full in advance of despatch.

10

Mating, Pregnancy and Whelping

The Right Time

The best time to breed from a bitch is usually on the second or third season, when she will be between about eighteen months and two-and-a-half years of age. Much depends on when she comes on heat for the first time and the frequency of heats, plus the time of year and whether the pups' arrival and despatch to new homes interferes with holidays. Many people like to get their priorities right and dispense with holidays in order to enjoy puppies to the full!

Holiday time, however, is not a good time for puppies to be ready for their new homes, although they are easier to rear in the summer. Sensible people will wait to take their purchase on return from holidays, and you may have to hold their puppy for several weeks. Avoid Christmas, with its irrational demands, and just afterwards when the pet market will be predictably slow and poor weather prevents babies being run outdoors.

The bitch must, of course, be fit and healthy, well exercised and not overweight in order to be in peak condition for mating. She must be free from skin diseases and parasites, and any necessary treatments should be carried out well in advance.

Preparation

First consult your veterinary surgeon for a suitable wormer and possibly a course of wheatgerm (vitamin E), which may aid fertility. You should also ensure that booster vaccinations are up to date, but this must be done before mating as afterwards it may damage the unborn puppies. Bathing should also be done in good time, and not after the season has started.

173

Check your bitch at regular intervals when her season is due so that you can be quite sure of the date it starts. Once a bitch has come into season she must be carefully supervised so that she does not get out. It is normal for bitches to be ready for mating somewhere between the tenth and fifteenth day, though there are variations to this. The coloured discharge should become straw-coloured to indicate when she is ready for mating, and this is generally found to be about the twelfth day.

Allow two to three days to ensure the bitch is properly on heat, then contact the owner of the chosen mate or kennel. If you have not previously discussed the possible mating, the owner will naturally need to approve the bitch and her breeding (pedigree) before allowing the dog to be used. If you are new or unfamiliar to breeding, leave it to the kennel owner to decide which dog seems compatible with your bitch. As you become experienced in breeding, you will come to know your own bitches, and learn the best day to take them to the dog. Even so, all bitches are individual.

As the predicted time draws near, you should examine her daily by wiping with cotton wool or a tissue to check when the discharge begins to pale. If you find it seems to be drying up and the vulva less swollen, you should ask to take her earlier, but if on the day before she is due to visit the dog, she is still heavily coloured, you should contact the stud owner and request a postponement. The vulva should be swollen and fluid when the bitch visits the dog, and most stud owners will be happy to advise about the suitable day.

The Mating

The matter of mating is not always as simple and easy as may be assumed from the strays in the street. There the bitch will have gone out on her peak day and may have given several dogs a run around before allowing one to mate her. It certainly should not be undertaken by the inexperienced without the supervision of someone more knowledgeable. The risks are too great, especially for the dog. A promising stud-dog's career could be ruined by a wrong move at a vital moment. There are some owners who, even after many years' breeding, prefer not to take control of the matings, but employ the help of a stud handler for the operation.

It is usual for the bitch to be taken to the stud-dog. She should not be fed before her visit to him, and should be given no more than a light meal early in the day if the visit is not to be for some hours. She should be allowed to relieve herself about twenty minutes before arrival.

A garage or quiet room may be set aside for the mating. When you have viewed the dog, and the owner has approved your bitch, leave her in his hands for the mating. It is better if an anxious owner is out of the way, for anxiety will be communicated to the bitch, and bitches are usually far less inhibited if they are on their own. A dog will have become accustomed to being attended by one handler and one particular assistant, so unless you are asked to hold the bitch, go and wait somewhere patiently and read a book!

The mating procedure is one which cannot be hurried and a time should be chosen when neither owner is under any pressure with regard to other commitments. Both dog and bitch should wear collars; it is far easier to restrain a bitch, who may make a sudden movement, with a fixed collar than it is with a slip-lead or check-chain. Before bringing the dog into the room, time should be taken for the handlers to become acquainted with the bitch. She will then be more relaxed and happy when meeting the dog. The bitch should be put on a table and examined. Then, while the assistant holds her head, the handler, with scrupulously clean hands and the middle finger smeared with petroleum jelly, can feel 'up and over' inside the vagina. The experienced handler can then tell whether the bitch is mateable; the petroleum jelly also acts as a lubricant. However, if you know the dog may be put off by it, wait to see if a mating can be effected without it.

Put the bitch on the ground and introduce the dog. The assistant should hold the bitch firmly on a short lead. Anticipate her reactions, for a maiden (previously unmated) or pet bitch may snap at the dog at first and a young male can be put off for life.

When the dog mounts the bitch, the assistant should hold her collar firmly with one hand and put the other underneath to support her. If the dog makes two or three unsuccessful attempts, the handler can move quietly in before he loses enthusiasm and, with a hand under the bitch, try to line up the vulva to the dog so that he can slip in. Once he has done so, press gently behind the dog's buttocks to ensure he penetrates. The penis will become enlarged and a 'tie' will take place. All this time the bitch must be firmly and carefully held quite still for if she should suddenly lurch forward or roll over, the dog may not care to make another attempt or may even be injured. While supporting the bitch, hold the dog on her for

175

half a minute, before allowing him to dismount. The dog will then turn and the two will be locked together tail to tail. The tie will usually last between ten and twenty minutes, but ties of a few minutes are quite satisfactory, while some even last an hour.

When the tie has been achieved, both dogs usually stand quietly together. Either the stud handler or the assistant should remain with the dogs, on their leads, while the other fetches the owner of the bitch just to witness the tie. It is possible for puppies to result from a mating where the partners have not tied. However, such a mating is not considered to be very satisfactory unless it is normal for that male and puppies have resulted on previous occasions.

If a dog makes several attempts to mate a bitch but does not seem to be making any progress, it may be that his height varies too much from that of the bitch or that her vulva is tucked down too low. In such cases a low platform, an inch or so high, could be used for one or other of them to stand on. It may be that the dog is getting over-anxious, in which case he should be taken outside to 'cool down'. A dog will sometimes seem to be standing too far away from the bitch to achieve a mating. In this case the bitch can be pushed gently back towards him, and it is a good idea if the procedure commences near a wall so that he can be backed up against it. A dog should not be permitted to extend himself unless he is inside the bitch, but should be pushed off her and prevented from starting again until any swelling has reduced.

Failure to get a mating may mean that the bitch needs to empty her bladder, or that she is not quite ready. It is often found that a bitch returning to the dog a day later will be much more responsive and better psychologically adjusted too.

When the mating is finished, the pair will separate naturally, and there is sometimes a loss of fluid. Though some operators still like to do it, it is not necessary to up-end the bitch to retain the fluid, as the important sperm-bearing part will have been transmitted at an earlier stage of the mating. Ensure the male has recovered before he returns to the kennel and allow the bitch to rest for a while.

The stud fee must be paid at the time of mating but any other arrangement should be put in writing. Sometimes a puppy is taken in lieu of fee, but such agreements are often unsatisfactory and can lead to bad feeling.

A copy of the pedigree of the stud-dog should be handed over, together with a Kennel Club form for puppy registration signed by the dog's owner, confirming the mating. The stud owner should of

Mrs J. Rowland's Sh.Ch. Perrytree The Dreamer, made up in 1991. (Tracy Morgan.)

course be informed of the result in due course. If the bitch fails to prove to be in whelp, a free return service is customarily given if the male is still in the owner's possession, though this should not be assumed as a right.

When a bitch fails to conceive, the dog should not automatically be blamed. It is much more likely that the bitch was not at the peak of her season when taken to the dog. Although it is not necessary to give a bitch two services, this is often done if the bitch has missed on a previous occasion. If two matings are given in order to increase the chance of fertilization, these should take place over two or three days.

Antenatal Care of the Bitch

After the mating, the bitch will still be attractive to males, so must be confined as usual until the season is over. She should not be

177

allowed to jump or leap about, but otherwise normal exercise can be undertaken until she will naturally slow down at about the seventh week. It is advisable not to show a bitch in whelp for fear of picking up an infection or causing extra stress. Also, some owners prefer not to bath a bitch once mated, for fear of her catching a chill, or perhaps slipping or struggling in the water and causing some injury. Her rear end can be sponged from time to time and dirty feet can be washed in a bowl.

If the bitch has been on wheatgerm, continue the course for two or three weeks after mating. Apart from this, the bitch will not require any special treatment until about the third or fourth week, when she should be wormed. It is advisable to ask the vet for a suitable wormer for an in-whelp bitch, and it is about this time that he may be able to diagnose pregnancy by palpation, though even the professional cannot always be sure. However, most breeders prefer to wait another week or two, when it will be obvious if the bitch is pregnant. There will be a rounding of the flanks, and the teats will enlarge and stand out.

There are, of course, scientific ways of determining the best time for mating and of pregnancy diagnosis. Vaginal smears or progesterone levels may be tested for the former; ultrasound or blood samples for the latter. Some methods have limitations or drawbacks, for instance where repeated testing is necessary; radiography is not satisfactory before the seventh week of pregnancy because of the slow development of foetal skeletons. Although for reasons such as reabsorption the final outcome cannot be guaranteed, it is true to say that existing methods have already proved of value to some breeders, and as advances in techniques are made, scientific tests will no doubt have an increasing part to play in dog breeding.

From about the fourth week, or when the bitch demands more, the quantity of food can be increased. It should be mainly in the form of protein, and meat is especially beneficial. The bitch does not require milk during pregnancy. It is more important to use a good-quality feed; liquids will play their part when the bitch is nursing the pups. There is, though, usually an increase in thirst which is natural to keep the kidneys functioning, and clean water should always be available. For this reason, and because of the increased pressure on the bladder from the growing pups, the bitch may want to pass water more frequently.

Calcium is important and should be added to the diet, but it must be one that contains vitamin D to aid assimilation. Take a look at the balanced vitamin and mineral supplements available in liquid, powder or tablet form. Seek the advice of your vet, breeder or stud-dog owner as to choice and stick to that one. Follow the maker's guidelines and do not be tempted to make any further additions or the balance will be upset. An overdose of supplements can be harmful. For bitches fed on complete diets, follow the manufacturer's instructions. If it is one for pregnant bitches, supplements are probably unnecessary.

With the extra food intake, the bitch may prefer to have her meals split in two. A bitch may occasionally refuse food during pregnancy, but if it is only once or twice, it should be nothing to worry about.

Sometimes a heavily pregnant bitch will lose a little colourless fluid from the vulva when she sits down, but if any discharge should be stained red or green, the vet should be consulted. Some owners fight shy of injections for a pregnant bitch for fear of harming the pups, but even if attending for an unrelated problem, the vet must be informed of the bitch's condition so that he can give appropriate treatment.

One of the disappointments for breeders is when a much hoped-for litter is reabsorbed by the dam. It occasionally happens that a bitch who appears nicely in whelp suddenly regains her normal shape. This probably happens before the bone of the puppies is formed and could be caused by injury or infection; there will be no other signs. Wheatgerm is said to help avoid reabsorption or abortion.

About ten days before the bitch is due to whelp, you can begin shortening some of her feathering, especially if she is very heavily coated. This can be done a little at a time, removing the hair particularly from around the teats so that the babies will have access. With the thinning scissors, the hair round the bitch's rear end can be reduced, as this will become soiled during whelping and afterwards. An excessive shirt front, too, can be tidied up. If your bitch is a show animal, you will need to do all this with some care. Most bitches drop their coat anyway after whelping, and since it often takes some while to regrow, all thoughts of showing must be discounted for some months. There are many preparations, costly and simple, said to aid coat growth, which have been tried with varying results.

The teats themselves will need a little conditioning at this stage. Sponge them down with soap and water and dry the bitch gently and quickly. Gently massage them with a little warm olive oil to make them supple. It is important to use only mild products, as some ointments or shampoos could be harmful to the bitch or unborn puppies. For the same reason, insecticides should not be used. The bitch should have been kept clear of parasites, but if any are evident at this stage, they must be picked off, or the vet asked for something suitable. The puppies could be born any time and inhalation or absorption of harmful chemicals while suckling must be avoided. Keep the teats clean.

The bitch should be encouraged to take regular and gentle exercise but as her time draws near, do not take her far from home.

Cocker Spaniels are usually easy whelpers and do not often have problems, but it would be as well to advise your vet of the impending whelping. Most bitches will get on with the job on their own, and it is best to leave them undisturbed as much as possible. The bitch, however, should be supervised, preferably by only one person, in case of any difficulties. The normal gestation period is sixty-three days (nine weeks) but bitches can whelp several days early so it is necessary to have everything prepared and the bitch settled in her home well in advance. If a pregnant bitch goes into a second day over her time with nothing happening, you should consult the vet.

The Whelping Box

From two or three weeks before the pups are due, your bitch should be getting accustomed to the whelping box during the daytime at least, then full-time for the last ten days. The box should be positioned in a quiet room or placed away from the traffic of the household and where other dogs cannot interfere, but where the bitch is quite contented. The box should be accessible in order to attend to the puppies or any problems during whelping and should have electric light available for inspection. Many litters are reared very satisfactorily indoors in a warm room. Warmth is essential for bringing up puppies and many breeders use an infra-red lamp, with dull emitter and wire guard, over the whelping box. It could be suspended by a chain from a beam or from an angle-bracket on the wall, but must, of course, be safely erected and the bitch has to be able to move away if she feels discomfort, leaving the litter under its heat.

The alternative is that to which many breeders, particularly of the smaller breeds, are reverting: the old idea of the closed-in whelping box. In this, the bitch has privacy and with the modern purpose-

180

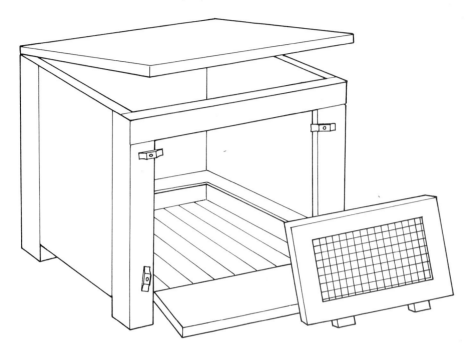

Closed-in whelping box with optional grille.

made bedding, generates her own heat, providing a satisfactory environment for the litter. Outside the box, normal room temperature would be sufficient.

Whichever method is used, the box must be large enough for the bitch to stretch out so that she can comfortably feed the litter, especially if it is a large one. It is amazing how quickly the puppies grow and how much room they take up just before they are completely weaned and while the dam still feeds them. The ideal bedding is a proprietary brand of fleecy blanket on a canvas backing through which puppies' urine or leaks from the bitch will drain on to a pad of newspaper placed beneath. It is machine-washable and quick drying, but two or three pieces of it will be required for frequent changing. The newspaper, too, must be changed often. Whatever type of bedding is used, it must be firm and lie flat. You must ensure that the bitch cannot scratch it up and smother a puppy underneath the folds.

There are purpose-built whelping boxes on the market in various materials from wood to PVC, but the average handyman should be able to put one together quite easily. The box should be at least 30 × 24in (76 × 60cm) and for the open type three sides should be about 12in (30cm) high. The sides of the closed-in version should be about 24in (60cm) high and it should have a hinged or removable lid and adequate ventilation. The box should have a low front for accessibility for the bitch who is heavy in whelp or in lactation, removable or hinged to allow the pups eventually to move freely in and out. A slatted front is ideal as the height can be adjusted as the puppies grow.

A small shelf or pig rail could be fixed around the inside a few inches from the floor to prevent the bitch crushing puppies against the wall. Even with such a bar, accidents can happen, and the owner must be ever watchful.

Some owners use a special electrically heated bed or pad in the early stages, ensuring of course that all plugs and cables are safely installed. Nonetheless, beware of the dam chewing the item!

The Whelping

It is a good idea to prepare in advance the equipment you may need: old clean newspaper, a cardboard box, hot-water bottle, puppy feeding bottle (which you may be able to get from the vet), together with milk powder suitable for infant puppies, two small blankets, several towels, cotton wool, small scissors, a kettle and a bowl of water and soap if these are not already to hand. For those who like to have things detailed, a thermometer, scales, notebook and pencil may be helpful. The bitch's temperature may drop to as low as 97 °F (36 °C) as an indication of impending birth.

The bitch will usually give some signal of the approaching whelping, which will in all probability take place at night. She will either refuse her food, or eat it and promptly vomit. She will probably be restless and scratch up the bedding, or sit and pant a little. She may frequently want to go out to spend a penny; always go with her in case she drops a puppy outside. At night, take a torch. It would be as well to take her on a lead because bitches are not unknown to dig at this stage and burrow their way under a shed or kennel in order to make a nest for the family, as they would in the wild. This early stage of labour can go on for twenty-four hours but no longer. She should then get down to the serious business; if she does not, consult a vet for advice. Make a note of the time contractions start;

the first puppy may then arrive in about twenty minutes or so, and it is quite normal for a bitch to give a yelp or little howl. If straining continues for an hour with no pups emerging, at any time during the whelping, seek veterinary advice.

The water bag will appear before the first puppy, which will follow within half an hour. Some owners are surprised at the deluge of water that gushes forth. Puppies will probably arrive at intervals of ten minutes to an hour, or the bitch may rest quietly between pups for up to two hours. If, however, she is restless but not straining, a walk round the garden or even a ride in the car will often get things moving. However, inactivity should not be allowed to continue for more than two hours, as it could be a symptom of inertia which is caused by a puppy that is wrongly positioned or by an obstruction. Immediate help should be sought.

The bitch can have the special bedding in the box to whelp on, or layered newspaper can be used. This can be removed a little at a time as it becomes soiled, but you must be tactful in your movements or the bitch may think you are taking a puppy away from her.

It is not unusual for a bitch to stand to deliver her pups (whelps). She will try to reach round to her rear end and, for a heavily laden bitch, this will become easier with each arrival. The 'pre-packed' pup will probably plop on the floor of the box, and the bitch will lick it and help it from the membrane bag as well as biting the umbilical cord. If she is getting on with it, do not interfere, but sometimes a bitch producing her first litter will not know what to do with the initial pup. In that case, you should tear the bag so the puppy can quickly get his first gulp of air, hold him upside down to drain away any fluid from the lungs and rub briskly with a towel. If the puppy is still attached to the afterbirth (placenta), the cord should be squeezed and cut about 2in (5cm) from the puppy. Some breeders prefer to tie it with cotton, then cut on the placenta side. The scissors should, of course, have been previously sterilized in a disinfectant solution, or by boiling for three minutes, then cooled.

Some people like to weigh each puppy at birth and keep a note of weights. This should be done as quickly as possible, and then the pup put back with the bitch to suckle. The whelps should be handled as little as possible during the first few days as normally the bitch will be very protective towards them and may resent any intrusion. She should be allowed to eat the afterbirths which will give her nourishment. However, if she has a large litter, one or two can be removed and disposed of as they tend to make the motions loose, which will in any case be black for a few days. The afterbirth is not always expelled at the same time as the puppy; it may come away later. Try to keep an account of the number passed, but it is not always easy to see what a bitch is doing when she is turned away from you into the corner of the box. You should have the bitch checked by the vet within twenty-four hours after whelping to ensure all the placentae have come away and that all is well. Some breeders like to give their bitches raspberry-leaf tablets for some weeks before whelping until one week after, as a birth aid and to help clear the placentae.

As a bitch will move around when attending to the next arrival, the first ones born may become scattered and drenched with the volume of green fluid which comes away with each birth. You may, therefore, like to place the first puppies in the cardboard box while this is in progress. Put them on the hot-water bottle which should be wrapped in a blanket, and cover them with another blanket. When she has dealt with the newly arrived puppy, the bitch will expect to have the others to nurse as well. If there are long intervals between arrivals, you will probably put them all back with her, but it is very much a matter over which you must use your discretion according to the reactions of the bitch. After the first couple of pups, the new mum may be grateful for a drink of warm milk with glucose or honey, especially if she has been without food for hours beforehand.

A few drops of brandy on the tongue may help to revive a puppy that is slow to get going. The puppies must be kept warm and it is essential they suckle within an hour or so. The colostrum, or first milk that the bitch produces, contains antibodies which help to protect the puppies from infection for their first six to twelve weeks. When the bitch has finished whelping, she should relax and be ready to settle down with her new family. You may be able to clean the box up at this stage, or if it causes too much disturbance to the bitch just clean round her. Put the puppies to her and then leave her to rest. After an hour or so she may like to go outside. Most bitches will be very devoted to their duties and only leave the box for brief intervals for the first couple of weeks. A bitch who is reluctant to go out may have to be lifted from the box and taken on a lead so that she has the opportunity to make herself comfortable. Give her a warm drink of milk and when she has settled down again, ensure the puppies are all suckling well.

For the first twenty-four hours after whelping, the mother should

Three-day old puppy. (Alan Carey.)

be kept on a light, mainly liquid diet, with clean water always available. She could have egg custard, milk pudding or some fish, and a plentiful supply of milk or invalid drink. The milk should be of the type specially formulated for lactating bitches and growing pups. As the days go by and her appetite increases with the demands of the litter, the bitch will need at least one pint of milk and one pound of meat per day with a good wholemeal biscuit. This food should be divided into four or five meals, and a breakfast cereal could be added to the milk drink. A good supply of meat will help the bitch to produce good-quality milk and the sucking action of the pups will encourage the flow. Calcium is important, so keep up the supplements according to the instructions. The bitch will be reluctant to get out of the box and you will not want the pups disturbed, so hold the food to her for the first few days.

It is fascinating to watch a good brood-bitch care for her litter – cleaning and feeding them and ensuring none strays too far from the warmth of her body. Clever mums hop in and out of the whelping box without disturbing the pups or treading on them, and settle themselves down to rest again behind them.

The bitch should be examined daily, and her teats and rear end sponged down and quickly dried, for she will want to leave the pups only for a minimum of time. However, a little gentle exercise round the garden twice a day should be encouraged to stretch the limbs and stimulate the bodily functions.

It is normal for a bitch to have a vaginal discharge for a week or so. If the discharge is foul-smelling or the bitch is unwell, you will need help promptly.

Complications

If there are any weak pups or any that seem to be sucking but are dissatisfied, check the mouths to make sure there are no cleft palates. A puppy with a cleft palate or any congenital abnormality should be destroyed. Make any such decisions at once and do not be persuaded into trying treatments. In this way, difficulties and heart-ache in the long run will be avoided. If there is a weakling or, in a large litter, one or two who are pushed out by the stronger ones, it is beneficial to supplementary feed them two or three times a day for a few days to build up their strength. It is also a good idea to take a lusty pup off a teat and hold the weak one on there so that you are sure he has a turn at the milk bar. Well-fed puppies will be happy and quiet.

Many breeders like to watch over their litters in the early stages to see that all is going well. It is most unfortunate to lose a whelp through the dam lying on it. This is where the pig rail is useful, for if a puppy should get behind the mother, there is less danger of his being crushed. However, if a puppy gets separated from the others, he will usually cry and a good mother will probably pick him up in her jaws and return him to the siblings.

If one puppy cries for no apparent reason, he could be troubled by wind. Pick him up and gently massage him soothingly. A few drops of gripe water as given to babies will probably do the trick. A bitch will clear up after the puppies in the nest by licking them. However, should the bedding be streaked with faeces or you see signs of loose motions, you should take some action. Again the gripe water may help and the bitch could be put on a bland diet for twenty-four hours. If the problem seems serious, the vet could supply some kaolin for the pups. As babies can deteriorate rapidly, one must always be vigilant.

It occasionally happens that a bitch will push out a weak puppy and refuse to have anything to do with him. In these cases, it is usually better to let nature take its course, for it may be that the puppy has a defect. Breeders will naturally strive to hand-rear such a puppy but, if successful and the puppy eventually appears to be quite normal, he should not be considered for future breeding. It may be a different matter when a healthy litter – through some misfortune with the dam, such as lack of milk – has to be hand-reared. Puppies will appear to be suckling but will cry and be dissatisfied. Successes have been achieved thanks to the breeder's efforts and devotion. Hand-rearing is hard work and time consuming, because puppies are dependent on the bottle for three weeks and must be fed every two hours, day and night, for the first week at least, then at slightly longer intervals. It does sometimes happen that a weak pup will die within a few days of birth, and inexperienced breeders should not regard themselves as failures if they lose one.

The majority of bitches know by instinct what to do during whelping and nursing, though some may require a little discreet assistance at times. Occasionally a bitch will completely ignore the puppies initially, possibly through fear or confusion. With the help of an assistant, hold the bitch down firmly but sympathetically and get the pups to suckle. When this has been done several times the bitch will probably become more tolerant. Other bitches are so devoted to their offspring that they become aggressive towards any attention, even from the owner. Provided the pups are obviously contented it is best not to interfere, and after a few days she will probably be less possessive.

Mastitis

If the bitch's milk comes in quickly after whelping and the pups are tiny or it is a small litter, the milk glands may become engorged which could lead to mastitis. Bathe the teats with a flannel wrung out from hot water and gently try to express some milk, at the same time massaging the teats into a good shape. Sometimes the teats are too flat and the puppies cannot get hold of them. This problem often occurs in the rear teats, and sometimes they are not even used. The matter often resolves itself as the pups become more vigorous, for they will take off sufficient milk at each feed for the glands to become softer. If the glands are hard and inflamed, advice should be promptly sought. Any treatment given to the bitch will of course go through to the puppies, and it has been found beneficial, should the bitch require antibiotics at any time during lactation, to give her a good teaspoonful of natural yoghurt, and to dab a little on the puppies' tongues too; this helps to replace the natural bacteria.

Fading Puppy Syndrome

As the name of this condition suggests, puppies begin to die for no apparent reason. It is depressing suddenly to lose what up to then appeared to be a perfectly healthy puppy, and heartbreaking to lose the whole litter one by one. It is important to see the vet right away and if he were to do a post-mortem on the first pup, he may be able to diagnose a cause. There still seems to be something of a mystery surrounding the matter. Though hepatitis could be responsible, the cause is probably multifactoral.

Eclampsia

This is the most frightening of the problems which could occur after whelping. It can happen at any time while the bitch is lactating, but seems more likely when strong puppies are putting greatest demand on the bitch at about three weeks of age, just before weaning starts. It is caused by a complete draining of the bitch's blood calcium and this must be replaced immediately by injection, *whatever time of day or night*, or the bitch may die. Though the bitch may have had regular calcium supplement, this does not guard against it.

The onset of eclampsia is signified by nervous behaviour of the bitch; she may stagger and appear completely disorientated and may even collapse. The puppies may have to be weaned off the bitch to avoid repetition.

Swimmers

If you should be unfortunate enough to have a 'swimmer' turn up in a litter, do not abandon hope immediately. A puppy with a flat chest and waving legs seems unable to support himself, but depending on the cause and extent of the condition, some help might be given. Typically recommended supplements for the puppy, from the time the problem is first noticed, are calcium with vitamin D, as already being given to the dam, plus vitamin E and halibut oil, all in appropriate dosages. Make sure the puppy gets his turn at the milk bar, and later be prepared to devise some practical walking aid, such as two posts laid down to form a channel for the struggling pup to walk along. Provided the chest eventually drops into a proper shape, the pup may be able to control his limbs without further problem.

Of Nails and Tails

As the pups suckle, they will use their forelegs to pummel against the dam, and with their very sharp nails they can cause a certain amount of soreness. From time to time, therefore, the toe nails should be blunted by nipping off the very tip with an ordinary pair of nail scissors.

Dew-Claws

Cocker Spaniel puppies rarely have hind dew-claws, but it is usual for those on the forelegs to be removed to prevent injury when, for instance, hunting around in the undergrowth. It should be done with sterilized curved scissors when the puppies are between three and five days old (at the same time as docking). The wound should be dabbed with permanganate of potash crystals. Novices should be shown how to do this before attempting it themselves.

Docking

This is the removal of a portion of the tail and should be done at the same time as the dew-claws. It is done between the third and fifth day before the bone sets, and when the tail is no more than cartilage. It is customary to dock about two-thirds of a Cocker Spaniel's tail.

At the 1988 Congress of the Spaniel Council of Europe, a resolution was passed unanimously regretting any prohibition of tail docking. Nonetheless, the UK Parliament will ban docking by lay persons from July 1993, and since the majority of breeders wish to retain the option of removing tails, the controversy continues.

In the meantime, it is advisable to have an experienced person, perhaps the stud-dog owner, to show you how to dock properly.

Vets can of course be contacted for the removal of dew-claws and for tail docking, and although they may be happy to remove dew-claws, some are reluctant to dock tails on ethical grounds. They may also feel that if they are unfamiliar with the finer points of a particular breed, they may be blamed for ruining a pup's show prospects!

The First Eight Weeks

For the first three weeks, all being well, the dam will take complete care of the litter, but it is your duty to keep a daily check on her. Her teats and rear end will require sponging, and her ears may need attention because they sometimes become a little sticky from all the clearing up she does. A gentle brushing and combing, too, will freshen her up.

The puppies also should be regularly inspected. Should the bitch fail to clean properly the behinds of one or two, you may need to swab with warm water and cotton wool; then smear the anus with petroleum jelly.

Some owners cover the floor of the box with hessian or sheeting, and if the floor is separate from the side panels, or if the box has a false floor, the covering can be anchored around it. Whatever type is used, the puppies must be able to get a foothold in order to move around easily. The purpose-made, fleecy bedding is usually very satisfactory for comfort and grip.

Although the temperature needs to be between 70 °F and 75 °F (21 °C and 24 °C) for the pups for the first few days, heating, if used, should be gradually reduced. You must use your judgement, taking account of external factors: you may perhaps turn it off in the daytime and, later, at night as well. The pups must be hardened off by degrees, for you are not raising hot-house plants.

The puppies' eyes open at ten to fourteen days. Sometimes there is a little dried mucus at the corners and again this should be washed away and smeared with petroleum jelly. The lighting should be subdued for the time being. The ears are undeveloped at birth and it is not until the pups are about three weeks old that they take notice of sounds.

From about two-and-a-half weeks they will be able to get up on their feet and toddle unsteadily. But it is after three weeks of age that they become more interesting. They will then be attempting to play with each other, make little yapping noises and begin to respond to movements as well as sounds. This is when they become real time-wasters! But time spent daily in socializing the puppies is time well spent. A puppy well-handled from an early age and exposed to household noises and movements should become a well-adjusted individual later.

They should now be able to move freely in and out of the whelping box on to newspaper spread next to it, which they will use as a toilet area. A pen might be erected around the box in case the pups stray too far. Until they become capable of finding their way back to the sleeping quarters, it might be wise to shut them in at night, but you will soon find that the more adventurous will climb out.

At three weeks, the pups can have their first attempt at lapping. Make up a small quantity of the powdered substitute bitch's milk and, ensuring it is not too hot, offer some to each puppy from a saucer. Dip your finger in the milk, then in the pup's mouth, and the pup will soon get the idea. Competition is often helpful, so a shallow dish could be used where several pups can be fed all together. The dish can be placed on a little stand or platform, so that it is raised a couple of inches from the floor. The pups are then less likely to step or overbalance into it as they sometimes do initially. It must be so arranged that they can feed comfortably.

Feed the puppies once a day for two days, then twice a day. Some milk will inevitably be wasted in the early stages. Once they get the idea of lapping, baby cereal or instant porridge can be added to make a thin gruel. Scrambled eggs or egg custard make good starters. Sometimes puppies take little interest until a little scraped raw meat is offered. Once feeding has got properly under way, the dam should be kept away from the litter for a while near feeding times, and also after her own meal, otherwise she may regurgitate it to them.

Gradually increase the quantity and number of feeds until, at five weeks, the pups are having four meals per day. At the same time the food given to the dam should be gradually decreased. The pups should be given two meat meals and two milky feeds daily. Plain boiled rice and finely chopped cooked chicken or fish could be included in the diet, and a fine puppy meal could be introduced about this time. Rice pudding could be given, but make it with skimmed milk. Dogs do not tolerate the lactose in cow's milk, which sometimes gives them diarrhoea. Eggs should be cooked.

At five weeks the mother should be kept away from the litter all day, but allowed back at night. Often the bitch has had enough of them by this stage and a low table or upturned box must be provided, or she must have free exit from the pen, so that she can escape from their needle-like teeth and fine claws if she wishes. After six weeks, weaning should be complete, the bitch only being permitted a playtime with the pups. Continued suckling would stimulate milk production, but with greatly reduced food intake and limited access to the litter, the milk supply should be drying up so the bitch can gradually regain her figure. She may be given perhaps half her normal maintenance diet for a few days.

It is hoped then that the bitch's milk will dry up naturally, but it may be necessary to get something from the vet, or you can help by adding a teaspoonful of Epsom Salts to the drinking water. The bitch may need to relieve herself urgently, so be watchful and, of course, the pups must not be allowed to suckle or they may be affected too. Bathing the teats with vinegar helps to reduce them. These measures need be taken for only two or three days.

When she has completely finished with the litter, the bitch will need to recover her condition. Worm her, bath her and put her on a good diet. A yeast supplement may be beneficial for the skin and coat, though some owners prefer to add a knob of sunflower margarine to the daily feed. If she has been a devoted mum she will not only have lost body, but may be missing the pups too. She will deserve sympathy while making the break, and may need extra attention in the way of exercise and recreation to divert her maternal instincts.

From six weeks, the pups will probably have a soaked biscuit meal with both meat feeds. As an alternative to fresh or cooked meat, many breeders prefer to use canned meat. A special-formula product for puppy rearing should be obtained. Directions may indicate that this should be used with a biscuit meal complement. Some mixer biscuits can be added dry to the meat and do not need to be pre-soaked.

Breeders these days are turning to complete feeds for puppy-rearing as well as for adult stock. There are numerous variations on the market, graded to suit the needs and age of the dog. With these types of food, it is even more important that puppies have water always available.

It is also important, when rearing puppies that may be going to pet homes, to keep in mind the general availability of products. It is probably best for a young puppy to be accustomed to the type of food that an average householder is likely to use and can obtain.

When the puppy leaves the breeder, he should be established on a feeding pattern, and a guide to the diet should be given to the new owners. He should also be accustomed to handling and grooming, and acclimatized to spending short periods out of doors, according to the weather.

The puppies should be wormed between three and four weeks and again at six and eight weeks of age, whether they show any signs of infestation or not. Wormers specifically for baby pups must be obtained from the vet or pet store. The dam should be removed for a couple of hours as it is better then for the owner rather than the bitch to clear up the puppies' excrement and dispose of it.

Because some puppies are more greedy or eat quicker than others, some breeders like to separate the litter to eat singly or in pairs of equal size and speed for the main meat meals. In this way it can be ensured that each pup gets his portion and supplements. Not all puppies will require the same amount of food. Quantities for each must be assessed by the individual's development.

Breeders who use circular troughs for feeding their puppies find it an easy way, as only one receptacle is used and all heads can dive in at once. Reservations have, however, been registered as this method may be responsible for undershot or wry mouths. It is thought that there is not enough space between the inner circle and the outer circle of the dish for the jaws of the bigger, growing puppy to work naturally, and the puppy therefore compensates by pushing the lower jaw forward or sideways.

If you intend to keep any puppies from the litter, eight weeks is a good age for you to make your choice, for at this age the puppy should be a little model of his mature self. However, you must also keep your customers happy; buyers often want to make bookings and leave deposits prior to that time, and you may anyway want to be sure that you have at least some confirmed sales.

You must write out the pedigree for each puppy in the litter, to hand over to the new owner. Blank pedigree forms are available from various sources, such as dog food manufacturers, the dog journals, pet shops, breed clubs or printers of canine stationery. Kennel owners often have their own printed pedigree forms.

It is your duty to endeavour to find suitable and long-lasting homes for the puppies you sell, and most breeders make it known that they will help to rehome the animal if the need should arise.

11

Health and Welfare

Cleanliness, exercise and a well-balanced diet are the first essentials for keeping your dog fit and healthy. A regular grooming programme is important, which should include the routine care of eyes, ears, teeth, nails and coat. This has already been described in Chapter 6 (*see* page 105). It is wise not to neglect the first signs that a dog may be feeling under the weather. Even in the best-regulated establishments, things sometimes go wrong and professional help is required.

When you have made the decision to become the owner of a pet, or you already own one and are moving to a new area, you should as a matter of priority locate a veterinary surgeon and keep the address and telephone number handy in case of emergency. However, in the normal course of events, your first visit to the vet will be for your puppy to be vaccinated.

Vaccinations

By the time the puppy is about twelve weeks of age, he will have lost the natural immunity passed on to him by the dam. Puppies are normally vaccinated about this age against canine distemper (including hardpad), infectious canine hepatitis, leptospirosis and canine parvovirus. Some boarding kennels insist on dogs also having prior vaccination against kennel cough.

The vet will advise on a vaccination programme, and the puppy must be kept away from other dogs, and areas where they have been, for ten to fourteen days after vaccinations have been completed. As the UK is free of rabies, vaccinations against the disease are not normally given. They are available only to dogs being exported, or to newly imported dogs who also have to undergo strict quarantine for six months.

Parasites

Worms

Worms can be controlled by regular worming with one of the preparations available. However, it may be harmful to dose an in-whelp bitch with some wormers, so prior consultation with the vet is recommended.

Roundworms (*Toxocara canis*) Most puppies have roundworms to a greater or lesser degree, so from the age of about three to four weeks, they should be dosed fortnightly until three months of age, then monthly until adult. Adult dogs should be treated every six months. There are effective remedies on the market and it is important to ensure that the type used is suitable for the age and weight of the puppy or dog. Your vet will be able to supply you with a suitable wormer.

Tapeworm (*Dipylidium*) There are three types of tapeworm that may affect the dog, but *Dipylidium* is the most common since its intermediate host is the flea, which is why it is important to keep your dog free of fleas. However, tapeworm is still less common than roundworm. If there is an unaccountable weight loss in an otherwise lively dog, tapeworm may be suspected, and an appropriate treatment for the problem may be given.

Fleas

These are reddish-black, fast-moving insects which, if your Cocker Spaniel has them, can easily be seen when using the No. 76 comb over head, back and flanks. The fleas leave black droppings which will at the same time comb out. The dog, any companions, bedding and immediate environment must be dusted, sprayed or washed with a suitable parasiticidal preparation. There are also available different insecticides to use in the kennel or house, as the flea breeds in the environment, in cracks between the floorboards or in the carpet. Cats can bring fleas to the house so it is as well to treat the cat at the same time, although you may need to use a different product as it may not be safe to treat dogs, puppies and cats with the same one.

Lice

These tiny, white or pale orange insects move slowly or sit very close to the skin in areas such as neck, armpits and ears, especially in the little fold at the back of the ear. They can be seen with the naked eye or magnifying glass. Dabbing benzyl benzoate right on to the infected places will quickly remove them, or insecticidal sprays or powder could be used. For a dog severely affected, bathing with a special wash would be more appropriate. Lice breed on the dog and the treatment must be repeated to ensure removal of all nits (or eggs) as these become attached to the hair. Other dogs must be treated too.

Harvest Mites

In late summer or autumn, the harvest mite sometimes attacks dogs. Field mice are their natural hosts. Mites are orange coloured and are found in the ear pockets or between the toes. Again benzyl benzoate is effective or ask the vet for a suitable treatment.

Ticks

Sometimes as big as a bean, these are large and white or greyish, but dark brown or black when distended with blood. They bury their heads deep into a dog's skin and must be very carefully removed. They must be dabbed with a swab of ether or surgical spirit which makes them loosen their hold so that they can then be removed with tweezers. If the head is not removed, an abscess could form. Their natural hosts are sheep and hedgehogs, so they are more common in rural areas, and the larvae can be picked up when the dogs run through grass or woods.

Ear Mites

A dark waxy discharge or canker may be caused by these parasites which live in the ear canal. They can set up violent irritation, which the dog will try to ease by shaking the head or rubbing it along the ground. Drops must be obtained for treatment which should be continued for some weeks to be effective. Other dogs and associating cats must also be treated. Note that a slight waxy secretion is normal and does not indicate mite infestation.

Rabbit Fur Mite (Cheyletiella)

The presence of this mite is indicated by skin scaling, mainly on the back, and it is sometimes known as 'walking dandruff'. As the mite has a long life cycle, treatment must be sustained. It can cause a rash to some people.

Mange

There are two types of mange: sarcoptic and demodectic. The first is caused by a mite which burrows into the skin and sets up intense irritation. It is very infectious; the dog and his contacts must be repeatedly washed with appropriate parasiticide, and the kennel and bedding thoroughly cleansed or destroyed. Demodectic mange is caused by mites living in the hair follicles. They are present on most dogs and normally cause no problem. However, should they start to multiply, they bring on a severe hair loss often accompanied by a secondary bacterial infection. A veterinary remedy should be promptly sought, and as there is thought to be an inherited connection, dogs who have suffered from it should not be bred from.

Allergies

Occasionally dogs can be hypersensitive to certain kinds of food, showing symptoms in the skin, or causing vomiting or diarrhoea. Skin allergy is a very complex subject and because there are numerous possibilities, causes are very difficult to identify. Some dogs are allergic to flea bites, while others have been found to be allergic to something in the household, such as a wool blanket, carpet, or carpet-cleaning product. Some dogs show a reaction, such as running eyes, to cigarette smoke.

The vet can give the dog something to relieve the irritation, and if you cannot easily find and remove the cause of the trouble, he may even refer the animal to a specialist.

Sickness and Diarrhoea

There can be many causes of either problem and often there is nothing to worry about. Sometimes something in the diet, such as

197

liver, may be responsible, or a sudden change of diet or overfeeding. It may be that the dog has been scavenging or has eaten something left by the cat! Most Cocker Spaniels are greedy and will plead for titbits, but do not be tempted to give dried fruit or nuts. Milk is not suitable for the adult dog and, except to give to a nursing mother, is best avoided. Stress or excitability can cause sickness or diarrhoea.

If the dog is not otherwise poorly, a fast of twenty-four hours for an adult dog, twelve hours for a youngster, should put the matter right, but water should always be available. Feed small amounts of boiled rice with cooked egg or fish, three or four times the following day. Chewing grass and bringing it promptly back is a natural way for the dog to clear away excess juices.

However, if the dog is retching, or diarrhoea persists and the animal is obviously unwell, seek veterinary attention, as it could be an indication of serious illness. Sickness and diarrhoea in a puppy should not be ignored as puppies can quickly dehydrate.

Interdigital Cysts

These are rare, but if you see the dog giving a lot of attention to his feet, you may find a swelling between the toes. It may respond to saline bathing, though in some cases lancing is necessary. The dog should be taken off exercise. It is not unknown for grass seeds to give similar symptoms and, if not removed, to work their way internally to other parts of the body.

Labial Eczema

Unfortunately, particles of food and moisture may collect in the loose folds of skin on the lower lips of some Cocker Spaniels, causing an infection. In very severe cases surgery to remove excess skin may be recommended, but the condition can certainly be relieved and kept under control by an attentive owner. The dog should be denied access to water at night-time, as it is important to give the affected area a chance to dry up. Cleanse and dry the skin thoroughly; then apply some medicated powder obtainable for pet purposes, or a mild talcum. Some owners use diluted hydrogen peroxide.

Anal Glands

These are scent glands situated one either side of the back passage and they normally empty when the dog passes faeces. If the dog scoots or rubs his rear end along the ground, or chases his tail, it may mean that the glands are blocked. (It is not, as is sometimes thought, a sign of worm infestation.) As the anal glands can become infected if left unattended, the vet will empty them. They may need emptying periodically and if you can be shown how to do this yourself, you may be able to attend to it. It is a good idea to ensure the dog has sufficient roughage in the diet to help the natural action of the glands.

Kennel Cough

Several viruses can cause kennel cough, which can be picked up at shows or boarding kennels and quickly spreads between contacts. Vaccinations are available, but are not long-term or all-embracing. A whole day's fast, with only honey and water to drink, followed by a herbal remedy may help to alleviate the symptoms.

Coprophagia

Eating faeces, a dog's own or his companions', is a very unpleasant habit, though it probably does less harm than some may imagine. A bitch will naturally clear up after her puppies, but it is important for the owner to take over the responsibility for this task promptly and thoroughly as soon as the litter becomes active and before the puppies learn to copy the dam. It sometimes occurs with kennelled dogs, perhaps through boredom, but it can become a habit with companion dogs too.

Gardens and kennel runs should, therefore, be scrupulously and regularly cleared in order to remove the opportunity. However, the dog may be seeking some vitamin or mineral in short supply in the diet, so a supplement may be introduced. Alternatively, it may be helpful to add baker's yeast or pineapple to the diet as this will make the faeces less attractive to him – but of course all the dogs in a kennel must be given it, or the offending dog will just discriminate in his choice!

Gender

The Bitch's Season

Bitches are 'in season' or 'on heat' twice a year, theoretically every six months, although intervals up to nine or ten months are not uncommon. The first sign may be a licking of the external organ, the vulva, which will begin to increase in size. This stage may take a few days or weeks during which time male dogs living with the bitch may take a greater than usual interest in her. The bitch can be said to be in season when she has a discharge of blood from the vulva. This stage is called pro-oestrus and usually lasts about nine days. Then comes the period of oestrus, when the discharge will be less profuse and paler in colour. It is during this time that ovulation occurs and the bitch will accept a dog for mating. The best time for mating is usually found to be between the tenth and fifteenth day.

The bitch will be attractive to male dogs for about three weeks from the first sign of discharge, so she should be confined during this time and, if exercised away from home, she should be kept on a lead and only taken to a quiet area. Not only may dogs be attentive to her, but she may have a desire to run off to seek a mate. Preparations can be given to the bitch or applied to her externally to allay the attention of male dogs, but their effectiveness with your bitch and the neighbouring dogs would need to be monitored, and they do not prevent her from being mated or from conceiving.

There are methods for controlling heat in bitches, but should you have any intention of breeding from your bitch at a later stage, it would be advisable to discuss the matter with your vet and a breeder before deciding on a course of action. Some methods disturb the natural cycle.

In a household with more than one bitch, one of them coming into season will often trigger another one to follow suit.

Neutering

If you wish to have your bitch spayed (which involves the removal of uterus and ovaries), you should first look into all the advantages and disadvantages. Discuss the matter with your vet and with someone of experience. It is of course a major operation and it may be preferable to delay it until the bitch is mature. There may be side effects: Cocker Spaniels tend to put on weight, so exercise and diet will need to be adjusted, and spaying makes a marked difference to the coat. If yours is a show bitch, you may think twice about it. If the bitch needs to be spayed for health reasons, you must of course follow the veterinary surgeon's advice.

A dog may be castrated (have the testicles surgically removed) to stop offensive behaviour, or to ease a domestic situation where a dog and bitch are living in the same household. Certainly it is preferable to have an animal neutered than to have unplanned puppies on the market. The dog rescue services have problem enough without adding further to the burden.

Provided the Kennel Club has been notified of the operation a neutered animal can be exhibited in the UK, but may be penalized.

Misalliance

If your bitch should accidentally get mated, or you suspect that she has, take her to the vet within forty-eight hours for an injection to prevent her conceiving. Should the misalliance occur after she has been mated by a chosen stud, the pregnancy should also be stopped. A more careful watch should be kept on the bitch in future, and on the household!

False or Phantom Pregnancy

This can occur with a bitch who has failed to conceive, and even with an unmated bitch. There are some bitches who, a couple of months after their season, will show all the signs of motherhood: making nests, brooding over toys and even producing milk. If the symptoms are mild, there is probably no need for treatment, but it can be helpful to increase the exercise and to feed only white meat and no cereals, so as to discourage the manufacture of milk. Raspberry leaf tablets, from the first day of season for bitches who are prone to phantom pregnancy, are said to be a preventative measure. As the condition may have a psychological connection, the bitch should be treated in a sensible but somewhat unsympathetic manner and have playthings removed.

Pyometra

If a bitch has an unpleasant-smelling discharge from the vulva, or is unwell with an increase in thirst, it could be pyometra, especially if this occurs a month or so after a season. It is important to contact the vet straight away. Sometimes the condition will respond to treatment, but it may be necessary to remove the uterus.

Mammary Tumours

These sometimes occur in an older bitch. Their growth should be monitored and veterinary advice sought as to their removal. They are less common in a spayed bitch.

First Aid

Temperature

The normal temperature of the adult dog is 100.9–101.7 °F (38.3 – 38.7 °C). The temperature is taken rectally, but it would be very unwise for a novice to attempt to do this without prior instruction because of the risk of the thermometer breaking and becoming irretrievable.

Heat Stroke

A common cause of heat stroke is leaving a dog in a car on a sunny day. Even with ventilation, the temperature inside a car can rise extremely rapidly, so a dog should never be left unattended in a car. Heat stroke will cause panting, distress, possibly collapse, and it can be fatal, so immediate action is necessary: cool the dog down by giving water to drink and dousing him with cold water from a hose or river, or by applying packs of ice. Do not cool a dog to below his normal body temperature. Even if the dog appears to have recovered after first aid, take him to the vet immediately as he may be suffering from shock.

Grass Seeds

In late summer when grass seeds are formed and dry, those especially of the barley type may cause a problem. The trailing ears of the Cocker Spaniel seem to attract the seeds, so if your dog shakes his head, examine him immediately as you may be able to remove the offending article. If, however, the seed or awn has reached the ear canal, any poking around may push it farther in, so take him to a vet. The dog will probably be frantic with the irritation caused, and anaesthesia may be necessary in order for the vet to remove the seed. To avoid the problem, exercise the dog on a short lead at that time of year, and keep the hair on the insides of the ear flap short and free of tangles. Grass seeds can also be troublesome to the feet. It is important, at home or in the kennel run, to cut the grass before it seeds.

Foreign Bodies

In the Eye   In the case of a foreign body or injury, flush out and wash the eye with warm water. The dog should be prevented from rubbing the eye, and taken to the vet without delay.

In the Mouth   If the dog is frantically pawing at his mouth, it may be that an object, such as a piece of stick, is wedged across the roof of the mouth. You will probably be able to remove it by gripping it, pushing it back and then pulling it out, though it may be necessary for the vet to do this under anaesthetic. Sometimes a piece of biscuit may get lodged between the back teeth and the cheeks. Gentle massage from outside will dislodge it. If a small object, such as a ball, should get stuck in the throat, it may be possible to move it by massaging behind the jaws. Otherwise, the dog should be taken promptly to the vet because the object could cause asphyxiation. Let the dog play only with large solid rubber balls.

Stings and Bites

These are often self-induced, as dogs are tempted to catch flying insects. Bathe any swelling near the head or neck with cold water or it could cause difficulty with breathing. Take the dog to the vet.

Poisons

There are many harmful things in daily life with which the dog of an unsuspecting owner may come into contact. Some bulbs and laburnam trees, for instance, are poisonous, and dogs should be kept away from areas where slug pellets have been laid or where garden sprays, rat poison or weedkillers have been used. Care must also be taken when exercising in case grass verges have been treated, or spray has spread from farmland. Be careful that a dog does not walk in such things as spilt anti-freeze or creosote. Besides being harmful to the paws, the dog will probably lick his feet and take the damage internally. If a problem is suspected, try to ascertain the type of poison swallowed. If it is non-corrosive, make the dog sick with a teaspoonful of salt or a crystal of washing soda *and* take him to the vet with as much information as possible on the likely source. If you suspect that the dog has swallowed a corrosive substance, do not make the dog sick, but give him milk before immediately taking him to the vet.

Road Accidents

If a dog is involved in a road accident, precautions should first be taken to ensure that you do not get bitten. An injured animal may bite with fear, so tie his muzzle with a tape or bandage; try to slide the dog (not by his legs in case they are injured) on to a blanket in order to lift him and carry him to the veterinary surgeon. If there is bleeding, apply a compress.

Alternative Remedies

If you feel inclined towards the ideas and principles of alternative medicine, it is well worth seeking advice, as there are many natural and herbal products becoming widely available. There are also specialists in homoeopathy and acupuncture for animals, and literature on these matters can also be found.

The Elderly Dog

The life of a Cocker Spaniel is usually eleven or twelve years, with dogs going on to fourteen not being remarkable. Very often they will continue with their accustomed exercise as they get into double figures, particularly if there is a young dog in the household too. However, as the dog begins to slow down, the diet and exercise must be adjusted accordingly. Cocker Spaniels tend to put on weight easily and obesity puts a strain on the heart. Easily digested nourishing food should be given, and it is probably better to divide the quantity and give it at two meals. Appropriate foods are available for the elderly dog. The dog's teeth should be regularly checked. Sight and hearing eventually deteriorate and sometimes sense of smell, but so long as the dog is in familiar surroundings, he will probably cope very well. By this stage of life, it would cause such a dog too much stress to go into boarding kennels, unless it were a kennel to which he is well accustomed and where he knows the staff well.

As the dog gets older, even greater care must be taken to ensure he is thoroughly dried after exercise, and swimming in cold weather should definitely be prevented. A natural fish oil with a rheumatism and arthritis formula may in any case prove beneficial to the ageing dog. You owe it to your dog to give him a happy 'retirement' in return for the companionship he has given you.

Some older Cocker Spaniels develop warts, especially around the head and ears. The warts do not usually cause any trouble except that care must be taken not to knock them when grooming, especially any hidden in the hair. However, if any enlarge around an eye or become too unsightly, the vet can treat them. An increase in thirst could indicate a kidney problem, or, in an unspayed bitch, pyometra might be suspected. In any case, consult your vet.

Euthanasia

Owners are thankful if the aged dog passes away naturally in his sleep, but if you have to face a decision, veterinary surgeons are usually sympathetic and will help you to an appropriate solution. Some people like to bury their favourite pets in the garden; otherwise the vet can arrange cremation or other disposal for you.

12

The Cocker Spaniel Around the World

North America

USA

Although a spaniel is reported to have voyaged to Massachusetts aboard the *Mayflower*, there is no indication of a link with the modern dog. However, it is known that in the late-nineteenth century, Mr Farrow exported from England a bitch, Chloe II, who was in whelp to Ch. Obo. She produced Obo II, a black dog who in due course became a champion. Braeside Betty, a blue-roan granddaughter of Rivington Bluecoat and of Toots, also made the journey across the Atlantic, and took championship honours. She was considered so excellent a specimen that it was said of her: 'Such dogs should never be allowed to leave the country.' Betty and Obo II, both strong in Obo blood, played important parts in the development of the Cocker Spaniel on the North American continent.

Obo II became a great-grandsire of Toronto, the black dog that Mr Phillips imported from Canada. Betty was already a proven brood at home, having produced Blue Peter, by Braeside Bustle. Blue Peter was the grandsire of Rivington Dora (*see* page 12). Solids and particolours of today all trace back to Toronto and Rivington Dora. Descending from Obo II as well as Betty through Robinhurst Foreglow came, in the 1920s, Red Brucie who is behind all American Cocker Spaniels. It can be said, therefore, that all English and American Cocker Spaniels have American Champions Obo II and Braeside Betty as ancestors.

Back in those early days, there was an interest in the Cocker Spaniel in Canada as well as in the USA. Cocker breeders in Canada, however, seemed to favour the larger dog, perhaps with the purpose in mind of usefulness in the field, not of reducing it solely to an exhibition dog. Felbrigg Mark, born in 1926, went out from England to start the Moray kennels in British Columbia, and he and several others who joined him became Canadian champions and are behind many of today's dogs.

In the USA though, breeders over the years focused their attentions on breeding the shorter-faced, smaller, glamorous dog, mainly of solid colour, while the British breeders, keeping working capabilities in mind, utilized a mixture of blood from other spaniels and setters to develop a slightly different, larger, dignified dog with a longer head. Some dogs were exported to the USA, but there were marked differences between the American type and the English type, although both were exhibited as Cocker Spaniels (the only division being between solid colour and particolour). It was almost pointless to show the English type as judges apparently favoured the American version.

However, in 1935 a sanctioned event for 'English' Cocker Spaniels was organized, mainly in order to evaluate the interest in the breed. No entry fees were paid and no prize money was given, but the host, Mr. E. Shippen Willing on whose Chester County estate it took place, entertained about seventy-five supporters to a beer and sandwich lunch. Forty Cocker Spaniels were entered, and many winners, including top dog Squirrel Run Invasion, were closely related to Luckystar of Ware.

The following year the American Kennel Club granted variety status to English Cocker Spaniels, and the Breed Standard as used in England was adopted. Thus, there were three varieties: solid colour, particolour and English type. Championship points were available for each variety, but only one Best of Breed went forward to the Group. Later that year, the English Cocker Spaniel Club of America (ECSCA) was founded. Members soon made a pledge against inter-breeding between the English type and the American type, and this move created a situation which necessitated the identification of one type from the other. It was a mammoth task which involved research back into pedigrees stretching over many years. Mrs Geraldine Dodge (Giralda), by then president of the English Cocker Spaniel Club of America, was instrumental in getting this work accomplished, which culminated in the publication of a volume which included the names of Cocker Spaniels registered since 1920 whose pedigrees proved pure English ancestry for at least five generations. Some British Cockers, who had a close relationship to American-bred dogs such as Robinhurst of Ware, had arrived in

207

the States but could not be accepted in the records because of their ties with the American variety.

The next task was to seek breed status separate from the American Cocker Spaniel. In order to help the matter, the Standard was rewritten with some slight alterations to distinguish it from the American variety, the main difference being the desired weight. (A height clause was added in 1955.) The Standard, together with the file of pure-bred English Cocker Spaniel pedigrees, provided the evidence presented to the American Kennel Club. It was 1946 by the time the AKC recognized the English-type Cocker as a distinct breed. Spaniels, English Cocker, appeared in the American Kennel Club *Stud Book Register* for the first time in January 1947.

Thus, Cocker Spaniels emanating from the same roots had diverged over the years and become two distinct and separate breeds. Here a problem arises in designation, for the Americans claimed to themselves their breed as the Cocker Spaniel, though it is known in other parts of the world as the American Cocker Spaniel. On the other hand, the breed known and loved in Britain and around the world as the Cocker Spaniel is in the USA and Canada referred to as the English Cocker Spaniel. To this day this causes confusion, particularly in regard to written matter, and even the *Kennel Gazette*, when listing twenty-five publications about the Cocker Spaniel, managed to include many which were in fact about Americans. The newcomer would do well, therefore, to check the location of publishers to ascertain whether literature concerns Cockers or American Cockers (or Cockers or English Cockers!)

In the 1930s, Mrs Dodge imported several Cocker Spaniels from the Blackmoor kennel in England. The lemon-and-white dog Am. Ch. Blackmoor Beacon of Giralda, a great-grandson of Ch. Invader of Ware, was an outstanding sire and appears in the pedigrees of the majority of modern American-bred English Cockers. Two sons of his, bred in England before Beacon's export, were to establish themselves in their own right when they joined their sire at Giralda. The lemon-and-white Am. Ch. Blackmoor Beaconlight of Giralda was the first English Cocker Spaniel to win Best in Show at an all-breed show in the continental United States, while his black-and-white brother Am. Ch. Blackmoor Beaconblaze of Giralda, CDX (Companion Dog Excellent), created records in obedience competition. The golden dog Am. Ch. Treetops Tristan of Giralda, a son of Bazel Otto, went out at the outbreak of war and is behind many solids and some particolours.

Via Canada, Miss Ethelwyn Harrison (Shikar Wyn) acquired a daughter of Falconers Cowslip, Falconers Chuza, who was the first English Cocker Spaniel to become both an American and a Canadian champion.

The first American-bred English Cocker Spaniel to complete a championship was a liver-roan dog, The Laird of Uxbridge, born in 1936. It is to be wondered whether the kennel name was chosen by his owner, Miss Doris Flagg, from the town in Middlesex close to the home of H.S. Lloyd from whom she purchased The Laird's dam Miss Trilby of Ware.

About this time, the Alberstan kennels of British Columbia were quite productive, their dogs going to homes in all corners of the States and several of them becoming Canadian or American champions. Many were descended from Luckystar of Ware through Can. Ch. Lucky Streak of Ware, and some are behind today's field trial winners in the UK by way of F.T.Ch. Young Punch of Elan.

One of the early Merryworth exports, a black-and-white-ticked dog called Merryworth Mariner, whose great-grandsire was Cobnar Critic, helped to establish the Surrey English Cocker Spaniels of Mrs Olga Hone Rogers and her daughter Anne Rogers Clark. In 1941, a blue-roan bitch, Am. Ch. Surrey Eventide, made breed history by being the first American-bred and the first bitch to take a Best in Show. A few years later, Am. Ch. Comanche of Ranch-Aero, a blue-roan great-grandson of Hubert Arthur's Harley Sandylands Flare, gave Anne her own first Best in Show win on her way to becoming one of the top professional handlers on the dog show scene.

In the 1950s, a grandson of Mariner, a black dog with white dot and dash marks on his throat, made a name for himself and for his owners Mr and Mrs Seymour F. Prager of the On Time kennels. His solid-colour ancestry was through Am. Ch. Lanehead Distinction of Giralda and Am. Ch. Sinner of Sauls. He was the aptly named Am. Ch. Surrey On Time Morse Code, who had quite a successful show career, always owner-handled; but it was as a sire that he is best remembered. His descendants are spread worldwide. Numerous particolours in the States can trace back to him and, especially as a forebear of Ger. Ch. and Sh.Ch. Lochranza Merryleaf Eigar, his influence on the solid Cocker Spaniel has been widespread. (*See* Chapter 2, page 35.)

About the same time, a couple of imports from England really hit the high spots. These were the black dog Am. and Can. Ch. Lymas Master Key and the blue-roan Am. Ch. Springbank Ace of Giralda (a

Ch. Colinwood Cowboy. (Thurse.)

Ch. Colinwood Cowboy grandson). The former had a total of twelve Best in Show wins in the United States and Canada, while Ace won ten Best in Shows and numerous groups.

It may be interesting for modern-day readers to note that at the English Cocker Spaniel Club of America National Specialty in 1953, both the top winners were liver roan. The dog, Am. Ch. Free Chase Pumpkin Coach, was Best of Breed, and the bitch, Am. Ch. On Time Susie Bell (a Morse Code daughter), was Best Opposite Sex. Susie Bell became a top-producing bitch.

The blue dog Am. Ch. Squirrel Run Confederate, a grandson of Sh.Ch. Tracey Witch of Ware, was just one of the successful English Cocker Spaniels from the kennels of Mr and Mrs S. Hallock du Pont, whose dogs were often handled by Anne Rogers. Confederate's great-grandson Am. Ch. Ascot's Donny of Squirrel Run was the sire of Dunelm Surrey Gambit, who started a later group of Surrey English Cocker Spaniels for Anne and James Edward Clark.

The Colinwood Cockers also made an impression on the Amer-

Ch. Blue Flash of Ide. (Fall.)

ican show scene, Ch. Colinwood Firebrand through his sons (five of whom became champions), and his litter-brother Colinwood Trigger who took up residence and not only became a Champion himself but was also the sire of eleven. A Ch. Colinwood Cowboy grandson also made his mark under the management of well-known handler Laddie Carswell. This was the tricolour Ch. Colinwood Son-of-a-Gun, who gained the American title in ten days, with two group wins, and went on to his Canadian title too. Before leaving England, he had sired Craigleith Geisha Girl, who produced Sh.Ch. Colinwood Cheyenne. In due time, Cheyenne followed in the steps of his grandsire and became champion both in the United States and Canada.

One of those sons of Firebrand, Am. Can. Ch. Colinwood Joker, became the maternal grandsire to Am. Ch. Glengladdon Lucky Star, who was an important representative of the breed in the early 1960s. Lucky Star, a blue roan belonging to Dr Donaldson Beale Cooper, was sired by Valstar Lucklena Minstrel, a full brother to Ch. Lucklena Musical Maid, and closely line-bred to Ch. Blue Flash of Ide. Thus, successful British lines were combined and are spread

211

Am. Ch. Glengladdon Lucky Star. (Acknowledgements to ECSCA, Inc.)

through the particoloured English Cocker Spaniels of North America today. It is interesting that Blue Flash's grandsire, Lucky Shandy of Merryworth, was also the sire of Merryworth Mariner. Lucky Star was handled by Jane Kamp Forsyth and created a record by winning Best of Breed at the American Spaniel Club Show on four occasions.

While many Colinwood particolours established themselves in the USA, the solid-colour breeding of the kennel was represented by such as Colinwood Kestrel, a black who became a champion there. He was royally bred from Sh.Ch. Glencora Black Ace and Sh.Ch. Colinwood Bunting.

A granddaughter of Colinwood Cowboy, Colinwood Woodroyd Carousel, for many years held the record for the top-producing bitch and helped Dr and Mrs Arthur B. Ferguson to become top breeders. One dog they bred was Am. Ch. Dunelm Galaxy, a grandson of both Carousel and Glengladdon Lucky Star. Born in 1964, he was one of the outstanding dogs of the breed. Through the ownerships of Evelyn Short and Ruth Cooper, he had a long and successful show career managed by Richard Bauer. His crowning achievement was Best in Show at Devon Dog Show Association in

Am. Ch. Ancram's Simon. (Evelyn Shafer.)

1969, defeating 1,634 dogs. He sired the staggering total of ninety-three champions and was the top sire in the breed until he was surpassed by his grandson, Am. Ch. Kenobo Capricorn in 1984. Descendants of Galaxy have even made their way across the Atlantic to find a new home and success on the Continent.

While Galaxy was making a name for himself as a super stud, Am. Ch. Ancram's Simon was knocking up some more than impressive wins. At the show of the American Spaniel Club in 1969 he made history by becoming the first English Cocker Spaniel to take Best in Show there. In fact, it was only the third time since the Club was founded nearly 100 years before, that any breed other than an American Cocker had taken the honour – and Simon did it twice! His total of eighteen all-breed Best in Show wins still stands as a record for the breed.

Both these dogs, Simon and Galaxy, really made the dog show world take notice of the English Cocker Spaniel. Simon's sire Am. Ch. Ancram's Oliver was home-bred from products of Mrs Joyce Scott-Paine's original import Ricmour Crystal Dawn who was of Ide

Sh.Ch. Astrawin Arkadina, dam of Astrawin Apollo, Dog of the Year All Breeds in Finland in 1975.

and Falconers breeding, her sire being Sh.Ch. Buryhill Cedar; Simon's dam was Am. Ch. Courtdale China Mink, a daughter of Sh.Ch. Courtdale Flag Lieutenant.

Meanwhile, the Fergusons were looking for suitable mates for their Galaxy daughters, and decided upon half-brother sons of Flag Lieutenant. They first imported the black-and-white Reklawholm Paul Jones and later the orange-roan Reklawholm Firebird, both closely related to Can. Ch. Craigleith Vagabond King on the dam's side, and both of whom gained their titles. Breeders in due course found Firebird a very useful sire and he was able to claim no fewer than fifty-eight champion offspring. Paul Jones is probably best remembered as being the sire of Dr Mary Livezey and Dr Jean Le Poidevin's blue-roan dog Am. Ch. Applewyn Angus, who finished his championship when still under nine months of age. Always in the hands of Dick Becker, he was Best in Show at twelve all-breed shows and was top English Cocker Spaniel three years running.

It was a few years after the two Reklawholm dogs had established themselves in America that their breeder, Mrs Prudence Walker,

214

Urug. Ch. Oaklands My Wild Irish Rose.

emigrated from England and settled herself in Canada. One of the dogs she took with her was the Irish-bred Copperally Minstrel of Reklawholm, who became a champion in America as well as Canada, and is in many of the Ranzfel pedigrees.

Another emigrant in the 1970s was Mrs Irene Martin, whose solid Cocker Spaniels were built up on the Lochranzas. Several of her dogs had been winners, notably Sh.Ch. Merryborne Simone who was Best of Breed at Crufts in 1971; exports to the Continent, Scandinavia and South America were also successful. After some of her dogs settled in the USA where they became champions, Mrs Martin followed too and made her way to California. The well-known red dog, Sh.Ch. Merryborne Big Shot, who went with her, soon added American and Canadian titles to his name.

A son of Am. Ch. Merryborne Mackeson, the black dog Tolgate Tamnkee Masterpiece, owned and bred by Mr and Mrs Joe D. Newell Jr, had a long and interesting show career, becoming an American and Mexican champion as well as being successful in the group ring.

One puppy who made the crossing prior to Mrs Martin was the black dog Merryborne Minstrel who became an American and Canadian champion. Through the interest and efforts of Minstrel's owner Deborah Mason and some other enthusiasts, working tests became available for Cocker Spaniels, and Minstrel was one of the first to be awarded the Working Dog Excellent (WDX) Certificate. He also attained his WS (Working Spaniel) title in Canada. He was sire of thirteen champions, including the group winner Ch. Braeside Dark O'The Moon, WDX, as well as others who inherited his abilities in the field.

Several Astrawins have made their way to the States and become champions there, and another solid export to make his home there was the golden dog Buff Tip of Broomleaf, a son of Butterprint of Broomleaf. He was sent out to join the Merrythought kennels of Mrs Collier Platt, whose interest in Cocker Spaniels goes right back to the founding of the ECSCA in the 1930s. Buff Tip completed American and Canadian championships, and probably his greatest win was defeating 216 exhibits at the ECSCA Specialty in 1978.

The Kenobo kennels of Mrs Helga Tustin have made a marked impression on English Cocker Spaniels. From a combination of Colinwood and Am. Ch. Dunelm Galaxy breeding, these dogs have created many records. Pride of place must go to the blue-roan dog Am. Ch. Kenobo Capricorn. Born in 1972 and co-owned by Mrs Tustin and Mrs Bonnie P. Threlfall, he sired the incredible number of 120 champions and is the all-time top-producing sire.

The breed's top-producing bitch, with twenty-one champions to her name, was the blue-roan Am. Ch. Somerset-Saga's Antigone, born in 1974, and line-bred to Am. Ch. Kenobo Constellation and Am. Ch. Maple Lawn Tortoise-Shell. Her son, by Am. Ch. Kenobo Rabbit of Nadou, Am. Ch. Somerset's Stage Door Review, had the distinction of going best all-breeds at the Raleigh Kennel Club Show in 1985. Beating 2,322 dogs made this the greatest triumph yet for an English Cocker Spaniel.

The well-travelled Am. Ch. Amawalk Cottleston Concorde, a son of Dunelm Galaxy, became a Champion in Venezuela and later returned to live in New York. His younger relation, Amawalk Perrocay Qeqertaq, not to be outdone, gained titles in America, Canada, Bermuda and the Bahamas, as well as becoming a Best in Show winner.

Undoubtedly, the personality of the 1980s was the blue-roan bitch Am. Ch. Olde Spice Sailors Beware, who was line-bred to Kenobo Capricorn. Sailors Beware swept to stardom, finishing her championship at the age of fourteen months with three Majors. She created a record by becoming the only exhibit ever to win the

ECSCA Specialty on three occasions. She also had three all-breed Best in Shows to her name. By all accounts the bitch has been much admired for her charming character as well as her looks. Credit for her outstanding achievements must go to her owner Miss Vicky Spice who not only bred her, but conditioned and handled her too.

Particolours, especially blue roan, have always been popular in the show ring, more so than the solids. This probably harks back to the days when the breed was considered a 'variety' of the American Cocker Spaniel whose breeders favoured solids, and it is likely that fanciers concentrated on other colours to help establish English Cocker Spaniels with a separate identity. The influence of the blue roans Galaxy and Simon, who had such an impact on the breed twenty years ago, has helped to keep the colour in prominence.

Canada

Dogs of the USA and Canada often move around and compete at each other's shows. One exhibitor and judge from Canada who became familiar to the show scene in the States was Miss Virginia Lyne (Ranzfel), who in 1976 had the honour of judging the ECSCA Speciality. Her interest started when she took back from England a black-and-white bitch Lochranza Ring Dove, who not only became a Canadian champion but, because her owner was keen on obedience too, also gained Canadian and American Companion Dog (CD) titles. Miss Lyne later imported dogs from Weirdene, Reklawholm and Colinwood. Am. Can. Ch. Colinwood Crofter (by Glencora Moyhill Mallory) sired Am. Can. Ch. Cullercoats Bumble Bee, who when put to Am. Can. Ch. Craigleith Magic Flute made a very successful combination which has many descendants in the ring. Mrs Patricia Power's successful Willowbrooks stemmed from her foundation imports Can. Ch. Cochise Carioca and Can. Ch. Cochise Cambyses, combined with the Colinwood dogs.

The Ranzfel dogs have made quite an impression on English Cocker Spaniels in America, Am. Can. Ch. Ranzfel Newsflash, Am. Can. TD (by Kenobo Capricorn) and Am. Can. Ch. Reklawholm Lyric of Ranzfel (by Sh.Ch. Leabank Levity) being high on the list of top-producing sires.

Of the solids in Canada, Am. Can. Ch. Sorbrook Dandylion, a red son of Sunglint of Sorbrook, made his mark. He and Am. Ch. Hubbestad Kermit played their part in producing Am. Can. Ch. Hobbithill Ashwood Hi Class, an outstanding red dog who was owner-handled to twenty-five Best in Show awards in Canada, a breed record, and was Top Show Dog of the Year All-Breeds in 1986. Kermit was a red dog by Nor. Ch. and Sh.Ch. Lochranza Man of Fashion, and bred by G. Flyckt Pedersen in Sweden.

Besides multiple Ch. Valsissimo of Misbourne of Wittersham, the breed has benefited from other imports of British blood by Eugene Phoa. Notable amongst these was the golden dog Sh.Ch. Bryansbrook High Society, who had won Best of Breed at Crufts in 1980. He was another son of Man of Fashion, and went on to complete championships in America as well as Canada. A golden grandson of Valsissimo, Am. Can. Ch. Wittersham's Emblem, has been going great guns with Best in Show wins to his credit.

It was not until the 1980s that the English Cocker Spaniel Club of Canada was set up to represent interests nationwide.

Europe

Cocker Spaniels were introduced to France about 1870 by M. Paul Caillard. The early imports included stock from the strains of Messrs. Burdett, Bullock and Boulton, and Fred III (a brother to Ch. Obo). The breed was registered in France from 1885 onwards. M. Caillard became a respected judge and it was from him that the novice Cocker men, including a young medical student Charles Paul, gained their knowledge. M. Caillard also initiated steps towards the separation of Cocker Spaniels from Field Spaniels, a process which was not complete until 1900.

Following the Paris Show of 1897, the Spaniel Club Français was formed and amongst its first officers were Messieurs Lamaignère, Thiollier, Servan and Hazard, and Baron Jaubert. They established Standards for each variety and resolved to encourage breeding and showing and to organize field trials. While the matter of field trials for spaniels was being discussed in England, the Spaniel Club Français put the idea into practice and organized one for 'the small English Spaniels' a year earlier than did the Sporting Spaniel Society.

After the First World War, English imports to France were crossed with the old working blood to advantage. An improvement was noted in looks, and dogs could still give a good account of themselves in the field. At field trials then, most competitors were show dogs too. In Germany, Cocker Spaniels were also used to aid the

Mrs R. Bryden's Sh.Ch. Scotswood Warlord (a son of Sh.Ch. Colinwood Jackdaw of Lochnell), sire of Sh.Ch. Bronze Knight of Broomleaf and behind many winners at home and abroad.

deerstalker, and in Switzerland they were considered excellent to accompany the shooting man in the mountains for a variety of birds, though they were more often used for hare.

In 1906, Dr Paul went to an English dog show for the first time. Many more visits followed by the man who was associated with the Spaniel Club Français for many years and was to become its President. In the 1930s he admired the uniformity of type and quality being shown, not then achieved by continental breeders. He also said: 'Besides this perfect ensemble of the dogs, I have always admired the exhibitors; the English exhibitor prepares his dog and handles it with faultless chic and if, in spite of all his efforts, he does not win, he leaves the ring quite calm and does not recriminate. In a word, he is a sport.'

Another regular visitor from France was C. Daniel-Lacombe who had the important Wilful kennel. (It was there, as well as at the Falconers kennel of Mrs Higgens, that Mrs Dorothy Trench, later

219

breeder of the Crosbeians, served her apprenticeship in the Cocker Spaniel world.) As a respected judge of the breed, M. Lacombe was invited to judge dogs at the Cocker Spaniel Club's Jubilee Show in 1952, and bitches at Crufts in 1956.

It was the wisdom of these two gentlemen which, through the Spaniel Club Français, directed improvement of the breed after the difficulties of the Second World War. Mme O. Nourry was secretary of the Club at that time, and was another campaigner on behalf of the merry Cocker and a noted author on the breed. As a result of their efforts, the Cocker Spaniel soon became a popular and much-loved dog in France.

Mme N. Lambert (des Petits Brigands) and a few other Belgians had managed to keep a small number of Cocker Spaniels, so that when importation could recommence in 1947, breeding was able to get under way again, and some good specimens were produced. Today there is considerable interest in the breed in Belgium and many owners from that country and Holland visit British shows.

In Holland, the first imported Cocker Spaniel was registered in 1890, and a Cocker Spaniel Club started in 1926 – initially for all spaniels. Baroness van Tindall and Mr and Mrs van Herwaarden (Wagtails) helped to found the Club, the latter's dogs being of particular importance to the breed. They imported the red dog Woodcock Memory, who then won Best in Show at the World Show in Frankfurt in 1935. He became the progenitor of red Cocker Spaniels in Holland. The particolour Ahoi Dazzle from Germany was another significant acquisition. In the 1950s, UK imports included Lovells Roundabout of Ide, Treetops Tigg and Lanehead Dainty.

Also influential was the Urtica kennel which commenced in the 1930s and established uniformity in particolours. Dutch Ch. Urtica's Noble was probably the most famous. There were also champion solids, and although not active at shows, Urticas were still being bred fifty years later.

Although Cocker Spaniels were not so popular with the shooting men because the terrain did not provide suitable cover for game, field trials were, after a lapse, started up again in the 1960s under the influence of Jhr van Asch van Wijck, so that a combination of both beauty and working abilities in the breed should be encouraged. As a consequence, Holland has produced in the last twenty-five years such international champions as Int. Dutch Ch. Harvey v.d. Malpey, Fr. Lux. and World Champion in 1974; his daughter

It. Fr. Int. Ch. Gaston delles Grandes Murailles.

Int. Fr. Ch. Aphrodite of the Cockerplace; Int. Dutch Ch. Cloris v.d. Wilgenstulp, Ger. Fr. Bel. Lux. and World Champion in 1981, and Int. Dutch Ch. Jacco v.d. Wilgenstulp, Fr. Bel. Champion, a son of Cochise Conundrum.

Cocker Spaniels are now one of the most popular breeds in Holland, about 800 of them being registered each year. The position in the top twenty list is dropping slightly, but breeders will not be too anxious about that for they have seen in other breeds the consequences of over-popularity with the public.

Cocker of the Year in Holland in 1989 and 1990 was Dutch Ch. Birchen Beau Brummel, World Champion 1990, Winner 1990, a red dog of European and UK stock. Closely challenging him was the top-winning bitch Dutch Ch. Speggle-Waggel's Haighla, Mon., Ger. and VDH Champion, Winner 1989, Bundessieger 1990. This black and white was also bred from a Continental combination, being by Dutch Ch. Hazari High Hope, Mon. and VDH Champion (an Echelon son), and through Tripols and other Dutch influence on the dam's side was a descendant of Matagowrie of Merrybray and Courtdale Sub-Lieutenant.

221

The solids and black and tans of the German Caterra Cocker Spaniels have for many years been successful both in the show ring and at field trials. In France, Les Terres Froides are examples of the dual role, while the long-lived golden Katouk of Ayodha (a kennel name known in the 1920s) became a champion in the ring and in the field in the 1960s, and was responsible for progeny that did likewise.

The kennel du Valclain of Dr and Mme M. Drouillard in France began in 1945 and was active for very many years. Amongst their winners in the 1960s was the black dog Magic Boy du Valclain, a son of Lochranza Wellington Boots. At that time they had dogs of Lochnell and Pelynt breeding too. Also prominent over the years have been L'Herbe Vive Cockers of Mme L. Fried, whose stock has proved itself in the field as well as in the ring.

Dogs from Colinwood, Broomleaf and Lochranza were the popular choice of overseas exhibitors especially in the 1950s and 1960s, while Henry The Heron was an important export to Germany from the Sixshot kennel. Frau Barbara Englaender took stock to Austria from Lochnell and Weirdene, and twenty years later, in 1990, the top-winning blue bitch Sh.Ch. Lindridge Vanity Fair joined her kennel. Courtdale Sub-Lieutenant, a Sh.Ch. Courtdale Flag Lieutenant son, became a champion for his owner Frau Schulz in Germany, and as a sire did much good for the breed, especially for type and temperament. The influence of this dog and others such as Ger. Ch. Maedown Macao, Bundessieger 1976 (by Ouainé Diogenes), and Matagowrie of Merrybray, also by Flag Lieutenant, spread far and wide through Europe. Yet another son of Flag Lieutenant was Scolys Submarine, who had a successful career and became a great favourite with Barbara Bargoin in Paris.

A son of Matagowrie, Merrybray Monarua, went to Miss Rosemary Charrington in Austria and sired for her the orange-roan Sandstorm of Hilltop, who became an international champion in 1977 and won awards in eight different countries. On his dam's side, Sandstorm descended from her original male import Inverneiti Orange Quill and the others with which she started twenty or so years earlier. Sandstorm's progeny became champions or had other show or field trial successes in many countries including Poland, Czechoslovakia, Hungary and Yugoslavia – a truly international influence.

To show the versatility of the show-bred Cocker Spaniel, a great grandson of Sandstorm, Int. Ch. Hi! Jack of Hilltop, belonging to

Fräulein Maria-Luise Doppelreiter took show titles in Austria, Yugoslavia and Germany, acquitted himself well at field trials and tracking tests, and was an Austrian obedience champion into the bargain!

Among other German kennels, vom Lerchenwald is well known for solids; Frau Cornelius's kennel is of long standing, Widukinds Favorit being one of her famous dogs of some years back. Craigleith Kingfisher made a name for himself in the ownership of Ruth Widmaier of the Akita kennel (now Atkia) when she was resident in Germany in the 1970s. Euro. Ch. Aro's Goldfinch, born in 1979 by Valdikler of Misbourne, was successful for Alfred Rodenbusch, who also had in his kennel Misbourne Cheeky Robin and champion Rockaydon bitches. His more recent acquisition, Bullpark Blue Lightning (by Normanview Midnight Runner of Classicway) has already been a big winner, while Classicway Chart Topper has won for Wolfgang Matzke.

Over the years, Italy has been home for many successful Cocker Spaniels, and particularly during the 1970s numerous titles from all over Europe, both in the ring and in the field, went to Italian-bred dogs. The names of Tabasco and Giuliana are still seen at shows today while Teco and Ghiardo were also prominent in their time.

In the 1960s, the Gibor kennel had imported, along with Broom-leaf and Lochranza stock, Craigleith The Blue Sailor from the Sh.Ch. Courtdale Flag Lieutenant–Ch. Craigleith Cinderella combination. This significant dog sired Gaston delle Grandes Murailles, a blue roan who was probably the most famous Cocker Spaniel on the Continent at the time. In the hands of breeder and writer Mrs Franca Simondetti, Gaston became an Italian, French and International champion, and Bundessieger in 1971 and 1972. This influential sire is behind many of the Grandes Murailles that have been so successful in taking show and field trial titles in various countries; in fact, no fewer than six from this kennel have become dual champions, i.e. with full titles in the show ring and in the field.

World Ch., Int. Ch. and Ita. Ch. Yagermaister della Giuliana was a leading show dog of his day. He was bred from a bitch from the kennel del Vecchio Mulino, which had been active especially with British imports.

So, too, was Pavone, winning championships with such dogs as Sh.Ch. Waving Petals of Weirdene and Woodcote Honey of Weirdene (both by Wells Fargo), Darnmill Doughboy of Ware and Craigleith Casanova (brother to The Blue Sailor). These four were all

*Black-and-tan dog It. Int.
Ch. Vuolly delle Grandes
Murailles. (David Dalton.)*

orange roan, a colour greatly favoured by their owner Mrs Adonella
de Conciliis. The kennel also housed the blue It. Ch. Sunday Boy of
Settnor (by Sh.Ch. Settnor Mallard of Merrybray, ex Ch. Saffron of
Settnor), who also figured in pedigrees of winning dogs. Influen-
cing the solids was another British export, Peelers Dark Justice.

Under the rules of the Italian Kennel Club (ENCI), a show dog
cannot be termed Champion without qualifying in an open field
trial; likewise, a Field Trial Champion must have been shown and
been awarded at least the qualification Very Good. Thus, breeders
have been obliged to maintain all-round high standards, with some
dogs, as mentioned, becoming dual champions.

The Barone Rosso kennel was well known for its field trial Cocker
Spaniels, while the long-established Nalu, Valdorcia, Fagiana and
Francini kennels continue with this activity.

The show at San Remo in Italy forms part of the Mediterranean
International Canine Week, the other countries concerned being
France and Monaco. Nice and Monte Carlo complete the trio of
venues. Exhibitors travel from far and wide to attend these shows
which have a truly cosmopolitan flavour, the top Cocker Spaniel
winners at the Monaco Kennel Club's show in 1991, for instance,

hailing from Denmark and Spain. From the former came the Best of Breed winning bitch Petit Don't Remember Me; the Spanish dog was British-bred Charbonnel Crackerjack, who has met with success in his new homeland as well as taking the CACIB at Monte Carlo.

The black bitch Sh.Ch. Merryborne Simone, Best of Breed at Crufts in 1971, had made her way to Spain and was followed by Helenwood Checkpoint, who sired many winners in his new country. He was a Nightskipper son and litter-brother to Sh.Ch. Helenwood Checkmate. Another dog by the same sire, Sp. Ch. Helenwood Fiddler on the Roof, also furthered the Nightskipper reputation by producing many champions on the Continent.

Among present-day British exports, Beligar Pause for Applause has become a champion in Spain and Portugal, and relatives of Sh.Ch. Cilleine Echelon and Sh.Ch. Quettadene Emblem are fostering the increasing interest in the breed in those countries.

Australia

In recent years, visiting judges have all expressed the view that the top winners in Australia could hold their own against any competition. This should not be surprising as stock has been exported to Australia for many years and a sound background of breeding has been built up there. The influence of British blood has been maintained by a number of dogs from noted kennels who have made the long journey in recent times. The progeny of Aust. Ch. Sorbrook Candle Glint (a Sunglint son) combined with home-bred stock has produced one particular dog who has caught the eye of several visiting judges. This is Aust. Ch. Bellesam Black Douglas who has consistently gone to the top at Cocker Spaniel Championship Shows in different states over the last few years.

One of the early arrivals on the Australian Cocker Spaniel scene was not a dog, but G. Penson Whitaker, who had been one of the first secretaries of the Cocker Spaniel Club before the First World War. He was a good advocate for the breed, for after his death nearly forty years later, V.A.H. Mathews said that he 'never tired of singing the praises of the Cocker'. Mr Mathews himself, who was considered an authority on the breed, was for thirty-five years president of the Cocker Spaniel Club of Victoria. About the time of its foundation, in 1931, he voiced a hope that breed clubs would be formed in all states of Australia in the interests of the merry Cocker

Spaniel. Nowadays, enthusiasm for the breed is such that some states can boast several clubs devoted to that objective. Mr Mathews was a careful student of the breed and, with a desire to help owners produce more and better Cocker Spaniels, wrote a comprehensive volume *The Cocker Spaniel* (*see* Further Reading).

Back in the 1920s, Mr Mathews had imported a blue-roan son of Ch. Invader of Ware and Bluebell of Felbrigg, namely Church Leigh Crusader. Crusader and Silver Templa of Ware, who went out to the Thaxted kennels of D.L. Braham a decade later, both became champions and had considerable influence on the breed in their day and on future generations.

Gordon Hampton's interest in Cocker Spaniels, and dogs in general, extends over a long period. He became an all-breeds judge as far back as 1940 and, later, with stock from Mr Braham, he bred several Farnham champions, an affix which has continued to have successes in the ring. He has been involved with the administration of dogdom and has served as an official for clubs in various states. He is known today as a well-travelled connoisseur of the Cocker Spaniel and an ambassador on behalf of the breed to many parts of the world.

In the 1950s, the blue-roan dog Aust. Ch. Sedora Syntax of Ware was a successful import and influenced the particolours. Aust. Ch. Broomleaf Kim of Churdles, a red son of Ch. Broomleaf Bonny Lad of Shillwater, did the same for solids, which were in a minority at that time. The use of his bloodlines and their own imported black dog Aust. Ch. Coffee Bean of Lochnell helped Mr and Mrs Harry Murray to establish their successful Koubla kennel. The show career in the 1980s of Aust. Ch. Marsue Gold Privilege, a son of their import Browster Welsh Treaty, was unequalled by any solid-coloured dog in Australia.

An orange-and-white dog, Aust. Ch. Mighty Rare of Ware, was the last of H.S. Lloyd's exports and went out to join the Dolgelly Cockers of Miss C.C. Jenkins. A son of Sh.Ch. Buryhill Cedar, he had a fantastic show career including Best in Show at Sydney Royal Show and was Dog of the Year in 1963. He was a devoted companion into old age and left his likeness on the breed by way of his progeny, which included twenty-six champions.

The involvement of Miss Jenkins as breeder, exhibitor and judge goes back nearly half a century. She has also taken over the role of author for the breed and her love of it has compelled her to produce the modern-day handbook *The Cocker Spaniel*.

Aust. Ch. Larkana Laurentian. (Classic.)

Probably the most outstanding dog over a long period was the Australian-bred blue-roan grandson of Mighty Rare, Aust. Ch. Larkana Laurentian. Besides being a great influence on the breed through his progeny, his total of seventy-five Best in Show awards was one to be envied.

About thirty years ago, Mrs Ethel Cunningham emigrated to Australia, and several of her Darnmill Cockers, carrying much of the Craigleith blood, were very successful in their new country.

From putting Aust. Ch. Colinwood Pawnee and Aust. Ch. and Sh.Ch. Winter Yana of Weirdene to the already-established Lambrigg line, an orange-roan dog, Aust. Ch. Dandaul Just-A-Jump, was produced. This dog had the distinction of going Best in Show at The Cocker Spaniel Club of Queensland Championship Shows on five consecutive occasions from 1968.

Aust. Ch. Brightleaf Bewinged (Michael M. Trafford.)

Another Weirdene to make an impression was Waymaster, who became a champion in New Zealand as well as Australia. From the same kennel went Wonder Boy of Weirdene, a brother to Sh.Ch. Wells Fargo of Weirdene. He linked in well with the stock which Mr and Mrs T. Bennett in New South Wales had from Craigleith. Mated to Aust. Ch. Craigleith Dream Girl (an orange-roan bitch from the top drawer, by Sh.Ch. Courtdale Flag Lieutenant, ex Ch. Craigleith Cinderella), Wonder Boy sired the orange-roan Royoni Rags to Riches. This latter dog became a prolific sire and, in turn, his grandson Aust. Ch. Royoni Ruly 'N' Truly was a noted winner. Over the last forty years, progeny from the Craigleith foundation has been supplemented by further imports to Royoni from the same kennel. From Dream Girl and the attractive tricolour Aust. Ch. Craigleith Ambassador to the present-day blue-roan Aust. Ch. Craigleith Kings Ransom, this is testimony indeed to satisfaction in the goods.

The dark-blue Australian-bred dog, Aust. Ch. Brightleaf Bewinged, seems to have been something of a legend in the 1970s.

He amassed a total of ninety-eight CCs, lived to a ripe old age, and sired fifty-six champions along the way. Bewinged was sired by Aust. Ch. Feenix Fly By Night and his dam (the orange-roan Aust. Ch. Brightleaf Be Gracious) was, interestingly, a granddaughter of the black Lochranza Monkspring Mandoline.

Adorable, Marsden, Kildonan and Teenalee are among current kennels which have been successfully breeding and exhibiting for a number of years. UK exports from Stonemill and Lochdene have proved successful for Clarevale; and Australian Champions Lochranza Go for Gold, Lochranza Hyte of Fashion, Colinwood Vital Spark and Colinwood Blaze have upheld the great traditions of their famous affixes in recent times, the latter with all-breed Best in Show wins to his credit. Three such wins and fifty CCs made Aust. and NZ Ch. Marquell Masterpiece (now 143 CCs) a Grand Champion in New Zealand.

13

The Cocker Spaniel at Work

In the Field

Show and working strains have gone their separate ways, but the show-bred animal has not developed into a toy breed as had been feared. It is in general a sturdy, good-looking dog with a lively, gentle nature, albeit more suited to the family home than the shooting field. The working Cocker Spaniel, on the other hand, has lost some of his looks in the quest for the intelligence and energy to fulfil the role of a highly skilled fast-moving gundog. Because of his particular merits, the Cocker Spaniel has been adopted by thousands who want him as a show dog or pet and who have no inclination or facilities to use him for work, and also by a minority who have the opportunity and the desire to train him to the gun. The divide between the two factions is distinct, but things were not always so.

Field trials were started in the latter part of the nineteenth century and it was, in fact, a Cocker Spaniel, Stylish Pride, who won the first trial for spaniels in 1899. This dog also won a special prize for the most obedient, keen and persevering puppy. By 1903, a stake solely for Cocker Spaniels was provided at The Spaniel Club's Trials, and it was gratifying to supporters of the day that several show-bred specimens competed and were amongst the winners, for some were of the opinion that a good-looking dog could also be a good worker.

It was noted that prize winners at trials were sired by such as Ch. Ben Bowdler and Ch. Rufus Bowdler. The close ties between show and working Cocker Spaniels of that time were exemplified at a trial in 1907 where awards went to three brothers from the same litter by Ch. Doony Swell, ex Ch. Rivington Ruth. One of them, Rivington Gunner, later became a champion himself. A liver-and-white bitch,

Grindon Mary, was in the same litter, and she subsequently became the dam of Grindon Gerald, the grandsire of Peacemaker of Ware, whose son Barnsford Brigadier sired F.T.Ch. Rivington Dazzle.

The descent from Rocklyn Magic, a kennel mate of Peacemaker, was also important as from this source came F.T.Ch. Elibank Attention, the winner of the first Field Trial Cocker Championship. Elson, Attention's son, sired F.T.Ch. Pat of Chrishall, who was claimed to be one of the outstanding sires of all time. Pat, together with his maternal grandsire Rivington Dazzle, played a crucial part in the development of the working Cocker Spaniel.

Nobel Nippy descended through Fulmer Ben and Ch. L'ile Beau Brummel from Fairholme Rally. Nippy was important as a sire and passed on considerable working qualities. Int. F.T.Ch. Barney of Ware, F.T.Ch. Auchencairn Jayne and F.T.Ch. Jig Time of Fews were among other successful descendants of Rally.

The great stud-dog Corn Crake was not only responsible for producing the handsome Southernwood Critic but from him have also descended F.T. Champions Dalshangan Peter Pan, Jazz and Tango of Fews.

For generations, show and working breeding was interlinked, many show dogs taking awards at trials. But with the two disciplines firmly apart, it became rare indeed to find show blood infiltrating that of the working Cocker Spaniel. Notable exceptions to this were F.T.Ch. Speckle of Ardoon (*see* page 50), and some Mansergh bitches of the last decade.

The person requiring a dog to be highly skilled in the shooting field will select one bred for that purpose from a shooting or field trial strain, and will be concerned only with the working qualities of the dog, paying no attention to appearance. There have always been, however, a minority who like their working dogs to bear some resemblance to the typical breed type. After all, the Breed Standard was based on the requirements of a shooting dog. They believe that inherent hunting instincts, perhaps one of the most important points for a worker, and other essential traits, though having lain dormant for some generations, can be developed to a satisfactory level for the average shooting man. Indeed, not a few show-bred pups, having been taken at an early age and trained in the right environment, have nicely proved the point!

Captain R. George, one-time president of The Cocker Spaniel Club, was a believer in the dual role of the breed, and his Nene Valley show winners were also trained gundogs. Over the years, there have occasionally been exhibitors eager to demonstrate that show Cocker Spaniels have not lost the power to work, and such dogs as Bradpark Bandboy and Coritan Love-In-The-Mist have even gained Certificates of Merit at field trials. Other owners take pleasure in training their show dogs to the gun in a non-competitive atmosphere.

Working Characteristics

As for the devotee of the working Cocker, there is no turning him. He regards the little dog as the shooting man's all-purpose companion and in this the Cocker Spaniel has no equal. Most spaniels range and quarter the ground, but Cockers seem to have particularly acute scenting powers and, therefore, game-finding ability. They hunt with enthusiasm, have the courage to face the most punishing cover and go under like eels where others may find it too dense to penetrate. Many have shown determination in following a runner (a wounded bird unable to fly) long distances in order to make a retrieve. Despite their small stature, they are strong for their size and seem quite capable of carrying all that is asked. Indeed their performance as retrievers is quite remarkable, and they even have no difficulty with a running cock. Apart from a disinclination to jump – maybe inherited from their short-legged ancestry – nothing would seem impossible to a Cocker Spaniel.

They show charming and affectionate characteristics which may belie their desire to have their own way. As with any member of the Cocker Spaniel family, it is important for them to be disciplined from an early age, and it has been said that with the right training, a Cocker can be a treasure and a pleasure in the shooting field.

In looks, the modern working Cocker Spaniel bears little resemblance to the show specimen. There is no type in the working strains; they are bred purely to satisfy working demands. Although the shoulders are well angulated for correct use of neck and head, broader shoulders than on the average exhibit may be the result of working over rough terrain. The shape of head does not compare with that expected in the show ring. The stop is less pronounced, shorter ears are higher set, the eyes are invariably tight and length of muzzle not shortened. They are not high on the leg, nor oversize. Although maintained on the lean side, they have well-sprung ribs to provide room for heart and lungs. A moderate length of loin and well-bent stifles permit the functioning of the muscular hindquar-

An eager field trial dog.
(Nicholas Meyjes.)

ters, something for which the structure of the over-short modern show dog allows no room. The build of the working dog is strong and slender, more athletic than aesthetic. Feathering and ear fringes are non-existent, for these would only become tangled in the undergrowth, and coats are sleek and weather-resistant. The tail of the working dog is not docked as short as seen in the ring, and so occasional damage and bleeding to the longer ones gives support to the practice of docking. The tail must, however, be a reasonable length so that it can be seen when the dog is working. It is an instrument for communication between the dog and his handler, and the handler can tell much by the tempo of the tail. Working Cocker Spaniels are alert and quiver with anticipation while waiting their chance to seek for game or to make a retrieve.

Colours are various, with black, solid liver, black and white, and liver and white not being uncommon. White markings, if only tail end or blaze on the head, are useful for picking out the dog in the bushes. Shooting is a high-risk occupation and the dog needs to be easily discernible.

A working Cocker Spaniel has a high opinion of himself and is

233

wholly self-reliant. He is extremely independent and tends to work on his own. He has no intention of paying heed to sign or signal from his handler, and because of this it is difficult to break his concentration. There is no alternative but to leave him to get on with it; it may be agonizing, but the bird will be delivered sure enough!

There does not seem to be prejudice against the working Cocker Spaniel as once there might have been. The modern worker is as good as any of his larger counterparts. Sportsmen have found that, tough for his size, he has the capacity to fulfil the role of all-round gundog, and more are now succumbing to his charm.

While the shooting man will seek a gundog of working ancestry, other buyers should be wary of purchasing a puppy from a game-keeper or from a breeder of field trial dogs, for a working dog may not be suited to becoming the average house pet. His highly developed hunting instincts and natural energy may be more than the pet owner can cope with. Whether his energies are channelled in the way of country pursuits or alternatively obedience or agility, it is essential that they should find an outlet; otherwise frustration will result. The prospective pet buyer must consider whether he has the right to deny the dog the opportunity to follow the instincts which have been bred into him for generations.

Training

The experts contend that training a Cocker Spaniel is an art of its own, and that while you can train a Springer, you can only guide a Cocker. You have to win his co-operation and avoid giving unnecessary orders. Because of the dog's independent spirit, the trainer should first perhaps teach himself to be restrained, and learn to act as if he is always in control.

As with any dog, the basic learning should start at an early age, with the aim that when he is in the shooting field, for the dog's own safety, he must be under control. He must learn to come and to sit in response to the whistle. The pup can start carrying soft objects short distances, but these retrieves should be limited until after teething. A glove or stuffed sock can be used in the beginning, making the dummy heavier and sewing on feathers as the pupil progresses. He must learn to pick up game, but the handler must be wary of using pigeons, unless wrapped in a nylon stocking, or the dog may be put off by getting a mouthful of feathers. Training should be fun and Cocker Spaniels usually enjoy searching for a dummy thrown in the bushes. The youngster must, however, learn to wait to fetch it until the command is given.

Most spaniels hunt instinctively and will quarter the ground, or work from side to side, in front of you in search of game. Out shooting, the dog is expected to quest within gunshot, so in training should keep within a range of about twenty-five yards. The trainer gives the command to drop or 'hup' to flush or shot, which will become second nature to the well-trained dog. A little at a time must be learned and much praise and encouragement given at each stage. Proceed slowly because until the mental capacity develops, the puppy cannot accept too much too soon. Gunfire must not be introduced too early and must be carefully done, at gradually decreasing distances.

Training a dog to the gun is a complex subject and books and videos are available for those intending serious study of the sport. Aspiring participants would do well to find a training club (though those for spaniels are comparatively few), or seek advice from a trainer or owner. Trialling people are a friendly bunch and many are willing to talk to the novice.

Field Trials

Field trials, which take place in the shooting season, are run on private ground by invitation of the landowner, and are wholly natural competitions. They have a fascination for a specialized section of the sporting community. The trialling world is tough and uncompromising. The rivalry is intense, but the sportsmanship is equal to it. The training programme necessary to reach trialling standard means very hard work over many months by handlers as well as dogs. Trials are notorious for the strain on the nerves, perhaps because a dog is involved and so much depends on each member of the partnership.

Amateurs successfully compete at trials and have made up champions, but few have proved themselves competitively to be in the class of John Kent, John Forbes, Reg Hill, Jimmy Wylie, Keith Chudley or Keith Erlandson.

Spaniel stakes are normally limited to sixteen runners and, irrespective of the number of stakes, not more than sixteen dogs may compete in one day at a field trial meeting. For spaniels there are two judges with an official 'gun', i.e. person firing the gun, accompanying each judge. Two dogs are tested at a time, one under each

Hard weather. (Nicholas Meyjes.)

judge. Judges, guns and handlers stand in a line and move forward with the work of the questing dogs. Spectators and other competitors must keep back behind the line. When the right-hand judge has seen the work of odd-numbered dogs, and the left-hand judge the even-numbered ones, the dogs will run under the other judge in the second round. Unless they request any dogs to run again, judges can then make the awards from first to fourth and, at their discretion, also give Diplomas of Merit at the Championship or Certificates of Merit in any other stake.

The spaniel should bravely investigate any cover, making sure no game is left undisturbed. Wind direction can affect the way in which the dog works his ground. The dog should stop on command when a bird is put up or at the sound of the shot. He should mark the fall (watch to see where the bird lands) and may be asked to retrieve that bird or a different one. If a dog fails to bring back the game, and a second dog is tried and successfully makes a retrieve, this constitutes an 'eye-wipe', and the first dog will be discarded. Running-in (going to retrieve before being given the command) or chasing and barking or whining are also eliminating faults. Credit will be given to the dog with game-finding ability, rather than the one who needs excessive whistles and hand signals to guide him through his task. A quick retrieve, delivering game undamaged to hand, completes the assignment. A certain degree of style and artistic impression is taken into consideration in Cocker Spaniel work.

Field Trial Champion

To become a Field Trial Champion (F.T.Ch.) a Cocker Spaniel must win two open stakes, whether for Cockers or open to any breed of spaniel, at two different field trials. There must be no fewer than ten competitors in the former and no fewer than fourteen in the latter. The winner of the Cocker Spaniel Championship automatically gains the title. A spaniel must pass a water test.

The Spaniel Championships

The Kennel Club runs championships annually for which eligibility is determined by previous wins in approved open stakes. There are two Spaniel Championships, one for Cocker Spaniels and one for spaniels other than Cocker. The winner of each becomes a field trial champion and to win the Championship is the pinnacle of achievement. In 1991, M.J. Perfect, a Metropolitan Police sergeant, handled his first working dog, lemon-and-white bitch Mymwood Eira, to win the Cocker Spaniel Championship and gain her title.

Famous Field Trial Champions

Field trialling was dominated for a very long time by the Elan dogs of Lt.-Com. E.A.J. Collard, and they have continued to have considerable influence to the present time. The first of his field trial champions was Young Punch of Elan, born in 1947. He was a grandson of F.T.Ch. Punch of Blair, the dog who had won the last two Spaniel Championships before the War. Punch of Blair was a grandson of F.T.Ch. Poddle Crunch and F.T.Ch. Poddle Crinkle belonging to Miss J. Wykeham-Musgrave. Crunch was by Pat of Chrishall and Crinkle by Rivington Dazzle.

The next Elan was F.T.Ch. Geisha Girl, whose sire F.T.Ch. Glennewton Julius was bred and owned by John Forbes, who in fact piloted so many of the Elans to victory. (Others have been handled

A competitor at the Cocker Spaniel Championship.

by Keith Chudley or by the Commander himself.) Geisha Girl produced F.T.Ch. Buoy of Elan, a dual winner of the Cocker Spaniel Championship and a dog who had a great impact on the breed. Other Cocker Spaniel Championship triumphs followed and Elan winners have continued to be produced (Elan Garbo became a field trial champion in 1991), making Commander Collard probably the most successful field trial Cocker Spaniel owner yet.

Glennewton Julius was also a grandson of Punch of Blair on his sire's side, and, through his maternal grandsire F.T.Ch. Druidaig Prince, had Elson, Nobel Nippy and Southernwood Critic as ancestors. Julius, therefore, combined all the foremost blood of earlier times and can be regarded as the major link between the pre-war and post-war eras. He and the Elans have formed the background to today's field trial Cocker Spaniels. Ardnamurchan Mac and his sire Templebar Blackie were descendants of Julius through Julius's son Merlin Micky and grandson Wilfred of Cromlix, all these being field trial champions and figuring prominently in the breeding of field trial winners. Mac sired F.T.Ch. Exton Jemima, just one of the many good winners bred by Mrs T.A. Watt from her old-established strain.

Mr R.F. Button and Golden Glimmer, a son of F.T.Ch. Jade of Livermere. (Alan Carey.)

The current chairman of the Kennel Club Field Trials Sub-Committee and new member of the General Committee, Denis Douglas, is a working-Cocker man. His first Cocker Spaniel was F.T. Ch. Jimmy of Elan (a great-grandson of F.T.Ch. Buoy of Elan), whom he took over from Lady Auckland of Cromlix, just before she died. Jimmy had won the Cocker Spaniel Championship in 1971. Mr Douglas then made up several field trial champions, but perhaps the greatest thrill was to handle F.T.Ch. Tayburn Cockle to win two successive Cocker Spaniel Championships.

Cockle's sire, F.T.Ch. Carswell Zero, was in fact a grandson of F.T.Ch. Jimmy of Elan, and in turn one of the sons of Zero, F.T.Ch. Bunter of Jordieland, became influential in the 1980s. Jordieland dogs have produced many field trial champions (including several for the Concraig kennel). From them, including Bunter, has come F.T.Ch. Jade of Livermere who is making an impression on the present-day field trial scene.

Mr and Mrs H.C. Gwynne's black bitch F.T.Ch. Gwibernant Snake produced a remarkable four field trial champions carrying the Wernffrwd affix, two to Bunter and two to Mac's grandson F.T.Ch. Rhu of Migdale, both Rhu and Snake having been bred by Keith Erlandson. It was Mr Erlandson who had handled Speckle of Ardoon to her exceptional feat of three consecutive Cocker Spaniel Championship wins in the 1970s.

Lasting Lines

The Headland affix must be amongst the oldest in Cocker Spaniels. Miss P.E. Brown's strain, mainly based on the Falconers line, has produced many good puppies, some of them becoming champions in different countries. At the same time, a working line was kept, based on the of Fews strain and going back to Nobel Nippy. However the dogs were bred, they all took their turn out shooting. The Headlands have produced many workers and field trial champions, often for other people, including F.T.Ch. Headland Hazel of Monnow (by. F.T.Ch. Buoy of Elan), who produced well herself, and is behind F.T.Ch. Helion Manor Tyhill, the sire of F.T.Ch. Sandringham Mango who was bred by H.M. The Queen.

The Mansergh line started in the 1930s and early on a litter by F.T.Ch. Poddle Crunch was bred. Major Roslin-Williams then got going in field trials, and within a few generations had bred F.T.Ch. Lash of Mansergh, who won the Spaniel Championship in 1949. Cockers with the Mansergh affix have bred on in other hands, producing several field trial champions. James Roslin-Williams now maintains the line primarily as a working kennel, the dogs competing only rarely. Seventeen generations have been bred from the foundation bitch, with all details carefully noted. The dogs are good companions and give pleasure by their support on shooting days.

Show Spaniels Field Day

In the late 1960s, this innovation was put into practice to enable show dogs to try for their qualifiers in the field at an event run especially for the purpose. However, it is still possible to attempt the Certificate at a proper field trial if preferred.

A spaniel is required to hunt, face cover and retrieve tenderly, and wherever possible should be tested on freshly shot game. The dog must not be gun-shy, and must not whine or bark while in the line, but absolute steadiness is not essential.

As the word 'qualifying' had caused some confusion in its various contexts, the Kennel Club decided to drop the term Qualifying Certificate and, in 1979, the name was changed to Show Gundog Working Certificate. Over the years many spaniels have gained this at the Field Day, but it is sad that few Cocker have been amongst them. In 1990, Miss Jo Walker's blue-roan dog Okell Outward Bound (by Sh.Ch. Dearnewood Star Venture), at only twelve and a

Kennelbourne Maybe, great-grandson of Sh.Ch. Wells Fargo of Weirdene. (Roger Chambers.)

half months of age, was the first Cocker Spaniel to gain the qualification for nine years. A year later, two more were successful, namely Mesdames Rice-Stringer and Hook's Kennelbourne Spot On (a grandson of Kennelbourne Maybe), and Mr and Mrs D. Bowkis's Crufts 1990 winner Ch. Bowiskey Boy Blue (by Sh.Ch. Lindridge Venture). Afterwards, Okell Outward Bound gained the necessary show wins to take the Champion title too.

Other Pursuits

Working Tests

Working tests are artificial competitions run on similar lines to a field trial, but dummies are thrown, blanks are fired, and often there is only one judge. They take place at any time. Dummies may be made using fur or feather, but canvas ones can be obtained if specified for competition. Some societies put on cold-game tests in the season, where previously shot game is used instead of dummies. It is at certain approved events of this type where the Show Gundog Working Certificate can be obtained.

While dyed-in-the-wool sportsmen may frown upon such activities as being too contrived, they nonetheless can be fun and give the dogs something to put their minds to. They are increasingly popular and moves are afoot to incorporate this activity under the authority of the Kennel Club. They may be held in less rural areas than are necessary for field trials, and within a fairly restricted space. Such tests are held at country fairs and this helps to bring the work of gundogs before the public as well as providing entertainment. Gundog working tests should not be confused with working trials, which are more akin to Obedience as undertaken in America.

Obedience

As with conformation shows, various types of obedience show are licensed by the Kennel Club, ranging from Sanction to Championship. Classes start with the straightforward Pre-Beginners, introducing Retrieve a Dumbell, Temperament Test, Scent Discrimination, Send Away and Distant Control, in varying stages, through to the advanced Test C. In the lowest class, the dog is tested in the Down position for two minutes, but by the time the senior class is reached the time is extended to ten minutes. More interest is being taken in obedience tests by Cocker owners, but the breed has not reached the heights it has in the USA.

Agility

Agility competition has become popular in recent years. It involves completing an obstacle course, where the dog must jump fences, balance on a see-saw and run through a tunnel, amongst other exercises. These are timed events and as the handler has to accompany the dog round the course, he or she must be fit too.

Cocker Spaniels are an awkward size for this sport as some do not fit within the height limit of 15in (31cm) for 'mini' competition, but a Cocker Spaniel named Turbo Toes did qualify for the first appearance of a mini challenge at Crufts in 1991. Calls, however, are being made for 'midi' contests at agility events.

Community Service

More and more, the dog is becoming useful to man in various worthwhile ways. While lovers of animals have long been aware of the companionship and comfort they can give, the medical profession has taken notice of their therapeutic value only in the last decade or so.

The charity PRO Dogs was at the forefront of promoting the benefits of dogs for people, and in 1983 started the PAT Dog Hospital Visiting Scheme. Applications can be made for suitable dogs to be accepted on the Pets As Therapy register so that both owner and dog volunteer to visit hospitals or residential homes on a regular basis. Dogs' visits have turned out to be a tonic without side-effects for the patients, with whom Cocker Spaniels have proved popular.

A Cocker Spaniel lover from the south of England, Mrs Anne Conway, has helped to publicize Hearing Dogs for the Deaf. She and her Cocker Spaniel, Lucy, who had already been trained for competitive obedience, gave public demonstrations to promote the work of, and raise money for, that organization.

By their very nature, many spaniels are suited to work with people with special needs or to be employed as sniffer dogs – to seek out drugs, dry rot or explosives. It may be that Cocker Spaniels will play a bigger role in these and other directions in the future.

North America

Formal field trials for English and American Cocker Spaniels ceased in 1964, though prior to that time there had been quite an interest in the breed for this purpose. An English Cocker became the first field trial champion Cocker in the US in the 1920s, and the Cinar kennel had many successes with stock descended from F.T.Ch. Rivington Dazzle and F.T.Ch. Pat of Chrishall.

In the 1940s, two English Cocker Spaniels accomplished a very rare feat and became dual champions, that is champions in the show ring as well as in the field. These were Arbury Squib, a liver dog bred in Ireland, and a black and white called Camino Boy. A little later, several field trial winners went out from England, including F.T.Ch. Shawfield Glenfire (who was by Blanco of Mansergh, ex F.T.Ch. Desire Me) and his son F.T.Ch. Greatford Meadowcourt Pin (ex F.T.Ch. Meadowcourt Breckonhill Beau), both of whom took titles in the country of their adoption.

Alas, the competitive interest waned and it was not until 1977 that enthusiasm for field work was renewed and the ECSCA introduced a working test. This is a relatively simple task requiring the dog to hunt and flush game and to retrieve, including from water. The dog must be under reasonable control and must not be gun-shy, but does not need to be steady to shot. Three dogs qualified on the first occasion, and these were also champions in the show ring. The ECSCA guidelines stipulate that, 'A dog which completes all parts of the test in a creditable manner should be awarded the Working Dog (WD) Certificate. A dog which completes all parts of the test in a superior manner . . . should be awarded the Working Dog Excellent (WDX) Certificate'.

There is, however, another scheme for the owner of the show-bred dog, who wants to prove his dog in the field. In the late 1980s, the AKC set up hunting tests for spaniels. Testing is done on three levels: Junior Hunter, Senior Hunter and Master Hunter, and 'while the tests are non-competitive, the dogs are scored on the various aspects of their performance'. (*The English Cocker Spaniel Handbook*.) Am. Ch. Ranzfel Quarrystone, CDX, TD, WDX, became the first English Cocker Spaniel to earn all three titles: JH, SH and MH.

There is now a small growing interest in the working English Cocker Spaniel and some field-trial-bred dogs have been sent over to the States in recent years, with some people setting up their own breeding programme. These dogs seem to be used solely as shooting companions.

In America, as in the UK, obedience training classes can be found in most populated areas, and to give one's English Cocker Spaniel training in basic obedience is a wise move no matter where one lives. For those who wish to train their dogs to a higher standard, obedience trials can be hard work but fun for both dog and handler.

In the UK, the ultimate title in obedience is Obedience Champion, but in America there are various titles that a dog can acquire on his way up to becoming Obedience Trial Champion. The first title is the Companion Dog (CD), which is a series of basic obedience tests, including 'Stand for Examination', where the judge touches the dog's head, body and quarters. This is a good exercise for a young dog learning to be handled in the show ring too. The Companion Dog Excellent (CDX) is an extended version of the CD and includes retrieving and jumping. A more advanced test is the Utility Dog

(UD) which involves scent discrimination as well as taking directions from a distance.

There is a further sport, tracking, which carries with it an AKC title Tracking Dog (TD). Because of the dog's acute scenting powers, tracking has been found to be one of the pursuits that English Cocker Spaniels thoroughly enjoy and for which they are particularly suited. It is, however, a sport which has its limitations on training, for areas of unused land are required, and an accomplice to lay the track. The track must then be left for some hours before the dog is put to it.

In the early stages of training, the track layer will leave some markers to point the course, but in a test the judge will have a map. The handler works the dog on a harness with 40ft (12m) of light line. The dog must follow the turns of the track and not be distracted by wildlife or other scents. For the Tracking Dog Excellent (TDX) title, the track covers more difficult terrain, and may cross bridges, fences and roads. In addition, the dog has to recover several items dropped along the way. Cross tracks are laid to cause confusion. Because spectators must be kept back from fouling the track, it is not a sport to attract the public, but those who participate in it seem to find it all-absorbing.

In the UK, the overall concept of obedience under Kennel Club rules is different. The aspects of jumping and tracking come under a pursuit quite separate from obedience, and that is working trials.

Before the Second World War, Am. Ch. Blackmoor Beaconblaze of Giralda was the first English Cocker Spaniel to gain a CD title. He was also the first dog of any breed to earn a perfect score and his record in obedience was remarkable. English Cocker Spaniels seem to have done well in obedience over the years, and several champions in the show ring have taken obedience titles too. Louise Shattuck's Carry On dogs have been successful in various areas of the sport, and excel particularly in tracking. Miss Shattuck has bred more English Cockers with obedience titles than anyone else. The Merrynook Cockers from Canada have also made an impression on the tracking scene in both countries. From such imports as Can. Ch. Peasemore Mary Poppins, CD, TDX, Am. Can. Ch. Courtdale Captain Kidd, CD, TD, and Can. Ch. Okell By Jupiter, TD, the Whittalls have produced several generations of successful competitors. These include Berm. Can. Ch. Merrynook Marsh Marigold and Can. Ch. Merrynook Saucy Sue, who were the first two English Cocker Spaniels to gain the American TDX title.

14

Breed Organizations

There are at present twenty-four clubs fostering the interests of the Cocker Spaniel in the UK, and these are listed in Appendix 1 (*see* page 249). They provide shows, information and instruction; a few stage field trials and working tests. Although others have come and gone, the principal breed organizations have played an indispensible part in creating the fabric of the Cocker Spaniel fraternity.

Successful club committees will strike a balance between members with lifelong knowledge and newcomers with fresh enthusiasm. A club must be receptive to new ideas, but in no way are these supposed to change the features or character of the breed, the interests of which must be paramount.

In organising shows, it is important to remember that their success depends upon the quality of the exhibits, not the profit made on the raffle!

The Cocker Spaniel Club

The Cocker Spaniel Club has promoted the welfare of the breed since the beginning of the century, and its founders would have been delighted to know that ninety years later, the Club is flourishing and serving a substantial membership in over thirty countries.

From the outset, the Club made it clear that its objectives were to promote the breeding of Cocker Spaniels; to publish a description of the true type, which it would urge breeders and judges to adopt as a standard of excellence; to establish field trials; to offer prizes at shows; and to adopt other means for the encouragement of the breed. These aims, encompassed by the first rule of the Club, have not changed; and in pursuing them, the Club has been highly successful, as the continued popularity of the breed bears witness.

Cocker Club Championship Show 1990. Best Puppy, Miss S.J.
Ellison's Withiflor Moonlighting; dog judge, Mrs P. Masters; Mrs
A. Hackett with Best in Show Lindridge Salute; Mrs K. Holmes
(chairman); bitch judge, Mrs P. Wise; Reserve Best in Show, Mrs
Hackett's Sh.Ch. Lindridge Vanity Fair; and Mr David Havell (Hon.
secretary). (Tracy Morgan.)

However, the breed was fortunate in having so many personalities willing to dedicate their time to the Club and its ideals.

It is active in shows, field trials and rescue, and has taken the initiative in, and helped to fund, various areas of veterinary research. Of particular merit is the continued production of a comprehensive year book, now running to nearly 300 pages. Year books, full of information, pictures and advertising from many countries, can be used to track the pedigrees and conformity of the leading specimens of the breed. The compilation of such books is a complex task, the importance of which is not often appreciated until decades later.

The Club's annual Championship Show is the highlight of the year for all enthusiasts, and has proved an event not to be missed by Cocker lovers the world over.

Mr H.S. Lloyd, Hon. secretary of the Cocker Spaniel Club for thirty-nine years, chairman 1961, with Mrs E. Lloyd (later president), and Mighty Rare of Ware.

The Breed Council

The increase in the number of breed clubs led to a demand for a co-ordinating body for exchange of information, and in 1968 the Cocker Spaniel Council was formed. Its aims were to enable all its member clubs to speak with one voice, to make recommendations to the Kennel Club and to maintain lists of judges. The Cocker Spaniel Club stood alone as the parent Club, having its own line of communication with the Kennel Club, and has continued to take independent action on matters concerning the breed. However, all the other clubs eventually joined the Council. A chairman holds office for three years, but Mrs Joyce Caddy is its long-serving secretary.

The Council represents the breed in the United Spaniel Association. Formed in 1971, this brings together clubs for all the spaniel breeds in the Gundog group and is a means of liaison with the Spaniel Council of Europe and its biennial European Congress.

Clubs and societies hold the future of the Cocker Spaniel in their hands. May they long protect this lovely breed with integrity.

Appendices

Appendix 1: Breed Clubs

The following is a list of the main Cocker Spaniel clubs. The Kennel Club will be able to supply the names and addresses of their current secretaries.

Black Cocker Spaniel Society
Cheshire Cocker Spaniel Club
Cocker Spaniel Club
Cocker Spaniel Club of Lancashire
Cocker Spaniel Club of Scotland
Coventry Cocker Spaniel Club
Devon and Cornwall Cocker Spaniel Club
East Anglian Cocker Spaniel Society
East of Scotland Cocker Spaniel Club
Hampshire and Sussex Cocker Spaniel Club
Home Counties Cocker Spaniel Club
London Cocker Spaniel Society
Midland Cocker Spaniel Club
North Midlands and Eastern Counties Cocker Spaniel Club
North of England Cocker Spaniel Association
North of Ireland Cocker Spaniel Club
North Wales Cocker Spaniel Club
Parti-Coloured Cocker Spaniel Club
Red and Golden Cocker Spaniel Club
Rotherham and District Cocker Spaniel Society
South Wales and Monmouthshire Cocker Spaniel Club
Ulster Cocker Spaniel Club
West of England Cocker Spaniel Club
Yorkshire Cocker Spaniel Club

Appendix 2: Useful Addresses

The Kennel Club
1 Clarges Street
Piccadilly
London W1Y 8AB

Irish Kennel Club Ltd
Fottrell House
Unit 36
Greenmount Office Park
Dublin 6

American Kennel Club
51 Madison Avenue
New York
NY 10010

Australian National Kennel Council
Royal Show Grounds
Ascot Vale
Victoria 3032

Féderation Cynologique Internationale
Rue Leopold 11
14 B-6530 Thuin
Belgium

Ministry of Agriculture, Fisheries and Food (Animal Export Division)
Government Buildings
Hook Rise South
Tolworth
Surbiton
Surrey KT6 7NF

PRO Dogs National Charity
4 New Road
Ditton
Aylesford
Kent ME20 6AD

Appendix 3: Pedigrees

Quettadene Memento
Black Dog

Owner: Mrs P. Lester

KCSB No. 5028BW
Born: 12.10.86

Sh. Ch. Broomleaf Bright Memory	Sh. Ch. Benedict of Broomleaf	Sh. Ch. Bronze Knight of Broomleaf	Sh. Ch. Scotswood Warlord
			Black Frost of Broomleaf
		Sh. Ch. Olanza Pipestrelle	Butterprint of Broomleaf
			Olanza Pipers Love
	Buttercandy of Broomleaf	Butterprint of Broomleaf	Southbank Bootbrush of Broomleaf
			Buttercup of Broomleaf
		Bronze Joy of Broomleaf	Broomleaf Grangehill Mark
			Brioche of Broomleaf
Quettadene Picturesque	Sh. Ch. Quettadene Emblem	Sh. Ch. Sorbrook Christmas Knight	Willowside Buffalo Bill
			Sorbrook Penny Royal
		Quettadene Fascination	Lochranza Go For Gold
			Quettadene Charisma
	Quettadene Ebony Bloom	Sh. Ch. Lochranza Newsprint	Butterprint of Broomleaf
			Sh. Ch. Lochranza Bittersweet
		Cornbow Tantaliza	Sorbrook Boomerang
			Mint Toes of Cornbow

251

Sh.Ch. Lindridge Venture
Blue Roan Dog

Owner: Mrs A. Hackett

KCSB No. 4332BV
Born: 29.10.85

Mistfall Meddler	Bitcon Silver Rebel	Ouainé Diogenes	Sh.Ch. Moyhill Maxwelton
			Ouaine Diadem
		Sh.Ch. Bitcon Silver Model	Ch. Scolys Starduster
			Sh.Ch. Bitcon Blue Model
	Sh.Ch. Mistfall Mood Indigo	Sh.Ch. Dearnewood Star Venture	Sh.Ch. Leabank Levity
			Scolys Silver Cygnet
		Snowgate Blue Lady	Leabank Luckstone
			Perambur Victoria Trudy
Sh.Ch. Lindridge Gypsy Girl	Styvechale Stormcloud	Sh.Ch. Normanview Thundercloud	Normanview Silver Waters
			Normanview Silver Salver
		Styvechale Silver Delight	Ch. Scolys Starduster
			Styvechale Sleigh Bells
	Sh.Ch. Lindridge Silver Charm	Sh.Ch. Chrisolin Cambiare of Styvechale	Scolys Strike Lucky
			Chrisolin Cantata
		Lindridge Spot-On	Stargazer of Quatford
			Lindridge Sweet Rhythm

Sh.Ch. Courtdale Flag Lieutenant
Light Blue Roan Dog

Owner: Mrs S.G. Jones

KCSB No. 578AX
Born: 3.1.63

Courtdale Colinwood Seahawk
- Ch. Colinwood Silver Lariot
  - Joywyns Blue Flash
    - Fantee Silver Sentinel
    - Cartref Charmer
  - Truslers Misty Morn
    - Ch. Colinwood Firebrand
    - Truslers Tracery
- Orburn Seafoam
  - Colinwood Darnmill Dandy Tim
    - Ch. Colinwood Silver Lariot
    - Darnmill Dana
  - Orburn Firefly
    - Colinwood Blaze Away
    - Orburn Sunshine Cutie

Courtdale Kinkellbridge Gina
- Sh.Ch. Wells Fargo of Weirdene
  - Weirdene Barnscar Fisher
    - Barnscar Ajax
    - Questing Seasprite
  - Weirdene Trech Zenda
    - Sh.Ch. Joywyns Blueboy of Ware
    - Talwen Riverbank Romana
- Kinkellbridge Toska
  - Kinkellbridge Bluebottle
    - Sh.Ch. Jaycee Marxedeson
    - Panda of Kinkellbridge
  - Kinkellbridge Sunflower
    - Donleen Questing Seacaptain
    - Kinkellbridge Sunset

Further Reading

Bower, John and Youngs, David *The Health of Your Dog* (The Crowood Press, 1989)

Cartledge, Joe and Liz (Editors) *The Complete Illustrated Cocker Spaniel* (Elbury Press, London, 1974)

de Casembroot, Judy *The Merry Cocker* (Rockliff, 1956)

Doxford, Kay *The Cocker Spaniel: Its Care and Training* (K. & R. Books Ltd., 1979)

English Cocker Spaniel Club of America, Inc. *The English Cocker Spaniel Handbook* (ECSCA Inc., Hales Corners, Wisconsin, 1989)

Fitch Daglish, E. *Training Your Dog* (W. & G. Foyle Ltd.) – A Foyles Handbook

Franklin, Eleanor and Turner, T. *Practical Dog Breeding and Genetics* (Popular Dogs Publishing Co. Ltd.)

Grayson, Peggy *A History of the Cocker Spaniel* (Grayson, 1992)

Jenkins C.C. *The Cocker Spaniel* (Jenkins, Kyneton, Australia, 1990)

Kane, Frank and Wise, Phyllis *A Dog Owner's Guide to American and English Cocker Spaniels* (Salamander Books Ltd., 1987)

Lloyd, H.S. *Cocker Spaniels* (W. & G. Foyle Ltd., 1978) – A Foyles Handbook

The Cocker Spaniel (Our Dogs Publishing Co. Ltd., 1948) – Five editions

Lucas-Lucas, Veronica *The Cocker Spaniel* (Popular Dogs Publishing Co. Ltd.) – Revised 1988 by Joyce Caddy

Mathews, V.A.H. *The Cocker Spaniel* (Oxford University Press, Melbourne, 1948)

Moxon, P.R.A. *Gundogs: Training and Field Trials* (Popular Dogs Publishing Co. Ltd.)

Some of these books are out of print, but are sometimes available through second-hand bookshops and stalls at shows.

Index